Legal Professionals Negotiating the Borders of Identity

This book uses a controversial criminal immigration court procedure along the México-U.S. border called Operation Streamline as a rich setting to understand the identity management strategies employed by lawyers and judges.

How do individuals negotiate situations in which their work-role identity is put in competition with their other social identities such as race/ethnicity, citizenship/generational status, and gender? By developing a new and integrative conceptualization of *competing identity management*, this book highlights the connection between micro level identities and macro level systems of structural racism, nationalism, and patriarchy. Through ethnographic observations and interviews, readers gain insight into the identity management strategies used by both Latino/a and non-Latino/a legal professionals of various citizenship/generational statuses and genders as they explain their participation in a program that represents many of the systemic inequalities that exist in the current U.S. criminal justice and immigration regimes.

The book will appeal to scholars of sociology, social psychology, critical criminology, racial/ethnic studies, and migration studies. Additionally, with clear descriptions of terminology and theories referenced, students can learn not only about Operation Streamline as a specific criminal immigration proceeding that exemplifies structural inequalities but also about how those inequalities are reproduced—often reluctantly—by the legal professionals involved.

Jessie K. Finch is the Chair of the Department of Sociology at Northern Arizona University and an Associate Teaching Professor. She studies migration, race and ethnicity, deviance, social psychology, emotions, culture, health, and pedagogy. She has a Ph.D. (2015) and M.A. (2011) in Sociology from the University of Arizona and a B.A. (2007) in Sociology and Music from the University of Tulsa. Jessie has published in peer-reviewed journals such as *Teaching Sociology, Race and Social Problems,* and *Sociological Spectrum* and has received grants from the National Science Foundation as well as the American Sociological Association. She is the co-editor of *Migrant Deaths in the Arizona Desert* (2016). She has also taught courses on immigration, race and ethnicity, deviance, research methods, popular culture, and happiness.

Routledge Critical Studies in Crime, Diversity and Criminal Justice

The works in this series strive to generate new conceptual and theoretical frameworks to address the legal, organisational and normative responses to the challenges that diversity and intersectionality present to criminal justice systems. This series aims to present cutting edge empirically informed theoretical works from both new and established scholars around the world.

Drawing upon a range of disciplines including sociology, law, history, economics, and social work, the series encourages different approaches to questions of mobility and exclusion with a cross-section of theorists, empiricists, and critical policy researchers. It will be key reading for scholars who are working in criminal justice, criminology, criminal law and human rights, as well as those in the fields of gender and LGBTI studies, migration studies, anthropology, refugee studies and post-colonial studies.

Edited by Patricia Faraldo Cabana, University of A Coruña, Spain
Nancy A Wonders, Northern Arizona University, USA

Women, Reentry and Employment
Criminalized and Employable?
Anita Grace

Race, Recognition and Retribution in Contemporary Youth Justice
The Intractability Malleability Thesis
Esmorie Miller

Legal Professionals Negotiating the Borders of Identity
Operation Streamline and Competing Identity Management
Jessie K. Finch

Campus Sexual Violence
A State of Institutionalized Sexual Terrorism
Sarah Prior and Brooke de Heer

For more information about this series, please visit: https://www.routledge.com/criminology/series/CDCJ

Legal Professionals Negotiating the Borders of Identity

Operation Streamline and Competing
Identity Management

Jessie K. Finch

Routledge
Taylor & Francis Group

LONDON AND NEW YORK

First published 2023
by Routledge
4 Park Square, Milton Park, Abingdon, Oxon OX14 4RN

and by Routledge
605 Third Avenue, New York, NY 10158

Routledge is an imprint of the Taylor & Francis Group, an informa business

British Library Cataloguing-in-Publication Data
A catalogue record for this book is available from the British Library

Library of Congress Cataloging-in-Publication Data
A catalog record has been requested for this book

ISBN: 978-1-032-22392-6 (hbk)
ISBN: 978-1-032-22394-0 (pbk)
ISBN: 978-1-003-27241-0 (ebk)

DOI: 10.4324/9781003272410

Typeset in Times New Roman
by KnowledgeWorks Global Ltd.

To all who migrate in search of a brighter future.

Contents

Figures

Tables

Acknowledgments

First and foremost, I thank my wonderful academic advisors for all the time, effort, and energy they have given to me and this project. Celestino Fernández has served as an inspiration, source of support, and all-around role model. Robin Stryker has provided a solid scholarly foundation and always-constructive feedback. Jane Zavisca has been a foundation of encouragement and an advocate. All of the patience and assistance from these and other friends have made this project possible.

I am also grateful to the sociology faculty at the University of Tulsa for inspiring in me the passion to pursue my academic career while equipping me with the tools to do so. I have been so lucky to have so many mentors and friends help me through this process as well, including Nancy Wonders, Emily Schneider, Wendy Roth, Kate Epstein, and others I am surely forgetting. I am also very appreciative of the excellent editorial team at Routledge.

Thank you so much to the friends and family who have given me unwavering love and support! I am ever in debt to the love of my life and my best friend, Neal Galloway, for all his patience and encouragement. My parents are my heroes.

I also owe an enormous debt of gratitude to the participants in this research, whose names here have all been changed to protect confidentiality. Their time, consideration, and hard work are not often appreciated, but they are vital parts of the current legal system—flawed though it may be. Their job is not easy, and they mostly do their best.

Much of this material is based upon work supported by the National Science Foundation Graduate Research Fellowship under Grant Number 2011100013 and the National Science Foundation Doctoral Dissertation Research Improvement Grant under Award Number SES-1433927. I also want to thank the generous support of P.E.O. Chapter EJ for their emotional and financial assistance through the P.E.O. Scholar Award.

I also want to thank Springer Nature and Lexington Books for allowing the republication of prior material. Some portions are reprinted/adapted by permission from Springer Nature Customer Service Centre GmbH: Springer Nature, "Competing Identity Standards and Managing Identity

Verification" by Jessie K. Finch and Robin Stryker, 2020, from *Identity and Symbolic Interaction: Deepening Foundations, Building Bridges.* Other portions are reprinted/adapted by permission from Rowman & Littlefield: Lexington Books, "Racialized Habitus in Criminal Immigration Defense Attorneys" by Jessie K. Finch, 2021, from *The Logic of Racial Practice: Explorations in the Habituation of Racism.*

INTRODUCTION

"A round-faced, Latino man, who cannot be over 30, escorts me into the Hon. William D. Browning Special Proceedings Courtroom. He is wearing the required indigo windbreaker with 'U.S. MARSHAL' printed on the back in large, silver, sans-serif font. As he opens the double doors, I smell body odor and alcohol-based hand sanitizer. He motions to the rows of hard wooden benches on the south side of the room. I see another marshal on the far side of the bar separating me from the rest of the courtroom. He is also young, but white, with a classic military crop, and he is more interested in his smart phone than the 68 men and two women defendants in handcuffs and foot shackles who sit on the North side of the courtroom. Sixteen of the Latino border-crosser defendants are seated in what would be a jury box in any other courtroom. Another 52 are on the same wooden benches at the opposite side of the viewing gallery. The two Latina border-crosser defendants are separated and sit on a center bench that is on the other side of the bar. I learn later that because their processing is separate from the men's, the women are required to sit in this different part of the courtroom. All 70 defendants are in the clothes that they crossed in; many wear shirts that feature American brands such as Miller Light, Hollister, Puma, Nike. They have not showered, brushed their hair, or in many cases, even called their families since their detainment within the last 48 hours. Their heads are adorned with black, plastic headsets that do not quite fit properly but are required in order to hear the courtroom translator. I count 11 other men and three women who mill about in suits between the front and back of the bar. They are a diverse group—from thirty-somethings to a man who looks feeble with age; white, Black, Latino/a. They talk to one another, often laughing or checking their phones. The gruff, overweight, Hispanic judge who enters along with me from the front of the courtroom looks to be in his early sixties. He calls order to the court. The attorneys find a table to sit at or sit in the center rows behind the bar. In a fast mumble, the judge begins to discuss the ins-and-outs of why we are all here today: 'Operation Streamline.'"—From Author Fieldnotes, April 17, 2013

DOI: 10.4324/9781003272410-1

"Zero Tolerance"

Operation Streamline is a "zero-tolerance" immigration policy in place in the United States since 2005 designed to increase the criminal prosecution of undocumented border-crossers. While some sectors' prosecutions have been on pause since March 2020 due to the COVID-19 pandemic, there has been no official termination of the program at the time of this writing. The program was designed to replace the "catch-and-release" strategy Border Patrol had more traditionally employed, in which apprehended border-crossers were voluntarily returned or deported through civil immigration proceedings, facing no criminal charges. To deal with the surge in criminal cases since Operation Streamline's implementation in Arizona specifically in 2008, the Tucson Federal District Court initiated a "streamlined" legal hearing that combines what regularly involves three to five court appearances for large groups of defendants called the Arizona Denial Prosecution Initiative. Consequently, every weekday, in the span of 30 minutes to 3.5 hours, up to 75 undocumented border-crossers—primarily Latinos from México—are charged with federal misdemeanors and sentenced from 30 to 180 days in prison, generally to be followed by formal deportation in civil court as well. The unique *en masse* nature of Operation Streamline as a criminal immigration proceeding as well as its compression of the legal process has created controversy, with many immigrant-rights groups and legal scholars criticizing those involved and calling for an end to the program. This book's double agenda is to explore how legal professionals understand their own participation in Operation Streamline at the micro level as well as discover how the program itself highlights the ways in which contemporary U.S. immigration governance is premised on criminalization and racialization at the macro level.

The contentious nature of Operation Streamline, particularly the way it has been targeted by activists—provides a site for observing heightened identity management among legal professionals such as judges and lawyers. In particular, the above-average number of Latino/a judges and lawyers who participate in Operation Streamline all take on a specific work-related *role identity* that entails assisting in the conviction and sentencing of border-crossers with whom they share one *social identity*—race/ethnicity—but do not share another social identity—citizenship. This book uses Operation Streamline to examine how individuals navigate situations that put their work-related role identity into competition with their social identities related to race/ethnicity, nationality, or citizenship/generational status. More broadly speaking, what happens when people who share a racial/ethnic social identity with those who are being oppressed participate in the systems that facilitate that oppression?

Operation Streamline provides an optimal setting to understand the strategies lawyers and judges who manage such delicate identity processes employ as broader structural power plays out in the courtroom. I examine how legal professionals assign salience to their various identities in line with their work, their race/ethnicity, their citizenship/generational status, and their gender. This context allows me to extend existing sociological research on identity by exploring a conceptualization of *competing identity management*, which assesses identity management strategies used by lawyers and judges to manage their multiple competing identities while seeking to comprehend under what circumstances these identities affect legal professionals' job-related interactions.

With racial/ethnic unrest once again taking center stage since 2020, how justice professionals deal with not only differences in race and ethnicity but also citizenship/generational status, gender, and other social identities is more relevant than ever. Additionally, Operation Streamline is a U.S. program, but it exemplifies some of the challenges that racial/ethnic and gender inequalities and other differences create for legal professionals who work in the global immigration system. The larger macro history of immigration-related racism and global structures of power inequality regularly play out in the micro setting of Operation Streamline. As such, this book builds on the literatures of social psychology and identity conflicts in justice settings as well as the increase of criminalizing immigration on a global scale. How legal professionals understand their own identities and how that impacts their work matters in how we understand the meaning of "justice" in programs like Operation Streamline, which are becoming increasingly more common both in the United States and internationally.

Aims of the Book

Broadly speaking, this book explores how legal professionals navigate their work-related role identities in a system that also brings up their social identities like race/ethnicity, citizenship/generational status, and gender. How lawyers and judges of different races/ethnicities, genders, and citizenship/generational statuses understand their work in a controversial program like Operation Streamline can also give us insight into other legal professions where these same factors may impact how justice gets carried out, such as policing and the U.S. Border Patrol. Additionally, these micro level insights are the daily consequences or macro level racialized state violence. Differences in identity management strategies for Latino/a and non-Latino/a respondents help demonstrate systemic racial/ethnic tension present in Operation Streamline, and these types of institutional racial/ethnic concerns also may be present in other justice professions such as local law enforcement, the Border Patrol, or Immigration and Customs Enforcement. As such, this specific case helps us to understand broader trends in social inequality and the justice system as well as the immigration system.

More specifically, the book asks the following research questions:

1   Do Latino/a lawyers and judges involved with Operation Streamline manage their potentially competing identities differently than non-Latino/as whose social identities do not compete with their work-related role identities?
2   Under what circumstances is a shared social identity with defendants detrimental or useful in the work-related role of these Latino/a lawyers and judges?

I employed a qualitative research design to investigate how Latino/a legal professionals manage their identities in Operation Streamline differently than non-Latino/a professionals and how this might affect their work. I used what Robin Stryker (1996) called strategic narrative to analyze (1) legal documents, media reports, and activist publications as well as (2) ethnographic observations of courtroom proceedings at the Evo A. DeConcini U.S. Courthouse in Tucson, Arizona, and (3) in-depth interviews with 45 defense attorneys and seven magistrate judges (both Latino/a and non-Latino/a). Strategic narrative is an iterative method that uses existing theory to shape expectations for analysis and then systematically incorporates empirical results in order to adjust and develop new theoretical understandings. Though initially designed for historical work, strategic narrative's analytic methodology—allowing for the "concurrent construction and mutual adjustment" of theory with empirical observations—is broadly appropriate for qualitative-interpretive analysis (Stryker 1996:304). It requires the explicit and precise operationalization of concepts, measures, and coding techniques as they inform—but do not preclude—further theoretical development. The use of coding categories created based on prior theory and the creation of new categories/modifications of prior categories based on the empirical analysis allows for and operationalizes the idea of iterative mutual adjustment of theory and data and of theoretically informed and delimited field research.

In 18 months of fieldwork, I observed 66 Operation Streamline procedures. I also interviewed as many attorneys and judges involved in the program as possible. This included federal public defenders (FPDs) as well as private attorneys contracted through the Criminal Justice Act (CJA) Panel who represent clients who cannot afford their own attorneys. The 45 attorneys interviewed represent approximately 70% of the CJA panel defense attorneys who regularly participated in Operation Streamline and about 15% of the FPD who participated in Operation Streamline regularly during my fieldwork period. I also interviewed seven out of the eight judges who presided over Operation Streamline during my fieldwork. None of the Special Assistant U.S. Attorneys (government prosecutors) would agree to interviews, as they had specific directions from the Border Patrol to direct inquiries to the Public Information Office. I was also able to interview seven out of the eight judges who presided over Operation Streamline during my fieldwork. One judge retired during my fieldwork and simply did not respond to multiple requests for an interview via e-mail or from other respondents I interviewed. All other judges, including the replacement for the retired judge who began in 2014, participated in my study.

Most of the Latino/a lawyers and judges I spoke with are of Mexican ancestry, although I use the broader term "Latino/a" to encompass other ancestries considered Latino/Hispanic in order to protect the confidentiality of the few respondents who were of other specific Central or South American ancestry. When confidentiality is not in question, I use respondents' descriptions of their own race/ethnicity, their own experiences, in their own words, and my own observations of their behavior in the courtroom to explore the different identity mechanisms and strategies of *competing identity management* and examine how different types of identities (social and role) become more relevant/influential and under what circumstances.

As we all do, Operation Streamline lawyers and judges have both role identities and social identities that they must manage. Role identity stems from what we think of as jobs—including attorney and judge—but can also include other social functions like parent or spouse (Stryker 1980). Here, I use the idea of a "work-related role identity" to specify the legal occupational/professional identity of attorneys and judges. Social identities, on the other hand, reflect socially recognized groups, statuses, and categories, such as race/ethnicity, citizenship/generational status or nationality, and gender (Tajfel 1981). In this book, I explore the connections between these two types of identities by investigating what I term *competing identity management* in a highly contentious case. Prior work connecting role and social identities (Stryker and Burke 2000) fails to explain situations such as Operation Streamline where role identity and social identity theories would each lead to different predicted identity management strategies. By bringing in additional cultural theories of identity as well as linking these mostly micro level identity theories to macro level ideas of immigration-related racism, critical criminology, and the broader "crimmigration" literature, I provide a more complete understanding of why power and systems of social inequality matter in how legal professionals complete their daily work.

I also expand other identity research concepts such as negotiated identifications, assigned versus asserted identities, and impression management to categorize various identity management strategies between competing social and role identities. These different mechanisms of *competing identity management* help elucidate how competing social and role identities affect attorneys' and judges' understandings of their own work in Operation Streamline—essentially using different justifications for their continued participation in legal and immigration systems that they know to be flawed. Because questions of law and migration cannot be separated from questions of power, the racial/ethnic social identity of attorneys impacts their work-related role as does their social identities of citizenship/generational status and gender. I explore how attorneys and judges with competing social and role identities (in this case, Latino/a attorneys and judges involved with Operation Streamline) use different strategies to manage these identities. By examining the differences both between and within social identity groups (Latino/as and non-Latino/as, different citizenship/generational statuses, and men- and women-identifying legal professionals) of Operation Streamline attorneys and judges, as well as exploring the situationality of both social and role identities, I find that macro systems of inequality (structural racism, nationalism, and patriarchy) impact legal professional's daily lives and work. This book then contributes broadly to future research on competing social and role identities, which operate in many other areas of life, as well as the literature on legal professionals operating within various overlapping structures of social inequality.

Additionally, the implications for legal professionals of different races, citizenship/generational statuses, or genders experiencing their work differently highlight the connection of daily legal work to larger structures of social inequality. This micro to macro connection is central to the conceptualization of *competing identity management* because the salience of different social identities in daily contexts is broadly based on who is privileged and who is oppressed by our current systems of structural inequality. In this manner, the ways in which courtroom actors experience Operation Streamline differently based on different social identities also affect the way they justify their participation in what they often know to be a "brutally flawed system" as Leonora, a Latina CJA attorney, called it. This daily identity management for legal professionals, then, reveals how race/ethnicity and other forms of power play out in both the criminal justice and immigration systems in the United States.

While Operation Streamline serves as a distilled microcosm of legal violence and immigration-based racism in the U.S. context, it also represents just one component of a broader, global pattern of growing crimmigration. Recent work in critical criminology, justice studies, and border criminology highlights the "Europeanization of Crimmigration" (Wonders 2017; Brandariz 2021) as well as the impact of nationalism on increased migrant criminalization worldwide (Koulish and van Der Woude 2020; Kubal and Olayo-Méndez 2020; Parmar 2020). This ever-expanding global network of crimmigration systems (Miller 2019) is also linked to neoliberalism (Wonders 2015; Wonders and Jones 2021) and militarization (Dunn 1996; Slack et al. 2016) as well as being based on nationalism and racial/ethnic hierarchies (Molina 2014; Bosworth, Parmar, and Vázquez 2018). As such, this study fits into a broader global context that can teach us about the entangled reality between systems of racial/ethnic, national, and patriarchal oppression and contemporary migration governance.

Terminology

This book uses several terms that have contested definitions. For example, the majority of people in the groups I term "Latino/a" usually prefer to identify themselves by their own specific country of origin or their national ancestry

(Pew Hispanic Center 2012). However, as in previous work (Anderson and Finch 2014), I use the term "Latino/a" to refer to people descended or migrated from any country in "Latin America," that is, México, Central America, South America, or elsewhere where Spanish or Portuguese is the dominant language. With the majority of my Latino/a respondents being of Mexican origin (as is typical of Arizona demographics [Pew Hispanic Center 2010]), identifying a respondent specifically by their country of origin would threaten confidentiality for those who did not claim that country. However, I do examine variation within this "Latino/a" group in detail responding to calls for scholars to examine critical within group differences of panethnic labels (Jiménez 2010).

I also refer to this shared social identity of Latino/a as a racial/ethnic group membership, though respondents generally used the term "race" in interviews. Social scientists suggest that Latino/as who are easily identifiable based on darker skin or other phenotypic markers, as well as cultural and language distinctions, are more subject to identity ascription (Lee and Bean 2007) and are thus becoming more racialized (Frank, Akresh, and Lu 2010). My findings support current literature on the racialization of Latino/as who previously have been seen primarily as only an ethnic group (Omi and Winant 1986; Bonilla-Silva 1997, 2014; Itzigsohn and Dore-Cabral 2000; Cobas, Duany, and Feagin 2009; Roth 2009). I thus also use race as shorthand for Latino/as, my social identity category of interest, despite the more complicated nature of the terms overall.

I also refer to respondents of any other race/ethnicity who did not identify as Latino/a (based on how it is defined above) as "non-Latino/a." While this is a very broad category, it is used to protect the confidentiality of the less than five out of 16 non-Latino/as who identified as Black or Asian with no Latino/a ancestry (see Appendix A for a full breakdown of interview respondents by race/ethnicity and sex/gender). The majority of non-Latino/as interviewed identified as white/Caucasian/Anglo. No respondents identified as mixed race/ethnicity or as multi-racial/ethnic. Given the historically racialized nature of the U.S. immigration system (Rodriguez and Menjívar 2009; Chacón 2009, 2012; Molina 2014; Golash-Boza 2015; Finch and Stryker 2020; Finch 2021), and the specific demographic breakdown of Operation Streamline defendants (almost exclusively Latino/a), the clear category of racial/ethnic interest from this study is the distinction between those who identify with some sort of Latino/a ancestry and those who do not.

There were no genderqueer or non-binary respondents in this study. As such, respondents who are women-identifying are termed women who are either Latina or non-Latina. Men-identifying respondents are called men who are either Latino or non-Latino. There are long-standing, systemic concerns around migration and patriarchy (Pessar 2005; Ochoa-O'Leary 2008; Donato and Gabaccia 2015; Boyd 2021) and issues of gender inequity abound in the legal professions (Siemsen 2004; Martin and Jurik 2006;

Helfgott et al. 2018; Batton and Wright 2019). Given the goal of this book to connect micro level identities with larger macro level systems of oppression, gender as a social identity is explored specifically in Chapter 7, but discussion on non-binary gender identities beyond men and women was not brought up by any respondents in the study and is thus not a central focus.

I use the term *undocumented border-crosser* to refer to those who have attempted to enter the United States without permission or proper legal documents. This term, in addition to labels such as "unauthorized" or "without legal status," is more accurate and more socially acceptable than some of the terms that respondents used such as "illegal immigrant," "illegal alien," or "criminal alien" (Weiner 2013; Abrego et al. 2017). Operation Streamline proceedings legally categorize the majority of defendants as "criminal aliens," but "undocumented border-crossers" is a more humane and academically accepted term than the federal legal vocabulary of "alien," a dated, racist, and tired term. Additionally, prior research on the term "criminal alien" in particular highlights the centrality of immigration-related racism that has developed in the United States in recent decades (Abrego et al. 2017).

Finally, terms surrounding generational status can be ambiguous in many literatures and there is much debate as to appropriate labels (Rumbaut 2004). In line with recent literature that calls for clearer distinctions, I consistently use the following definitions to describe what I call the citizenship/generational social identity status of my research respondents:

- "Naturalized/migrated themselves later in life"—this population migrated to the United States after the age of 12 and therefore "always have a point of reference in the countries they left behind" (Portes and Rumbaut 2001:17). While others have labeled this group "first-generation," I use this more specific term in order to differentiate from people who migrated at a younger age.
- "1.5-generation"—people who migrated to the United States before they were 12. This group not only had little choice about migration but also generally identifies with the culture of the United States more so than their country of origin.
- "Second-generation"—those who are born in the United States as children of immigrants. These people completely "grow up American [...] their common point of reference is life in this country" (Portes and Rumbaut 2001:17).
- "Third-generation-plus"—those with migrant roots (e.g., most Americans) who no longer associate themselves with a foreign nationality. This is the least ambiguous term of the four.

Taking into account the constantly evolving generationally related language used by immigration scholars, I also use these four terms based on my respondents' descriptions of themselves. That is, the four distinctions above became relevant in strategic analysis and in the ways that respondents discussed their own immigration history.

My final note on terminology pertains to pseudonyms, which I have used for all respondents. Materials that I publicly accessed (such as media reports where my respondents were named by their real names) have been disguised or edited to protect the confidentiality of my respondents.

Summary

To explore the ways in which *competing identity management* plays out in the micro setting of Operation Streamline, as well as what that tells us about the macro level state of the current U.S. immigration regime, I start in Chapter 1 with the empirical foundation for this case study. The development and early history of Operation Streamline help to explain how this case so potently highlights competition between role and social identities. In particular, given the historical context of the United States' "crimmigration regime" (Stumpf 2006; Abrego et al. 2017), as well as the racial/ethnic social hierarchy in the United States upon which immigration policy is based (Molina 2014; Golash-Boza 2015), legal professionals who have a racial/ethnic social identity of Latino/a are continually being asked to carry out legal violence (Menjívar and Abrego 2012) on primarily Latino/a defendants in Operation Streamline.

Chapter 2 presents relevant prior literature on identity and develops the conceptualization of *competing identity management* between social and role identities. With such an abundance of identity literature, some theorists have begun to question identity's analytical utility as a concept (Brubaker and Cooper 2000). Thus, in the first part of Chapter 2, I systematize and prioritize prior conceptions of identity—drawing from social psychological and cultural models to outline the identity management strategies used by legal professionals in Operation Streamline. In the second part of Chapter 2, I provide a summary of key findings pulled from this literature to begin outlining *competing identity management* as an "umbrella" perspective to integrate prior work—most heavily drawing from Stryker's (1980) role identity and Tajfel's (1981) social identity.

I also reference Appendix A in Chapter 2, which describes the research design, the various qualitative data sources, and the method of analysis (strategic narrative) used for this book. I employed a mixed-method qualitative research design (18 months of ethnographic observations; 52 in-depth interviews; and content analyses on over 80 documents) to systematically assess strategies used by lawyers and judges to manage these multiple conflicting identities while investigating under what circumstances these identities affect job-related interactions. I use the analytical method of strategic narrative (Stryker 1996) and explain its unique importance for the analysis done here. It should be noted that judges (7 interviews) and attorneys (45 interviews) were grouped together in the analysis based on the similarity of themes found in their respective group data. That is to say, judges and lawyers generally both had the same experiences in dealing with their work-related roles in Operation Streamline and managing their competing role and social identities. I do highlight when there were minor variations between the two groups in the manuscript, but these differences were minimal.

Chapters 3–5 present the variation in work-related role strain, social and role identity competition, and identity management strategies between Latino/a and non-Latino/a attorneys and judges who participate in Operation Streamline proceedings. I find that compared to non-Latino/a legal professionals, Latino/a attorneys and judges use certain, distinct types of identity management strategies to manage their competing identities of being Latino/a (social identity) and being a legal professional involved in Operation Streamline (work-related role identity). Linking this micro level identity management with structural macro level forces, I attribute this variation in identity management strategies to the influence of structural racism in both the U.S. immigration and the U.S. criminal justice systems broadly as well as the reproduction of racial/ethnic inequality in Operation Streamline specifically (Boyce and Launius 2013; De La Rosa 2019; Finch and Stryker 2020; Finch 2021; Sarabia and Perales 2021).

First, in Chapter 3, I use the concept of "role strain" as a mechanism to explain this variation in identity management by racial/ethnic social identity. While all attorneys and judges in Operation Streamline experienced some work-related role strain, Latino/a respondents—who are presumed by those who are not directly involved in Operation Streamline (such as activists, courtroom observers, and the media) to show solidarity and care more about substantive justice for undocumented border-crossers because of their shared racial/ethnic social identity—experienced more strain. I found that Latino/a attorney and judges demonstrated more concerns about substantive justice in Operation Streamline (thus, showing more work-related role strain) because they share a racial/ethnic social identity with defendants. This in turn resulted in increased competition between their social identity and the substantive justice pole of their work-related role identity. As such, despite macro level identity strain, legal violence (Menjívar and Abrego 2012) and immigration-related racism (Molina 2014; Golash-Boza 2015) are reproduced in Operation Streamline even if by legal professionals who are somewhat reluctant to do so based on their own sense of racial/ethnic social identity.

Distinct identity management strategies between Latino/as and non-Latino/as are the further result of this work-related role strain as well as the competition between social and role identity. Chapter 4 explores the use of in-group and out-group social identity strategies and Chapter 5 explores how different groups negotiate their identifications with time, place, and language to manage work-related role strain and competing role and social identities.

Next, in Chapters 6–8, I examine the variation *within* the group of Latino/a attorneys and judges who participate in Operation Streamline. Panethnic assumptions about Latino/as have contributed to a lack of distinction in prior literature about the importance of citizenship/generational status identity within this racial/ethnic social identity group. In Chapter 6, I address this issue in an examination of how attorneys' and judges' citizenship/generational status impacts the salience of their racial/ethnic social identity and in turn their work-related role strain, identity competition, and identity management strategies.

Based on the relative importance of citizenship/generational status in the legal context, I find naturalized citizens (those who migrated themselves later in life) were more likely to differentiate themselves from the undocumented border-crossers they defend because of their recent Americanized status. Similarly, respondents of the third-generation-plus—who are distanced from the actual immigration experience—also want to differentiate themselves from defendants. These naturalized/migrated themselves later in life and third-generation-plus citizenship/generational status social identities thus result in a thin/assigned sense of Latino/a social identity—that is, a less salient racial/ethnic social identity. In turn, their thin and assigned racial/ethnic social identities decrease their work-related role strain and their subsequent competition between social and role identities as well as influencing their identity management strategies.

In contrast, I find that 1.5- and 2nd-generation Latino/as who have a more immediate connection to the struggle of migrants while still holding a solid Americanized frame of reference have more salient, thicker, and asserted racial/ethnic social identities of Latino/a. This in turn leads to more work-related role strain and more competition between social and role identities, necessitating identity management strategies different from those deployed by those Latino/as who were naturalized/migrated themselves later in life and those who have been in the United States from the third-generation-plus.

As such, the Latino/a legal professionals who were naturalized/migrated themselves later in life and those from the third-generation-plus carry out the immigration-based legal violence and racism (Menjívar and Abrego 2012; Golash-Boza 2015) represented by Operation Streamline with less identity conflict than 1.5- and 2nd-generation Latino/a legal professionals because they are less likely to personally identify with Operation Streamline defendants and thus hold a less salient racial/ethnic social identity.

Chapter 7 focuses on gender as a social identity that is also relevant, especially for Latina legal professionals working in Operation Streamline. Through interviews with respondents and field observations, it became clear that although the social identity of gender is less salient than the social identity of race/ethnicity, it could not be ignored when it came time for strategic analysis. This is consistent with the analytic technique of strategic narrative, which, similar to Burawoy's (2009) extended case method, draws on prior theory to focus and form expectations for the analysis but also facilitates new, empirically grounded insights and ideas (Stryker 1996). Issues of benevolent sexism (Glick and Fiske 1997, 2011) by men legal professionals were clear across racial/ethnic identities, but especially pronounced in Latinos. Latina legal professionals also faced specific issues dealing with emotional boundaries, authority, and their own activist pasts. Given the United States' broadly overlapping systems of inequality in the matrix of domination and the importance of intersectionality (Crenshaw 1989, 2017; Hill Collins 1990), as well as specific gendered inequalities that prior scholars have explored in both the immigration system (Pessar 2005; Ochoa-O'Leary 2008; Donato and Gabaccia 2015; Boyd 2021) and in the criminal justice system (Bloom 2003; Haney 2010; Chesney-Lind and Pasko 2012; Belknap 2020)—particularly for legal professionals (Siemsen 2004; Martin and Jurik 2006; Helfgott et al. 2018; Batton and Wright 2019)—the power differentials faced by the Latina respondents merited special attention.

Then, in Chapter 8, I explore the situationality of both role and social identities, which is particularly relevant to Latino/a respondents with thick/asserted identities from the 1.5- and 2nd-generation. By situationality, I mean how objective circumstances or certain situational conditions change respondents' social identity salience, experiences of work-related role strain, social and role identity competition, and identity management strategies. This integration and expansion of Stryker's (1980) situationality of role identity help recognize circumstances in which certain types of both social and role identities are highlighted or downplayed. Specifically, I investigated two different situations: (1) times when 1.5- and 2nd-generation Latino/a attorneys and judges have to defend their work in Operation Streamline to extra-legal critiques from activists and the media and (2) times when 1.5- and 2nd-generation Latino/a attorneys and judges have to talk about their daily work interactions with Operation Streamline defendants. I find that those with thick/asserted Latino/a legal professionals (those from 1.5- and 2nd-generation) vary in their identity management strategies based on these two situational contexts. This clearly demonstrates the racialized nature of U.S. immigration systems broadly (Rodriguez and Menjívar 2009; Chacón 2009, 2012; Molina 2014; Golash-Boza 2015) and Operation Streamline specifically (De La Rosa 2019; Finch 2021; Sarabia and Perales 2021) because those respondents with the strongest sense of a Latino/a racial/ethnic social identity go through extra identity management to justify their participation in this hyper-visible version of anti-Latino/a state violence.

Finally, in the Conclusion, I first provide a summary of the main findings on *competing identity management* in the case of Operation Streamline and then discuss potential generalization of these findings to demonstrate the framework and basic tenets of *competing identity management* more broadly. I also demonstrate that these identity-based insights help to reveal the oppressive and racially problematic nature of contemporary migration governance, linking the micro level day-to-day work of legal professionals with the macro level systems of inequality in which they operate. The identity management strategies used by legal professionals in Operation Streamline demonstrate how immigration-based racism and inequality get reproduced even by actors who are in many cases reluctant participants. I also discuss the limitations of this particular project while looking to future directions of how to continue to build a conceptualization of *competing identity management*, and one that is applicable to situations beyond Operation Streamline.

Next, I turn toward more applied contributions, exploring how the findings from this book can contribute to helping those involved in Operation Streamline better manage identities in ways that might improve their own well-being, their job performance, and their promotion of substantive justice—specifically as their identities are critiqued by those "outsiders" who are not directly involved in Operation Streamline (activists/media/scholars). I also include broader global comparisons of other programs and policy implications for how to end deterrence-focused programs like Operation Streamline and begin to dismantle the racialized U.S. crimmigration regime.

The conclusions of this book demonstrate that various social identities, particularly racial/ethnic identities, influence the work of legal professionals in criminal immigration proceedings. Latino/a lawyers and judges involved with Operation Streamline manage their competing social and role identities differently than non-Latino/as whose social identities do not compete with their work-related role identities because contemporary migration governance is tragically rife with racialized legal violence (Chacón 2009, 2012; Menjívar and Abrego 2012; Molina 2014; Golash-Boza 2015). These different identity management strategies reveal major differences between respondents based on racial/ethnic social identity, citizenship/generational status, as well as gender—linked to intersectionality and patriarchy in U.S. immigration and legal systems. Micro level identity management, such as legal professionals' justifications for participating in Operation Streamline and their ability to cope with work-related stress, is influenced by macro level structural inequality.

I also find that Latino/a lawyers and judges with higher racial/ethnic social identity salience involved with Operation Streamline manage their competing social and role identities differently than those with lower racial/ethnic social identity salience. This demonstrates variation *within* racial/ethnic social identity, especially when combined with the social identity of citizenship/generational status. Finally, I demonstrate that situationality is a factor in identity management because a shared social identity with defendants seems to be useful in the daily work of Latino/a lawyers and judges, but often detrimental in how they are perceived by activists and the media as well as others who are not directly involved in Operation Streamline.

From this case, I create an outline for *competing identity management*, integrating prior literatures on social and role identities. I elaborate mechanisms of some identity management processes while also developing grounded hypotheses on which to base future research. Exploring how even reluctant actors reproduce social inequality at the micro level may help improve how macro level criminal justice systems and immigration systems deal with the structural racism surrounding immigration "crimes" and *en masse* proceedings, such as in Operation Streamline. Because proposed "comprehensive immigration reform" has historically suggested expanding programs like Operation Streamline, research to understand the broader effects of the program on legal professionals is especially important not only to social scientists but to society at large. The fact that there is a difference in identity management strategies for Latino/a and non-Latino/a respondents helps demonstrate there is in fact underlying racialized state violence committed through Operation Streamline and that mass criminalization programs of migrants should no longer be a primary component of U.S. policy. Indeed, to improve justice for all in contemporary immigration governance, the COVID-19 "pause" on Operation Streamline should serve as the program's death knell.

References

Abrego, Leisy, Mat Coleman, Daniel Martínez, Cecilia Menjívar, and Jeremy Slack. 2017. "Making Immigrants into Criminals: Legal Processes of Criminalization in the Post-IIRIRA Era." *Journal on Migration and Human Security* 5(3):694–715. https://doi.org/10.1177/233150241700500308.

Anderson, Kathryn F., and Jessie K. Finch. 2014. "Racially Charged Legislation and Latino/A Health Disparities: The Case of Arizona's S.B. 1070." *Sociological Spectrum* 34(6):526–48. https://doi.org/10.1080/02732173.2014.947452.

Batton, Candice, and Emily M. Wright. 2019. "Patriarchy and the Structure of Employment in Criminal Justice: Differences in the Experiences of Men and Women Working in the Legal Profession, Corrections, and Law Enforcement." *Feminist Criminology* 14(3):287–306. https://doi.org/10.1177/1557085118769749.

Belknap, Joanne. 2020. *The Invisible Woman: Gender, Crime, and Justice.* Thousand Oaks, CA: Sage Publications.

Bloom, Barbara E., Ed. 2003. *Gendered Justice: Addressing Female Offenders.* Durham, NC: Carolina Academic Press.

Bonilla-Silva, Eduardo. 1997. "Rethinking Racism: Toward A Structural Interpretation." *American Sociological Review* 62(3):465–80. https://doi.org/10.2307/2657316.

Bonilla-Silva, Eduardo. 2014. *Racism without Racists: Color-Blind Racism and the Persistence.*

Bosworth, Mary, Alpa Parmar, and Yolanda Vázquez. 2018. *Race, Criminal Justice, and Migration Control: Enforcing the Boundaries of Belonging.* Oxford: Oxford University Press.

Boyce, Geoffrey, and Sarah Launius. 2013. "Warehousing the Poor: How Federal Prosecution Initiatives Like "Operation Streamline" Hurt Immigrants, Drive

Mass Incarceration and Damage U.S. Communities." Retrieved January 15, 2022. https://dspace.hampshire.edu/bitstream/10009/935/1/popdev_differentakes_082.pdf.

Boyd, Monica. 2021. "Women, Gender, and Migration Trends in a Global World" Pp. 19–36 in *The Palgrave Handbook of Gender and Migration*, Mora, Claudia, and Piper, Nicola, Eds. New York, NY: Palgrave Macmillan.

Brandariz, José A. 2021. "Criminalization Or Instrumentalism? New Trends in the Field of Border Criminology." *Theoretical Criminology*. https://doi.org/10.1177/13624806211009158.

Brubaker, Rodgers, and Fredrick Cooper. 2000. "Beyond 'Identity'." *Theory and Society* 29(1):1–47. https://www.jstor.org/stable/3108478.

Burawoy, Michael. 2009. *The Extended Case Method: Four Countries, Four Decades, Four Great Transformations, and One Theoretical Tradition*. Berkeley, CA: University of California Press.

Chacón, Jennifer M. 2009. "Managing Migration Through Crime." *Columbia Law Review Sidebar* 109:135–48. http://dx.doi.org/10.2139/ssrn.2033931.

Chacón, Jennifer M. 2012. "Overcriminalizing Immigration." *Journal of Criminal Law and Criminology* 102(3):613–52. https://scholarlycommons.law.northwestern.edu/jclc/vol102/iss3/5.

Chesney-Lind, Meda, and Lisa Pasko. 2012. *The Female Offender: Girls, Women, and Crime*. Thousand Oaks, CA: Sage Publications.

Cobas, José A., Jorge Duany, and Joe R. Feagin. 2009. *How the United States Racializes Latinos: White Hegemony and Its Consequences*. Boulder, CO: Paradigm Publishers.

Crenshaw, Kimberlé. 1989. "Demarginalizing the Intersection of Race and Sex: A Black Feminist Critique of Antidiscrimination Doctrine, Feminist Theory and Antiracist Politics." *University of Chicago Legal Forum* 140:139–68.

Crenshaw, Kimberlé W. 2017. *On Intersectionality: Essential Writings*. New York, NY: The New Press.

De La Rosa, Bill. 2019. "Criminalization, Social Exclusion, and Punishment: The United States Prosecution of Migrants Under Operation Streamline." MSC Criminology and Criminal Justice, 2018-19, Dissertation Submission. https://www.law.ox.ac.uk/sites/files/oxlaw/bill_de_la_rosa_msc_dissertation.pdf.

Donato, Katharine M., and Donna Gabaccia. 2015. *Gender and International Migration*. New York, NY: Russell Sage Foundation.

Dunn, Timothy J. 1996. *The Militarization of the U.S.-Mexico Border, 1978-1992: Low-Intensity Conflict Doctrine Comes Home*. Austin, TX: CMAS Books, University of Texas at Austin.

Finch, Jessie K. 2021. "Racialized Habitus in Criminal Immigration Defense Attorneys" Pp. 165–84 in *The Logic of Racial Practice: Explorations in the Habituation of Racism*, Bahler, Brock, Ed. Lanham, MD: Lexington Books.

Finch, Jessie K., and Robin Stryker. 2020. "Competing Identity Standards and Managing Identity Verification" Pp. 119–48 in *Identity and Symbolic Interaction: Deepening Foundations; Building Bridges*, Serpe, Richard T., Stryker, Robin, and Powell, Brian, Eds. New York, NY: Springer.

Frank, Reanne, Ilana R. Akresh, and Bo Lu. 2010. "Latino/a Immigrants and the U.S. Racial Order: How and Where Do They Fit In?" *American Sociological Review* 75(3):378–401. https://doi.org/10.1177/0003122410372216.

Glick, Peter, and Susan T. Fiske. 1997. "Hostile and Benevolent Sexism Measuring Ambivalent Sexist Attitudes Toward Women." *Psychology of Women Quarterly* 21(1):119–35. https://doi.org/10.1111/j.1471-6402.1997.tb00104.x.

Glick, Peter, and Susan T. Fiske. 2011. "Ambivalent Sexism Revisited." *Psychology of Women Quarterly* 35(3):530–5. https://doi.org/10.1177/0361684311414832.

Golash-Boza, Tanya M. 2015. *Immigration Nation: Raids, Detentions, and Deportations in Post-9/11 America.* Boulder, CO: Paradigm Press.

Haney, Lynne. 2010. *Offending Women: Power, Punishment, and the Regulation of Desire.* Berkeley, CA: University of California Press.

Helfgott, Jacqueline B., Elaine Gunnison, Autumn Murtagh, and Bridgette Navejar. 2018. "Badasses: The Rise of Women in Criminal Justice." *Women and Criminal Justice* 28(4):235–61. https://doi.org/10.1080/08974454.2018.1468296.

Hill Collins, Patricia. 1990. *Black Feminist Thought: Knowledge, Consciousness, and the Politics of Empowerment.* New York, NY: Routledge.

Itzigsohn, Jose, and Carlos Dore-Cabral. 2000. "Competing Identities? Race, Ethnicity and Panethnicity Among Dominicans in the United States." *Sociological Forum* 15(2)225–47. https://www.jstor.org/stable/684815.

Jiménez, Tomás R. 2010. *Replenished Ethnicity: Mexican Americans, Immigration, and Identity.* Berkeley, CA: University of California Press.

Koulish, Robert, and Maartje van Der Woude. 2020. *Crimmigrant Nations: Resurgent Nationalism and the Closing of Borders.* New York, NY: Fordham University Press.

Kubal, Agnieszka, and Alejandro Olayo-Méndez. 2020. "Mirrors of Justice? Undocumented Immigrants in Courts in the United States and Russia" Pp. 198–224 in *Crimmigrant Nations: Resurgent Nationalism and the Closing of Borders,* Koulish, Robert, and van Der Woude, Maartje, Eds. New York, NY: Fordham University Press.

Lee, Jennifer, and Frank D. Bean. 2007. "Reinventing the Color Line Immigration and America's New Racial/Ethnic Divide." *Social Forces* 86(2):561–86. https://doi.org/10.1093/sf/86.2.561.

Martin, Susan E., and Nancy C. Jurik. 2006. *Doing Justice, Doing Gender: Women in Legal and Criminal Justice Occupations.* Thousand Oaks, CA: Sage Publications.

Menjívar, Cecilia and Abrego, Leisy J. 2012. "Legal Violence: Immigration Law and the Lives of Central American Immigrants." *American Journal of Sociology* 117(5):1380–421. https://doi.org/10.1086/663575.

Miller, Todd. 2019. *Empire of Borders: The Expansion of the U.S. Border Around the World.* New York, NY: Verso Books.

Molina, Natalia. 2014. *How Race Is Made in America: Immigration, Citizenship, and the Historical Power of Racial Scripts.* Los Angeles, CA: University of California Press.

Ochoa-O'Leary, Anna. 2008. "Close Encounters of the Deadly Kind: Gender, Migration, and Border (In)Security." *Migration Letters* 5(2):111–21. https://doi.org/10.33182/ml.v5i2.47.

Omi, Michael, and Howard Winant. 1986. *Racial Formation in the United States: From the 1960s to the 1990s.* New York, NY: Routledge and Kegan Paul.

Parmar, Alpa. 2020. "Arresting (Non)Citizenship: The Policing Migration Nexus of Nationality, Race, and Criminalization." *Theoretical Criminology* 24(1):28–49. https://doi.org/10.1177/1362480619850800.

Pessar, Patricia. 2005. "Women, Gender, and International Migration Across and Beyond the Americas: Inequalities and Limited Empowerment." Population Division of the Department of Economic and Social Affairs, United Nations Secretariat. Retrieved January 15, 2022. www.un.org/esa/population/migration/turin/symposium_turin files/p08_pessar.pdf.

Pew Hispanic Center. 2010. "Demography Profile of Hispanics in Arizona." Retrieved January 15, 2022. http://www.pewhispanic.org/states/state/az/.

Pew Hispanic Center. 2012. "When Labels Don't Fit: Hispanics and Their Views of Identity." Retrieved October 23, 2012. http://www.pewhispanic.org/files/2012/04/phc-hispanic-identity.pdf.

Portes, Alejandro, and Rubén G. Rumbaut. 2001. *Legacies: The Story of the Immigrant Second Generation.* Berkeley, CA: University of California Press.

Rodriguez, Nestor P., and Cecilia Menjívar. 2009. "Central American Immigrants and Racialization in A Post-Civil Rights Era" Pp. 183–99 in *How the United States Racializes Latinos: White Hegemony and Its Consequences*, Cobas, José A., Duany, Jorge, and Feagin, Joe R., Eds. Boulder, CO: Paradigm Publishers.

Roth, Wendy D. 2009. "'Latino/a Before the World': The Transnational Extension of Panethnicity." *Ethnic and Racial Studies* 32(6):927–47. https://doi.org/10.1080/01419870802245042.

Rumbaut, Rubén G. 2004. "Ages, Life Stages, and Generational Cohorts: Decomposing the Immigrant First and Second Generations in the United States." *International Migration Review* 38(3):1160–205. https://www.jstor.org/stable/27645429.

Sarabia, Heidy, and Maria Perales. 2021. "Operation Streamline: Producing Legal Violence, Racialized Illegality, and Perpetual Exclusion" Pp. 403–15 in *Race and Ethnicity in the U.S.: the Sociological Mindful Approach*, Brooks, Jacqueline, Sarabia, Heidy, and Ida, Aya Kimura, Eds. San Diego, CA: Cognella Academic Publishing.

Siemsen, Cynthia. 2004. *Emotional Trials: The Moral Dilemmas of Women Criminal Defense Attorneys.* Boston, MA: Northeastern University Press.

Slack, Jeremy, Daniel E. Martínez, Alison Elizabeth Lee, and Scott Whiteford. 2016. "The Geography of Border Militarization: Violence, Death and Health in Mexico and the United States." *Journal of Latin American Geography* 7–32. https://www.jstor.org/stable/43964648.

Stryker, Robin. 1996. "Beyond History Versus Theory: Strategic Narrative and Sociological Explanation." *Sociological Methods and Research* 24(3):304–52. https://doi.org/10.1177/0049124196024003003.

Stryker, Sheldon. 1980. *Symbolic Interactionism: A Social Structural Version.* Menlo Park, CA: Benjamin/Cummings Publishing Company.

Stryker, Sheldon, and Peter J. Burke. 2000. "The Past, Present, and Future of an Identity Theory." *Social Psychology Quarterly* 63(4):284–97. https://doi.org/10.2307/2695840.

Stumpf, Juliet. 2006. "The Crimmigration Crisis: Immigrants, Crime and Sovereign Power." *American University Law Review* 56(2):367–419. http://digitalcommons.wcl.american.edu/aulr/vol56/iss2/3.

Tajfel, Henri. 1981. *Human Groups and Social Categories: Studies in Social Psychology.* Cambridge, UK: Cambridge University Press.

Weiner, Rachel. 2013. "AP Drops 'Illegal Immigrant' From Stylebook." *The Washington Post.* Retrieved January 15, 2022. http://www.washingtonpost.com/blogs/post-politics/wp/2013/04/02/ap-drops-illegal-immigrant-from-stylebook/.

Wonders, Nancy. 2015. "Transforming Borders from Below" Pp. 190–8 in *Rethinking Border Control for a Globalizing World: A Preferred Future*, Weber, Leanne, Ed. New York, NY: Routledge.

Wonders, Nancy A. 2017. "Sitting on the Fence—Spain's Delicate Balance: Bordering, Multiscalar Challenges, and Crimmigration." *European Journal of Criminology* 14(1):7–26. https://doi.org/10.1177/1477370816640140.

Wonders, Nancy A., and Lynn Jones. 2021. "Challenging the Borders of Difference and Inequality: Power in Migration as a Social Movement for Global Justice" Pp. 296–313 in *Handbook of Migration and Global Justice*, Weber, Leanne, and Tazreiter, Claudia, Eds. Cheltenham, UK: Edward Elgar Publishing.

1 OPERATION STREAMLINE

"Dear Operation Streamline Lawyer,

> I am writing because I think you care as much as I do about justice for defendants who appear in court. Operation Streamline was invented purely for the mass prosecution of immigrants as criminals. This fast-track system is wrong and must be stopped. I ask you to resign your participation in this court proceeding that that [sic] has huge costs for our country in terms of violated constitutional principles and millions of dollars a year in court and prison costs. I urge you to resign from your participation in Operation Streamline, and to encourage your colleagues to join you.
>
> Thank you.
> *[Member of the End Operation Streamline Coalition]"*
> *—Email Correspondence in Author Fieldnotes, February 19, 2014*

Criminal Immigration Prosecutions

Nearly every attorney and judge who worked in Operation Streamline during my fieldwork period received the above email message asking them to resign from the program—sometimes receiving this same text with a different signature up to 40 times in one day. This email was part of an online petition campaign headed by the End Streamline Coalition—a group of activists mainly formed from members of several other immigrants' right groups (including Coalición de Derechos Humanos; No More Deaths/*No Más Muertes*; Tucson Samaritans; and Humane Borders) with the expressed mission of stopping Operation Streamline proceedings in Tucson. Every time the online petition received an electronic signature, this email was sent to a list of Tucson attorneys and magistrate judges that activists had compiled based on who they knew worked in Operation Streamline.

The activist perspective on Operation Streamline is uniformly negative, though defense attorneys and judges who received this email or other

DOI: 10.4324/9781003272410-2

activist material insisted that these groups did not understand "the system" and that they were targeting the wrong people. While higher-level officials, such as prior U.S. Attorney Generals Eric Holder or Jeff Sessions, have also received emails about ending Operation Streamline, and protests have been held to attract national media attention, the majority of activist group activities have focused on individual legal professionals involved in Operation Streamline as the main targets of these social movement tactics. Indeed, these activist critics regularly fail to grasp some of the more nuanced legal aspects of the proceedings and often do not understand the nature of criminal immigration changes over time. However, their complaints about the growing criminalization of immigration policy as well as the racialized nature of these criminal immigration proceedings are supported by legal and social science scholars (Golash-Boza 2015; Abrego et al. 2017)

This chapter first lays out the historical context in which Operation Streamline was developed, a post-9/11 world bent on zero tolerance and closed borders. Next, I describe the program specifically as it developed in Tucson, Arizona, and explain how it has evolved over time. Following that, I demonstrate how Operation Streamline provides a specific example of competing role identities and social identities. The ways in which legal professionals navigate this particular federal immigration program at the micro level thus illustrate how racial/ethnic inequality is inherently built into both our immigration and our criminal justice systems at the macro level.

The Roots of Operation Streamline

Growing literatures on "making immigrants into criminals," "crimmigration," and the "criminalization of immigration" show the powerful structural interplay of race, immigration, law, and the criminal justice system, particularly for Latino/a people (Stumpf 2006; García Hernández 2015; Abrego et al. 2017). The militarization and criminalization of migration that have occurred in the past 50 or so years have been a clear indication that the institutions, laws, and policies that govern migration into the United States are part of a larger structurally racist society. In particular, Latino/a people, who have made up the growing share of immigrants into the United States in the past 50 years, have been subject to increased racialization and, thus, increased discrimination and criminalization in the U.S. immigration system (Lee and Bean 2007; Chacón 2009, 2012; Golash-Boza 2015).

In 2005, the Department of Homeland Security and the Department of Justice came together to develop and enforce a "zero-tolerance" criminal immigration policy called Operation Streamline. For most of U.S. history, the majority of those caught entering the United States without proper documentation were either voluntarily repatriated or to be tried in *civil* proceedings and then deported. This meant migrants did not consistently face criminal charges or spend time in prison for unauthorized crossing violations before 2005. Operation Streamline, however, standardized the criminal prosecution of undocumented border-crossers under criminal laws that have been in existence since 1952, U.S. Criminal Code, Title 8, Subsection 1325: Improper Entry by Alien (commonly called "illegal entry") and Subsection 1326: Reentry of Removed Aliens (commonly referred to as "illegal re-entry").

The designers of Operation Streamline, members of the executive branch under Republican President George W. Bush, hoped to achieve what legal scholars refer to as both general and specific deterrence (Stafford and Warr 1993). By criminally punishing offenders who were caught crossing without permission, the program creators sought to deter these specific individuals from coming back again personally, but they also hoped that the program would serve as a deterrent for others who had yet to attempt to cross the border, knowing incarceration was a serious possible consequence.

Operation Streamline was (and continues to be) a central part of the Border Patrol's "Consequence Delivery System," where the agency no longer emphasized voluntary returns and instead focused on three punishment outcomes: (1) Formal Removals (either before a judge through the civil immigration system or using Expedited Removals); (2) Remote Repatriation (returning migrants to different ports of entry from where they were apprehended; this includes the Alien Transfer Exit Program (ATEP) and the Mexican Interior Repatriation Program (MIRP); and (3) federal criminal charges through Operation Streamline. These changes created a dramatic increase in criminal immigration prosecutions of over 45% between 2005 and 2012 (Seghetti 2014; Argueta 2016).

Since then, prosecutions of undocumented border-crossers have soared, with the majority of convictions coming from Operation Streamline due to the *en masse* nature of the program. Between 2000 and 2010, federal prosecutions for petty immigration-related offenses increased by over 330% (Lydgate 2010). For example, in 2012, immigration-related offenses—such as illegal entry or reentry after removal—accounted for 40% of all federal criminal cases in the United States—doubling from 24% the previous decade in 2002 (U.S. Attorneys' Office 2002, 2012). In fiscal year 2019, before the COVID-19 pandemic forced Operation Streamline to be "placed on pause" (Murillo and Birmingham 2020:1), the total percentage of all federal criminal cases in the United States related to immigration was up to 44% (U.S. Attorneys' Office 2019). In raw numbers, there were 30,665 immigration-related cases filed in 2019 at the federal level, compared with the next two highest categories of "Violent Crime—Total" at 15,899 and "All Drug Offenses—Total" at 13,704 (U.S. Attorneys' Office 2019). This means the United States filed more immigration-related cases in 2019 than cases about drugs or violent crime *combined*. Even in 2020, where Operation Streamline was not in full operation in all districts because of COVID-19, immigration-related cases still made up 42% of all federal cases filed (U.S. Attorneys' Office 2020).

These staggering numbers, along with the continued large volume of undocumented border-crossers apprehended by the Border Patrol pre-COVID-19, necessitated that courts that participated in Operation Streamline adjust their usual procedures and start *en masse* group proceedings that combine several court appearances for defendants. These controversial procedures have since become common practice in many border-adjacent court districts in the Southwest. Criticized by activists, scholars, and politicians alike as "assembly-line" justice (Lydgate 2010), "an inferior standard of due process" (Grassroots Leadership 2012), and "a bastardization of the American legal system" (End Operation Streamline Coalition Activist, Fieldnotes August 25, 2014), under the policy large groups of migrants in courtrooms across the nation go through a compressed procedure, spending just one day at the courthouse. The program began in Del Rio, Texas, but up to 8 of the 11 federal court districts along the México-U.S. border have had some version of Operation Streamline in place. The Alpine District in Texas and both districts in California have opted out, with California's U.S. Attorney at the time, Carol Lam, citing the need to pursue "high impact cases" and not "low level narcotics and immigration crimes" (Moore 2009).

I selected the Border Patrol's "Tucson Sector" in part because, since its implementation of Operation Streamline in Arizona in 2008, it has frequently had the highest number of migrant apprehensions and the highest number of immigrant defendants charged with petty misdemeanors in the country (U.S. Department of Justice 2010). The Arizona Denial Prosecution Initiative, the state of Arizona's name for its modified version of Operation Streamline, allows the Tucson Federal District Court to implement a legal hearing that is streamlined in two ways. First, it combines three to five court appearances (initial appearance, preliminary hearing, detention hearing, change-of-plea proceeding, and sentencing) into one court appearance. Second, the court processes the cases of up to 70 defendants in just one day, in what is known as an *en masse* hearing.

The 70-person-per-day proceeding occurs at 1:30 pm five days a week, Monday to Friday, at the Evo A. DeConcini U.S. Courthouse located in downtown Tucson. That is to say, every weekday in Tucson, 70 undocumented border-crossers—primarily Latinos from México—are convicted of federal misdemeanors and given sentences between 30 and 180 days in jail as part of Operation Streamline. As of March 2013, over 73,000 people had been processed through Operation Streamline in Tucson alone (Trevizo 2013). Continuing these estimates, a likely 150,000 people have been tried through Operation Streamline in the Tucson sector, and in my fieldwork of 66 observations, I personally saw over 4,200 migrants turned into criminals in the eyes of the state.

Arizona Denial Prosecution Initiative, Tucson, AZ

Operation Streamline is touted as a "zero-tolerance" policy; however, in reviewing the number of border-crossers within the U.S. Border Patrol defined "Tucson Sector," this claim is overblown. Operation Streamline does criminalize more migrants than any preceding policy in history, but it, too, faces constraints in exactly how many migrants can be prosecuted and what types of migrants have been targeted to go through the program. Due to constraints in personnel, physical holding spaces, and budgets, the program has never been able to prosecute more than 70 migrants a day in Tucson, which, according to 2010 estimates, represents just 12%–17.5% of illegal entries in the Tucson Sector (Gambino 2010). Still, there is frequently talk of expansion for the program. For example, in June of 2013, the immigration reform bill that was passed by the Senate and stalled in the House called for expanding the capacity of Operation Streamline in Tucson to 210 defendants a day. Almost all of the legal professional respondents I interviewed stated that processing 70 defendants per day is already pushing the limits of the system and that an increase is impossible. As such, the program is actually more like an "80% tolerance" policy, rather than "zero tolerance." Nonetheless, Operation Streamline still represents approximately 18,000 migrants prosecuted in Tucson each year before the COVID-19 pandemic "temporarily" halted the program.

Recognizing the numeric limitations of Operation Streamline, the designers of Tucson's program at first emphasized the prosecution of first-time border-crossers—that is, those who Border Patrol had never apprehended before. The ostensible reason for this was to maximize deterrence. Hypothetically, targeting first-time border-crossers would deter *any* potential migrants seeking to cross. This logic was part of the "get-tough-on-immigration" approach deployed by the Bush Administration, especially after criticism of Border Patrol's more lenient "catch-and-release" strategy.

The goal of deterrence, however, has not been particularly successful. Numerous critiques have been lodged, including from the Tucson Federal Public Defenders office, questioning the program's effectiveness at deterrence as well as its exorbitant cost (McCombs 2007a, 2007b, 2009, 2010; Buentello et al, 2010; Lydgate 2010; Robbins 2010a, 2010b, 2010c; Grassroots Leadership 2012). Most recently, Corradini et al. (2018) suggest in their report for the Vera Institute of Justice that many sectors were already showing decreased apprehensions before Operation Streamline and there is no statistical evidence of migrants being deterred by the threat of criminalization.

After a change of leadership in the U.S. Attorney's Office for the District of Arizona in 2013, the program shifted its focus to migrants who had prior criminal convictions in the United States—commonly referred to in legal parlance as "criminal aliens." While the term has been used to suggest that the program targets dangerous or violent criminals, the attorney and judge respondents in this study suggested to me that defendants' prior convictions regularly consisted of prior 1325 illegal entry violations through Operation Streamline. That is, they were being criminally punished again for additional attempts at undocumented entry. Indeed, the term "criminal alien" is itself strategic symbolic violence that is meant to "other" unauthorized border-crossers (Abrego et al. 2017). Given this potentially high rate of

recidivism, Operation Streamline seems to fail at deterrence while also per-
petuating negative stereotypes about violent or dangerous immigrants.

In addition to changing the target populations who go through Operation
Streamline, the daily ins and outs of the procedures have also changed over
time. The original proceedings in early 2008 were less scripted than when
I completed my observations. Both attorneys and judges had more autonomy over the defense and sentencing. Attorneys were able to argue for sentence variations based on mitigating circumstances (such as the existence
of minor children who were U.S. citizens or a threat to safety in the home
country) and judges were in charge of delivering sentences, many of whom
gave time-served to first-time offenders when Arizona's program was not
yet targeting those with a prior conviction, which mitigated the immediate
impact on the migrants somewhat. As the program progressed and became
more and more standardized and "streamlined," these unscripted portions
fell away. The proceeding I regularly observed was done almost exclusively through the use of Change of Plea Agreements, in which government
prosecutors used very specific "equations" to stipulate sentencing. Judges
became figureheads who merely assured defendants understood the plea
they were entering instead of deciding sentences. Average sentences now
range between 30 and 180 days.

Based on my fieldwork talking to attorneys and judges, the "equation"
used to provide sentencing for defendants is in the hands of the prosecutors and is continually evolving, but generally, lower sentences mean less
prior immigration and criminal history. One defense attorney who had been
involved with Operation Streamline since its inception told me, "30 days
always means the only thing they have is one prior deportation, no criminal
history. It *always* means that. That's the one thing you can guess" (Mickey,
non-Latino, Criminal Justice Act (CJA) panel attorney). Generally, this sentence is doubled to 60 days if the defendant had previously gone through a
remote repatriation program, whether it be Alien Transfer Exit Program
(ATEP) or Mexican Interior Repatriation Program (MIRP). These programs send migrants back to locations distant from where they were apprehended in hopes of them not returning to the United States. Beyond these
two clear-cut distinctions, each case is handled based on specific priors
(adding 15–30 days for certain misdemeanors; more time for felonies, etc.)
and days are added until defendants max out at 180.

One thing that has remained relatively constant is that the public
Operation Streamline proceeding held daily at the Evo A. DeConcini Federal
Courthouse in downtown Tucson has always been visually quite startling.
As Hector, a Latino CJA attorney, described it, Operation Streamline has
the most "distressing optics" of any U.S. courtroom, especially for those
without prior courtroom experience—which includes most observers (activists and others). Figure 1.1 shows the layout of the courtroom during the
proceeding on most days during my fieldwork.

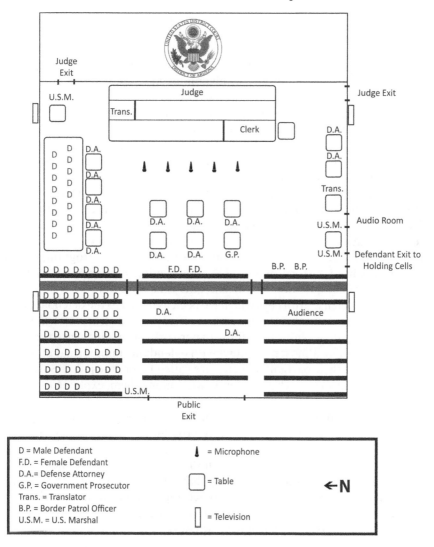

Figure 1.1 Operation Streamline Courtroom Layout

All 70 defendants are seated on the north side of the William D. Browning Special Proceedings Courtroom on the second floor of the building. Watched closely by numerous Border Patrol Agents and U.S. Marshals, the mostly men defendants spill out from the jury box into the north-side gallery. Women defendants sit separately on the center bench in front of the bar.

All defendants are wearing the same clothes as when they were apprehended, usually stained and disheveled. While most migrants do carry a change of clothes and toiletries on their crossing, these defendants have not been permitted to shower or allowed to change clothes, as their belongings are usually taken by Border Patrol Agents upon apprehension. Additionally, because the prosecution is required to have them appear in court within 48 hours for Probable Cause Presentations, they are not processed into the Department of Correction orange jumpsuits so ubiquitous in federal courtrooms. They also wear ill-fitting headsets provided by the court, as proceedings occur in English, but the translator is transmitted into these wireless devices.

As with all other defendants in the federal courthouse, though, the migrant defendants all wear numerous chains—wrist manacles, leg irons, and belly chains. These restraints clink and clang loudly as the U.S. Marshals or Border Patrol Agents lead migrants in front of the judge in groups of five to eight where microphones are set up for them. Almost every external media source and activist publication mentions the use of chains as a particularly distressing aspect of Operation Streamline since its inception, connoting dehumanization, criminality, and even direct references to chattel slavery. These chains alone symbolize the oppressive nature of the program, linked to the racialized history of the U.S. immigration and criminal systems (Golash-Boza 2015; Bosworth, Parmar, and Vázquez 2018).

The 12–15 defense attorneys who have been assigned to the defendants are scattered throughout the courtroom and often seem distracted or indifferent—checking their phones, shuffling paperwork, or reading newspapers or novels. They make almost no contact with defendants until formal proceedings begin and their particular clients are called before the judge. Solomón, a Latino CJA attorney, who frequently was among them, explained:

> [Activists] complain about attorneys sometimes filling out a paper [form] while somebody else is being brought up front for their sentencing. Well, guess what? That individual who is sitting back there, doing paperwork, has nothing to do with that case that is before the judge at that time. There is no reason why that attorney should be wasting his or her time paying attention to something that has nothing to do with them. Now, when my client is up front, when I have to go up, then my full attention is to my client and the court.

Solomón rightly points out that attorneys have no particular reason to pay attention to the rote sentencing of someone who is not their client and who they will never see again, but activists suggest that this distraction demonstrates a lack of caring or respect for the defendants and the court. For myself, after the first several observations of courtroom proceedings, I wondered how it was possible to ignore the human misery before us all. However, after 66 observations, I also felt that it might be necessary to do so, lest attorneys burn out completely.

Proceedings also vary based on the different judges presiding. Due to the oddity of *en masse* proceedings—and although much of the organization and structure are standardized and standardization increased over time—there is no singular script for judges to follow. Judges vary most significantly in the number of questions they ask defendants. For example, in September 2013, I saw one magistrate, Judge Ochoa, asking each defendant only two "yes/no" questions before sentencing them. In the subsequent week, a different judge on Operation Streamline duty asked defendants 25 questions, some open-ended or requiring longer responses, some individually and some in groups.

This kind of variation leads observers (be they activists or otherwise) to perceive the process differently based on which judge is presiding. For example, Judge Ochoa, given his speed and air of disinterest, has a reputation of being gruff, while Judge Darrell is seen as the most empathetic, perhaps because she often gives individual defendants the chance to speak. The variation in judicial oversight of Operation Streamline proceedings remains in spite of several Ninth Circuit Court of Appeals rulings (*U.S. v. Roblero-Solis, 2009; U.S. v. Escamilla-Rojas, 2011; U.S. v. Arqueta-Ramos, 2013*) on how such proceedings can be carried out. These appeal cases did stop judges from taking pleas *en masse* and affirmed that judges needed to complete individual questioning but, attempting to bring in Rule 11 and 5th and 6th Amendment complaints, did not significantly alter the proceedings.

This variation in the program overtime and across judges has often been overlooked by the media and by activist groups. These critics regularly fail to grasp some of the more nuanced legal aspects of the proceedings and often do not understand the nature of these changes over time. Much of the activist criticism of the program can be outdated, based on its initial setup rather than the evolved change-of-plea version of the program and many activists or media representatives view only one proceeding before critiquing the program. While knowing of these changes would likely not stop the activist critiques of the program, it could assist in social movement strategies.

These activist groups have chosen tactics that focus not on larger systematic concerns of criminal immigration patterns but instead target the individual legal professionals who are involved in the Operation Streamline program. That is, activists have primarily emphasized their problems with the individual lawyers and judges who participate in Operation Streamline in Tucson, instead of using other possible tactics that would have broader systemic focus (such as concerns around the bureaucratization of the legal system or the criminalization of immigration as a form of social control). While some activists have participated in letter-writing campaigns to higher-level officials—such as the U.S. Attorney General's office or Arizona Legislative Representatives—or have held protests to attract national media attention, the majority of activist group activities have chosen to focus on the individual legal professionals involved in Operation Streamline as the main targets of their social movement tactics, as seen in the emails and flyers directed at legal professionals. As demonstrated below, external critiques of Operation Streamline (from both activists and the media) have focused on the legal professionals involved and have created the very heightened sense of identity management done by the lawyers and judges, which is the main topic of this research.

Operation Streamline as a Case of *Competing Identity Management*

Work-Related Role Identities

The email that appears at the opening of this chapter questions the professional, work-related role identities of the attorneys and judges that receive it. By asking attorneys and judges to recuse themselves due to the problematic nature of Operation Streamline, it emphasizes caring about "justice for defendants" as an essential work-related role expectation for legal professionals involved in Operation Streamline. In addition to calling the program "wrong" and the driver of "millions of dollars a year in court and prison costs," it calls the "fast-track" system a "violat[ion of] constitutional principles." These legally pointed critiques, however unsophisticated, demonstrate the issue of role strain for legal professionals involved in Operation Streamline. The writers of the email are calling upon work-related behavioral expectations of attorneys and judges. In doing so, they are indicating that Operation Streamline legal professionals may not be fulfilling their work-related ethical obligations and thus failing at their role.

All attorneys and judges involved in Operation Streamline are faced with work-related role strain, or inconsistencies of behavioral expectations within their role as legal professionals. In this case, a major inconsistency exists between "formal-rational" or procedural justice (completing the daily legal work of Operation Streamline) and "substantive-rational" or reasonable justice, whereby legal professionals are expected to actually provide their defendants with a fair outcome (Weber 1978). Prior literature reveals these two poles of justice create work-related role strain for attorneys and judges in other situations, such as restorative justice programs (Olson and Dzur 2003) or sentencing consideration (Longfei 2018), particularly in examining how legal institutions do or do not support ideological assumptions of legal professionals (Blumberg 1967).

Formal-rational justice represents a "status-neutral" enactment of the legal system—essentially just following the formally laid out legal rules and proceedings—or going by the book. Substantive justice, on the other hand, interprets the law using extra-legal norms and values, such as a broader sense of what is right and wrong. These two poles often exist in tension (Lempert and Sanders 1986; Stryker 2007) and are central to the work-related role strain felt by attorneys and judges involved in Operation Streamline. Operation Streamline currently complies with *formal* justice requirements, but most of those who are not directly involved in Operation Streamline (and many insiders) see it as lacking *substantive* justice—that is to say, it "often just feels wrong," as Jesús, a Latino CJA attorney described it. Activists interrogate the work-related role identities and role-related behavioral expectations of Operation Streamline attorneys and judges by emphasizing the lack of substantive justice in this program, creating work-related role strain for legal professionals.

The mass email is only one of many requests most respondents receive to resign their post. For example, a respondent showed me one letter from the End Streamline Coalition that claims in bold lettering: "It is a fundamental responsibility of every judge and magistrate to refuse to participate in any proceeding that does not comport with constitutional, ethical, or due process principles." Use of the term "responsibility" clearly connotes a work-related role expectation of substantive justice that is being violated by Operation Streamline judges in the eyes of these activists.

The stated aim of these tactics is to end the program by eliminating all of the attorneys and judges who could participate in the proceedings through their voluntary resignations. Perhaps recognizing that the mass emails had no effect they could discern—that is no attorneys of judges left the program—in a later campaign, a few members of the End Streamline Coalition, acting without the full support of the group, set up "StreamlineLawyers. com." This website, which is no longer actively maintained, listed the names of about 35 Operation Streamline CJA panel attorneys under the caption: "Can you trust them to defend you?" These lawyers' names were posted below accusations that they were breaking the Arizona Rules of Professional Conduct and violating the "principles of the law" by participating in Operation Streamline. The now-defunct website also provided a link where visitors could file a complaint with the American Bar Association against these attorneys. Using attorneys' own professional organizations against them and mobilizing attorneys' code of ethical conduct presented a particularly pointed challenge of the work-related role identity of these attorneys. Several of the respondents in this study were among the listed attorneys on the site. Figure 1.2 provides one slide from the opening page of the website questioning the constitutionality of Operation Streamline lawyers' work.

The same group circulated a paper flyer in downtown Tucson on several occasions naming and picturing one specific attorney involved in Operation Streamline as well. This particularly personal attack seen in Figure 1.3

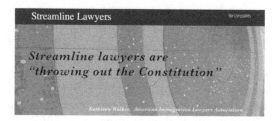

Figure 1.2 StreamlineLawyers.com (2014) Screenshot

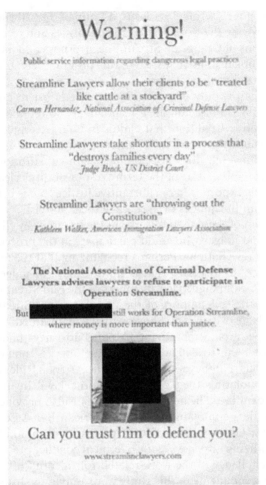

Figure 1.3 Flyer Targeting Operation Streamline Attorney

called out the attorney for continuing to work in "Operation Streamline, where money is more important than justice."

   With these tactics, the activist groups are highlighting legal profession-als' role identities and asking if they comply with what the general pub-lic should expect from an attorney or judge. Questioning the work-related role of those involved in Operation Streamline—asking if they are ethical, professional, and trustworthy—highlights the public's role expectations for these defense attorneys and magistrate judges. As expected, when I began my research, and as will be demonstrated through the findings, these tactics have caused those involved Operation Streamline to engage in extra identity management in consideration of what it means to fulfill their work-related role in Operation Streamline. However, more than just their work-related role identity is also called into question.

Social Identities

In addition to the challenges posed to professional, work-related role identities, activist groups, and media coverage of Operation Streamline bring up the racialized nature of the proceedings in their rhetoric. This is also in line with prior social science literature on immigration as a racialized project in the United States (Chacón 2009, 2012; Menjívar and Abrego 2012; Molina 2014; Golash-Boza 2015). This critique brings in racial/ethnic social identity expectations that may compete with work-related role identity (attorney or judge) expectations. For example, reporting for an online progressive news source called *Truthout*, McNeil (2013) quotes an attorney who quit doing Operation Streamline proceedings in Tucson because "they are not doing Streamline on anyone else but Mexican citizens. It is shocking and it is appalling, and it is disgusting. Underlying it is xenophobia and racism and disregard of rights of people that fit a general description" (2). While making a "separate but unequal" comparison between how Operation Streamline and Jim Crow laws treat specific racial/ ethnic groups, the article brings to the forefront the racial/ethnic component underlying Operation Streamline. In practice, Operation Streamline is indeed a specialized program designed for Spanish-speaking defendants violating sub-sections 1325 and 1326, though it has no overt nationality or racial/ethnic requirement. Many of the legal professionals I interviewed were quick to explain that the *en masse* prosecution of noncitizens "who all happen to be non-white" (Harry, non-Latino, CJA) is merely a byproduct of living close to the México-U.S. border. This justification of course ignores the long history of immigration-based racism in the United States, from 1790's H.R. 40 Naturalization Bill that restricted citizenship to those met the categorization of "free white person;" to the Chinese Exclusion Act (1882) and the Oriental Exclusion Act (1924); to the Bracero Program (1942–1964) and Operation Wetback (1950–1954).

Some media coverage specifically suggested that Latino/a attorneys and judges in particular should be loath to participate in Operation Streamline based on their racial/ethnic social identity. Indeed, contemporary Latino/a identity construction is frequently interwoven with issues of migration (Ochoa 2004; Cobas, Duany, and Feagin 2009; Roth 2009; Jiménez 2010; Martínez and Gonzalez 2021). The racialized history of immigration and the complexity of Latino/a racial/ethnic social identity demonstrates the necessity of this research to examine the additional behavioral standards that come from *competing identity management* of one's work-related role and one's social identity, specifically if one is a Latino/a attorney or judge involved in a racialized immigration proceeding.

Several respondents shared with me an article by journalist Max Blumenthal that asks if Latino/a attorneys and judges should demand even higher levels of justice because of their shared social identity with border-crossers. In his blog, Blumenthal (2010) discusses a Latina federal public defender (FPD), who said, with tears in her eyes, in answer to why she continues to work on Operation Streamline, "we're all parasites." She and a more activist-focused county public defender who was also Latina led him through his visit to Operation Streamline. These guides were, he observed, "the only Latinas in the room not in chains" during the proceeding (Blumenthal 2010:5). He provides the FPD's personal immigration history—that she is a second-generation Mexican-American—and he emphasizes her distress at "watching an entire class of people get stripped of their constitutional rights" (Blumenthal 2010:6). Again, the issue of the race/ethnicity of defendants is central, but it is also linked to the race/ethnicity of the attorneys and judges involved. This article and others like it suggest that one way social and role identities compete is that they intensify work-related role identity behavioral expectations for Latino/a attorneys and judges more than for attorneys and judges of other races/ethnicities. That is, work-related role expectations (especially substantive justice) are more stringent for some attorneys and judges (Latino/as) than others based on their race/ethnicity as a competing social identity. More broadly speaking, critics argue it should be harder for people who share a racial/ethnic social identity with those who are being prosecuted to justify their continued participation in Operation Streamline.

Media mentions of race/ethnicity concur with much of the activist conversation I heard while at Operation Streamline proceedings. Many anti-Streamline activists suggest that the problematic *en masse* and compressed proceeding of Operation Streamline happen because of systematic racism within the broader criminal justice system (and in larger society). One particularly outspoken activist who regularly attends Operation Streamline as a witness for her socially active church explained to me that the "railroading" of defendants through Operation Streamline should be of concern to all citizens: "How long before these unconstitutional practices move from the mostly-Mexican and all-brown population of these immigration proceedings to all U.S. citizens? Hardly any time at all, I am guessing" (Fieldnotes November 14, 2014). Her projection indeed matches documented trends in the increase of rapid-resolution proceedings, or "rocket-dockets" as one of my respondents called them. For example, there have been studies on the upsurge of federal plea agreements (Wright 2005; Crespo 2018) and other rapid resolution proceedings that are similar in structure to Operation Streamline for non-immigration populations (Perschbacher and Bassett 2004). This also aligns with large-scale patterns of increased policing of low-level offenses (Kohler-Hausmann 2018). As such, Operation Streamline is an immigration-based example of larger trends in punishment and social control of increasing plea agreements and hurried proceedings.

The issues surrounding the social identity of race/ethnicity heavily overlap with the social identity of citizenship/generational status as well. Activists attending hearings emphasized that Operation Streamline is a harbinger, and the offensive treatment of noncitizens will soon transgress the boundary and threaten citizens. The *Truthout* piece emphasizes the racism inherent in targeting "Mexican citizens" as a group. Other media reports also emphasize the use of citizenship/generational status as a social identity group in addition to race/ethnicity. One article lumps the problematic nature of Operation Streamline proceedings together with other instances of "illegal policing and civil rights abuses" that citizens tolerate because they target "immigrants and noncitizens" (Editorial Board of the New York Times 2013). This interpretation puts the social identity of citizenship/generational status above racial/ethnic social identity. In the case of Latino/a attorneys and judges in Operation Streamline, this nationality difference implies that as U.S. citizens and not themselves immigrants, they can use their social identity of citizenship/generational status to distance themselves from their defendants. Chapter 6 further discusses the implications of the social identity of citizenship/generational status for Operation Streamline legal professionals.

Another social identity that overlaps frequently with race/ethnicity is gender, particularly when we think of the inherently intersectional nature of identities (Crenshaw 1989; Hill Collins 1990, 2017). Numerous media articles on Operation Streamline noted the presence of just a few Latina defendants, separated out from the mostly Latino migrant border-crossers. While gender impacts the defendants, it also affects the legal professionals. Women magistrate judges were consistently called more empathetic and compassionate in media and activist conversations than men judges. Women attorneys also emphasized that their work-related role is inherently intertwined with their gender social identity, particularly when dealing with men clients and their activist pasts. Chapter 7 focuses on issues of the social identity of gender for Operation Streamline legal professionals.

Summary

A critical historical analysis of Operation Streamline broadly, as well as the development of the Arizona Denial Prosecution Initiative in Tucson specifically, demonstrates these programs to be the product of an increasingly criminalized and racialized immigration regime. These larger macro systems then impact the ways in which legal professionals implement this policy day after day, year after year. Forces of history come to bear on contemporary understandings of both work-related role identities for attorneys and judges and social identities such as race/ethnicity, citizenship/generational status, and gender, as will be further explored in later chapters.

Given the controversy Operation Streamline has created among activists and in the media, there is evidence of increased scrutiny of the attorneys and judges involved in Operation Streamline proceedings. This scrutiny comes both from media/activist critiques that invoke expectations for professional conduct—representing work-related role identity—and from critiques on the racialized, citizenship-based, and gendered nature of the proceedings—highlighting social identities. Thus, Operation Streamline serves as a case where participants must carefully manage potentially competing identities—the social identities of race/ethnicity, citizenship/generational status, and gender as well as the work-related role identity of their legal profession. This book, therefore, explores the ways attorneys and judges manage their work-related role strain as well as their competing role identities and social identities. All Operation Streamline attorneys and judges experience work-related role strain because activists, media, and scholars frequently argue that participating in the program violates norms of substantive justice. For Latino/a attorneys and judges though, their social identity intensifies this strain. I examine how each group manages this strain and how other social identities such as citizenship/generational status and gender have an impact as well. Exploration of this case helps us to understand how attorneys and judges justify their participation in these flawed systems and how even reluctant individuals sustain systemic inequalities.

References

Abrego, Leisy, Mat Coleman, Daniel Martínez, Cecilia Menjívar, and Jeremy Slack. 2017. "Making Immigrants into Criminals: Legal Processes of Criminalization in the Post-IIRIRA Era." *Journal on Migration and Human Security* 5(3):694–715. https://doi.org/10.1177/233150241700500308.

Argueta, Carla. 2016. "Border Security: Immigration Enforcement Between Ports of Entry." Library of Congress. Congressional Research Service. Retrieved January 15, 2022. https://www.fas.org/sgp/crs/homesec/r42138.pdf.

Blumberg, Abraham S. 1967. "The Practice of Law as Confidence Game: Organizational Cooptation of a Profession." *Law and Society Review* 1(2):15–39. https://doi.org/10.2307/3052933.

Blumenthal, Max. 2010. ""We're All Parasites." This Is Operation Streamline." February 15, 2010. maxblumenthal.com. Retrieved May 3, 2014. http://maxblumenthal.com/2010/02/were-all-parasites-this-is-operation-streamline/.

Bosworth, Mary, Alpa Parmar, and Yolanda Vázquez. 2018. *Race, Criminal Justice, and Migration Control: Enforcing the Boundaries of Belonging*. Oxford: Oxford University Press.

Buentello, Tara, Sarah V. Carswell, Nicholas Hudson, and Bob Libal. 2010. "Operation Streamline: Drowning Justice and Draining Dollars Along the Rio Grande," Grassroots Leadership. Retrieved January 15, 2022. http://grassrootsleadership.org/sites/default/files/uploads/operation-streamline-green-paper.pdf.

Chacón, Jennifer M. 2009. "Managing Migration Through Crime." *Columbia Law Review Sidebar* 109:135–48. http://dx.doi.org/10.2139/ssrn.2033931.

Chacón, Jennifer M. 2012. "Overcriminalizing Immigration." *Journal of Criminal Law and Criminology* 102(3):613–52. https://scholarlycommons.law.northwestern.edu/jclc/vol102/iss3/5.

Cobas, José A., Jorge Duany, and Joe R. Feagin. 2009. *How the United States Racializes Latinos: White Hegemony and Its Consequences.* Boulder, CO: Paradigm Publishers.

Corradini, Michael, Jonathan Allen Kringen, Laura Simich, Karen Berberich, and Meredith Emigh. 2018. "Operation Streamline: No Evidence That Criminal Prosecution Deters Migration." Vera Institute of Justice. Retrieved January 15, 2022. https://www.immigrationresearch.org/system/files/operation_streamline.pdf.

Crenshaw, Kimberlé W. 2017. *On Intersectionality: Essential Writings.* New York, NY: The New Press.

Crenshaw, Kimberlé. 1989. "Demarginalizing the Intersection of Race and Sex: A Black Feminist Critique of Antidiscrimination Doctrine, Feminist Theory and Antiracist Politics." *University of Chicago Legal Forum* 140:139–68.

Crespo, Andrew Manuel. 2018. "The Hidden Law of Plea Bargaining." *Columbia Law Review* 118(5):1303–1424. http://nrs.harvard.edu/urn-3:HUL.InstRepos:37122603.

Editorial Board of the New York Times. 2013. "Not One More." October 27, 2013. nytimes.org. Retrieved January 15, 2022. http://nyti.ms/16fajbd.

Gambino, Lauren. 2010. "Program Prosecutes Illegal Immigrants Before Deporting Them," Arizona State University. News21. Retrieved January 15, 2022. http://asu.news21.com/2010/prosecuting-illegal-immigrants.

García Hernández, Cesar Cuauhtemoc. 2015. *Crimmigration Law.* Chicago, IL: American Bar Association.

Golash-Boza, Tanya Maria. 2015. *Immigration Nation: Raids, Detentions, and Deportations in Post-9/11 America.* Boulder, CO: Paradigm Press.

Grassroots Leadership. 2012. "Operation Streamline: Costs and Consequences" Retrieved January 15, 2022. http://grassrootsleadership.org/sites/default/files/uploads/grl_sept2012_report-final.pdf.

Hill Collins, Patricia. 1990. *Black Feminist Thought: Knowledge, Consciousness, and the Politics of Empowerment.* New York, NY: Routledge.

Jiménez, Tomás R. 2010. *Replenished Ethnicity: Mexican Americans, Immigration, and Identity.* Berkeley, CA: University of California Press.

Kohler-Hausmann, Issa. 2018. *Misdemeanorland.* Princeton, NJ: Princeton University Press.

Lee, Jennifer, and Frank D. Bean. 2007. "Reinventing the Color Line Immigration and America's New Racial/Ethnic Divide." *Social Forces* 86(2):561–86. https://doi.org/10.1093/sf/86.2.561.

Lempert, Richard, and Joseph Sanders. 1986. *An Invitation to Law and Social Science: Desert, Disputes and Distribution.* New York, NY: Longman.

Longfei, S. O. N. G. 2018. "A Comparative Study of the Formal Rule of Law and the Substantive Rule of Law." *Canadian Social Science* 14(3):11–8. http://dx.doi.org/10.3968/10230.

Lydgate, Joanna Jacobbi. 2010. "Assembly-Line Justice: A Review of Operation Streamline." Chief Justice Earl Warren Institute on Race, Ethnicity, and Diversity at the University of California, Berkley Law School. Retrieved January 15, 2022. http://www.law.berkeley.edu/files/operation_streamline_policy_brief.pdf.

Martínez, Daniel E., and Kelsey E. Gonzalez. 2021. "Panethnicity as a Reactive Identity: Primary Panethnic Identification Among Latino-Hispanics in the United States." *Ethnic and Racial Studies* 44(4):595–617. https://doi.org/10.1080/01419870.2020.1752392.

McCombs, Brady. 2007a. "Jail Time in Store for All AZ Crossers." October 25, 2007. *Arizona Daily Star*. Retrieved January 15, 2022. http://azstarnet.com/news/local/border/jail-time-in-store-for-all-az-crossers/article_b10a5bc4-a1d0-564d-b0b5-fc8d1048d757.html.

McCombs, Brady. 2007b. "Bp May Have to Rein in Its Zero-Tolerance Plan." November 23, 2007. *Arizona Daily Star*. Retrieved January 15, 2022. http://azstarnet.com/news/local/crime/bp-may-have-to-rein-in-its-zero-tolerance-plan/article_4d83c082-7537-56e1-b919-2fa8365900e5.html.

McCombs, Brady. 2009. "Hearings for Entrants Taking More Time." December 13, 2009. *Arizona Daily Star*. Retrieved January 15, 2022. http://azstarnet.com/news/local/border/hearings-for-entrants-taking-more-time/article_b141f49b-8d5d-5106-bdcb-8eedf6c170d8.html.

McCombs, Brady. 2010. "Border Boletín: A Close Look at Operation Streamline (Updated Again)." September 13, 2010. *Arizona Daily Star*. Retrieved January 15, 2022. http://azstarnet.com/news/blogs/border-boletin/article_2f2d7ea8-bf5e-11df-a3ef-001cc4c002e0.html.

McNeil, S. Truthout "Streamlined Deportation: "No One Here in This Room Can Help You."" January 3, 2013. truthout.org. Retrieved January 15, 2022. http://truth-out.org/news/item/13580-streamlined-deportation-no-one-here-in-this-room-can-help-you.

Menjívar, Cecilia and Abrego, Leisy J. 2012. "Legal Violence: Immigration Law and the Lives of Central American Immigrants." *American Journal of Sociology* 117(5):1380–1421. https://doi.org/10.1086/663575.

Molina, Natalia. 2014. *How Race Is Made in America: Immigration, Citizenship, and the Historical Power of Racial Scripts*. Los Angeles, CA: University of California Press.

Moore, Solomon. 2009. "Push on Immigration Crimes Is Said to Shift Focus." *The New York Times*. A1. Retrieved January 15, 2022. http://www.nytimes.com/2009/01/12/us/12prosecute.html?pagewanted=all&_r=0.

Murillo, Lupita, and Paul Birmingham. 2020. "Digging Deeper: Procedures at Federal Courthouse Impacted by Covid-19." KVOA News 4 Tucson, March 23, 2020. Retrieved January 15, 2022: https://www.kvoa.com/coronavirus/digging-deeper-procedures-at-federal-courthouse-impacted-by-covid-19/article_1520b702-3f8b-567e-9030-05ba7d546d87.html.

Ochoa, Gilda L. 2004. *Becoming Neighbors in a Mexican American Community: Power, Conflict, and Solidarity*. Austin, TX: University of Texas Press.

Olson, Susan M., and Albert W. Dzur. 2003. "Reconstructing Professional Roles in Restorative Justice Programs." *Utah Law Review* 1:57–89.

Perschbacher, Rex R., and Debra Lyn Bassett. 2004. "The End of Law" *Boston University Legal Review* 84:1–62.

Robbins, Ted. 2010a. "Border Patrol Program Raises Due Process Concerns" September 14, 2010. npr.org. Retrieved January 15, 2022. http://www.npr.org/templates/story/story.php?storyid=129780261.

Robbins, Ted. 2010b. "Claims of Border Program Success Are Unproven" September 13, 2010. npr.org. Retrieved January 15, 2022. http://www.npr.org/templates/story/story.php?storyid=129827870.

Robbins, Ted. 2010c. "Border Convictions: High Stakes, Unknown Price" September 14, 2010. npr.org. Retrieved January 15, 2022. http://www.npr.org/templates/story/story.php?storyid=129829950.

Roth, Wendy D. 2009. "'Latino/a Before the World': The Transnational Extension of Panethnicity." *Ethnic and Racial Studies* 32(6):927–47. https://doi.org/10.1080/01419870802245042.

Seghetti, Lisa. 2014. "Border Security: Immigration Enforcement Between Ports of Entry." Library of Congress. Congressional Research Service. Retrieved January 15, 2022. https://trac.syr.edu/immigration/library/p10204.pdf.

Stafford, Mark C., and Mark Warr. 1993. "A Reconceptualization of General and Specific Deterrence." *Journal of Research in Crime and Delinquency* 30(2):123–35. https://doi.org/10.1177/0022427893030002001.

Streamlinelawyers.com. 2014. Members of the End Streamline Coalition. Retrieved May 3, 2014. https://www.streamlinelawyers.com.

Stryker, Robin. 2007. "Half Empty, Half Full, Or Neither: Law, Inequality, and Social Change in Capitalist Democracies." *Annual Review of Law and Social Science* 3(1):69–97. https://doi.org/10.1146/annurev.lawsocsci.3.081806.112728.

Stumpf, Juliet. 2006. "The Crimmigration Crisis: Immigrants, Crime and Sovereign Power." *American University Law Review* 56(2):367–419. http://digitalcommons.wcl.american.edu/aulr/vol56/iss2/3.

Trevizo, Perla. 2013. "'Operation Streamline' Takes Hard Line on Illegal Border Crossers." March 24, 2013. *Arizona Daily Star*. Retrieved January 15, 2022. http://azstarnet.com/news/local/border/operation-streamline-takes-hard-line-on-illegal-border-crossers/article_35cb6dc5-45e3-55e5-b471-c1dd2a72bc31.html.

U.S. Attorneys' Office. 2002. "Annual Statistical Report, Fiscal Year 2002." Retrieved January 15, 2022. https://www.justice.gov/sites/default/files/usao/legacy/2006/09/21/02_stat_book.pdf.

U.S. Attorneys' Office. 2012. "Annual Statistical Report, Fiscal Year 2012." Retrieved January 15, 2022. http://www.justice.gov/usao/reading_room/reports/asr2012/12statrpt.pdf.

U.S. Attorneys' Office. 2019. "Annual Statistical Report, Fiscal Year 2019." Retrieved January 15, 2022. https://www.justice.gov/usao/page/file/1285951/download.

U.S. Attorneys' Office. 2020. "Annual Statistical Report, Fiscal Year 2020." Retrieved January 15, 2022. https://www.justice.gov/usao/page/file/1390446/download.

U.S. Department of Justice. 2010. "Immigration Offenders in the Federal Justice System, 2010." Retrieved January 15, 2022. http://www.bjs.gov/content/pub/pdf/iofjs10.pdf

Weber, Max. 1978. *Economy and Society: An Outline of Interpretive Sociology*. In Roth, Guenther and Claus Wittich, Eds. Berkeley, CA: University of California Press.

Wright, Ronald. 2005. "Trial Distortion and the End of Innocence in Federal Criminal Justice" *University of Pennsylvania Law Review* 154:79–156. https://doi.org/10.2307/25047583.

2 COMPETING IDENTITY MANAGEMENT

In researching attorneys' and judges' identity management in Operation Streamline, I build on an integrative framework of identity research from social psychology and the sociology of culture to develop a conceptualization of *competing identity management* (see Table 2.1). Using an integrated methodology (detailed in Appendix A) for observing and analyzing identity management strategies, I highlight mechanisms by which competing social and role identities are managed as well as specific situations and other factors that influence these identities.

Identity is a core construct in sociological social psychology and there have been a variety of works that theorize how identities affect personal interaction (Owens 2003). Most centrally, I integrate the traditions of *role identity*—a structural symbolic interactionist strain of identity theory originally developed by Stryker (1980) and expanded by Snow (with Anderson 1987; with McAdam 2000), with *social identity theory*—a categorical view of identity developed by Tajfel (1981, 1982). Furthermore, I integrate two cultural approaches to identity (Cornell and Hartman 1998; Glaeser 2000) dealing with nationality/citizenship and race/ethnicity with the above social psychological views. I then use Goffman's (1959, 1967) work on impression management and interaction rituals as an additional way to examine the enactment of identity.

Structural Symbolic Interactionism: Role Identity and Processes

This book draws on a host of theorists who have started to plot the map of human identity. The first of these comes from sociological social psychologist Sheldon Stryker (1980, 1987) who developed a structuralist view of symbolic interactionism that relies heavily on role theory. Roles are defined as relatively stable parts of social structure that individuals play out and that come replete with behavioral expectations. A single individual may play a number of roles—for example, an attorney may also be a parent, a citizen, and a volunteer soccer coach. Though social behavior is never fully determined by these roles, much of individuals' social interaction is based on the

DOI: 10.4324/9781003272410-3

Table 2.1 Overview of Identity Literature

Author	Theory/approach	Concepts used	Observable mechanisms	Application to Operation Streamline
Stryker (1980); and McCall and Simmons (1978)	Role identity theory: structural symbolic interactionism	Role; role strain; salience; situationality	Behavioral expectations; commitment; role playing vs. role making; psychological compartmentalization; bargaining; withdrawal	"Lawyer" or "Judge" Work Role (Defined in opposition to "defendants" or "border-crossers")
Snow and Anderson (1987) and Snow and McAdam (2000)	Role identity theory: processual/negotiated symbolic interactionism	—	Distancing; embracement; fictive story telling; identity construction; identity avowal; identity amplification; identity consolidation; identity extension; identity transformation	Lawyers' and Judges' use of "Identity Work"
Tajfel (1981, 1982) and Tajfel and Turner (1986)	Social identity theory	Social identities	Demonstration of group/ category membership; in-group similarities; out-group differences; in-group preference; out-group discrimination	Racial/ethnic identity; national/citizenship identity
Cornell and Hartman (1998)	Social constructionism approach	—	Thick vs. thin identities; assigned vs. asserted identities	Occupational construction site of identity
Glaeser (2000)	Analytical theory of identity construction	Negotiated identifications; non-negotiated identifications	Identifications with spaces, times, other people, beliefs, ideas, morals, or values	Lawyers' and judges' identifications
Goffman (1959, 1967)	Presentation of self; interaction rituals	Presentation of self; interaction rituals	Impression management; deference and demeanor	Lawyers' and judges' interaction rituals

behavior expectations associated with given roles; to cite a bland example, attorneys wear suits.

Stryker makes a distinction between incidents when an individual merely "plays" a role—following expected behaviors closely—or when they "make" a role—stretching or manipulating it (Stryker 1980:55). For example, an attorney may wear just a simple black or navy suit to fit in to their work-related role, or they make expand their repertoire to less conservative, but still formal suits with pinstripes or plaid patterns. The social structures in which roles are embedded influence the degree to which there is freedom allowed in role making. The work-related roles of "lawyer" and "judges" are also embedded in a larger criminal justice system, a bureaucratic structure that might not allow for much role "making." Because attorneys and judges have fairly strict ethical rules set out by the bar in their state, they have limited option to "make" their behavior around certain courtroom etiquette or legal proceedings (much to the dismay of activists). This lack of structural control may exacerbate work-related role strain because there are very limited ways in which the attorneys and judges can support Operation Streamline defendants. Identity management strategies may become needed if one has difficulties being involved in such a controversial proceeding as Operation Streamline.

The average person holds numerous role identities, typically organized in terms of role salience and role commitment. *Salience* varies situationally. For example, a person may be a mother, a wife, an attorney, and a citizen. When she is interacting with her child, her mother role may be the most salient. When she is on a date with her spouse, her wife role becomes more salient. When she is at work, her attorney role is most salient. When she pays her taxes, her citizenship/generational status social identity is most salient, although the U.S. tax structure dictates that her occupation, parenthood, and marital status are still salient as well.

Commitment also varies situationally. Renouncing motherhood is far less common than renouncing wifehood (divorce), and an attorney may not experience significant identity change by switching firms. Renouncing citizenship is for many people a costly step. Thus, their ascending order of commitment for this one individual may be attorney, wife, citizen, mother. As such, salience and commitment can vary situationally as the role identity at hand is "called-up" by structural circumstances (Stryker 1980:61).

In light of widespread agreement that occupation is often salient in social interaction (Stryker 1980; Stryker and Serpe 1994; Jackson, Thoits, and Taylor 1995; Stryker and Burke 2000), the work-related role identity of "lawyer" or "judge" is highly salient for the respondents I spoke with who were involved in Operation Streamline. Most of these attorneys and judges first and foremost emphasized their own commitment to their occupational role in their interviews as a way of downplaying work-related role conflict.

Salience and commitment in different situations can affect issues of role conflict. *Role conflict* occurs when the variety of roles an individual has impose contrary behaviors expectations on that person. For example, a judge who is also an activist may feel that this second role requires compassion for immigrants but that the role of judge requires application of the law barring them. If they feel that "judge" has greater salience in the courtroom but feel more commitment to their role as activist, this may determine how they resolve the conflict.

Relatedly, *role strain* occurs when individuals work to fulfill multiple conflicting role obligations within a single role. As mentioned, all attorneys and judges involved in Operation Streamline are faced with work-related role strain as they participate in the "formal-rational" or procedural justice parts of legally completing their daily work with defendants while perhaps not feeling as if they truly provide their defendants with "substantive-rational" or extra-legal justice (Weber 1978). These two "poles" of justice require an attorney or judge to manage their work-related role identity in such a way that shows their alternating allegiance to either obligation if they are not aligned in the situation at hand.

Additionally, roles frequently come in pairs or sets—such as parent and children or teacher and students (Merton 1957). Operation Streamline attorneys' and judges' roles are defined partially in contrast to "defendants" or "border-crossers"—those who enter the country without proper documentation ("illegally") and whom lawyers are tasked with defending and judges with presiding over their plea agreements and sentencing. Defendants, lawyers, and judges in the Operation Streamline criminal hearings all have typical role behaviors, norms, obligations, and expectations in their interaction with one another. This role set provides certain behavioral expectations, for example, judges are the figures of authority, defense attorneys are meant to defend clients, and clients are accused of illegal actions.

Here, I focus on work-related role strain within the professional role of being an attorney or judge in the context of Operation Streamline. The obligation to enact proscribed formal justice and promote substantive justice can readily create a strain within Operation Streamline; activists' efforts to convince attorneys or judges to refuse to participate in the program trade on the idea that this strain is excessive and can be martialed for reform. For Operation Streamline attorneys and judges, work-related role strain results from trying to comply with both poles of justice as part of work-related role expectations. Because those who are not directly involved in Operation Streamline (such as activists, courtroom observers, and the media) have so often suggested that Operation Streamline lacks substantive justice, attorneys and judges involved in Operation Streamline are subject to higher levels of work-related role strain between these two poles of formal and substantive justice than lawyers and judges involved in other kinds of proceedings.

There are also several key management strategies for role strain, such as withdrawal, varying commitment, psychological compartmentalization, and bargaining (Stryker and Macke 1978; Stryker 1980; Thoits 1983, 1986; Jackson, Thoits, and Taylor 1995). Withdrawal from the role creating the strain in this case would manifest by attorneys or judges no longer participating in Operation Streamline. Attorneys or judges may display variation in commitment by highlighting that they only participate in Operation Streamline one day a week or one week a month. Psychological compartmentalization is defined as diminishing or denying the importance of one or another aspect of the role causing strain. An attorney or judge who compartmentalizes might make that evident by saying substantive justice is not something they think about very often. Bargaining refers to enhancing the importance of one or another aspect of the role causing strain. For example, an attorney or judge who is bargaining to lessen work-related role strain might highlight how "formal-rational" or procedural justice is more central to the legal system than substantive justice, saying "we are a system of laws." The work-related role strain attorneys and judges who participate in Operation Streamline feel might lead them to manifest all four of these strategies.

Social Identity

Existing in parallel to Stryker's role identity theory, social identity theory was developed by Henri Tajfel (1981, 1982) and examines the effect of categorical group membership on individuals' identity. Social identities can be thought of as cognitive tools that individuals can use to divide, organize, and classify the social environment (Owens 2003). Coming from psychological social psychology, these social identities, Tajfel claims, improve self-esteem by emphasizing the value of members of certain in-groups categorically. In contrast to role identity theory, which requires structure and interaction, Tajfel sought to explain large-scale, inter-group conflict via these categorically based identities.

However, Tajfel's *categorical* social identity theory has been applied to smaller, *interactive* groups as well (Hogg et al. 2004). As such, social identities can be based on minimal group membership criteria or on long-standing national or racial/ethnic divides. These social identities also go beyond mere categorization to effect processes of social action. In explaining Tajfel's (1970) theory, Hogg and Williams (2000) write that "motivational processes affect, and are affected by, group, intergroup, and societal processes, to make people behave and think about themselves and others in ways that are generally characteristics of groups and specifically shaped by the social context" (81). Thus, it suggests membership in a larger group can create in an individual a social identity that can help explain the behavior of that individual.

Tajfel also claims that people frequently demonstrate their membership in the groups to which they belong. They do so through a variety of in-group and out-group distinctions. Members of an in-group will share common markers (in-group similarities), while others do not share these markers (out-group difference). In the case of racial/ethnic identities, this may be phenotypic markers, patterns of speech or dress, or shared cultural traditions. Additionally, once membership is marked, individuals will likely show loyalty, preference, and favoritism toward those in their group and show bias, discrimination, and negativity toward those outside of their group.

Social identities also vary in their value based on given situations, similar to the role strain and salience we see with role identities. In my research setting, several social identities dramatically impact the work of lawyers and judges who take part in Operation Streamline proceedings, even though they all share the same work-related role identity. The social identity I explore most in this study is race/ethnicity—I examine the distinctions in the behaviors of Latino/a attorneys and judges and those of other races/ethnicities. Based on the history of racism as well as the current U.S. racial/ethnic hegemony where Latino/as are being increasingly racialized (Cobas, Duany, and Feagin 2009), this identity comes strongly into play for Operation Streamline attorneys and judges, resulting in group differences between Latino/a legal professionals and non-Latino/as (Chapters 3 and 4).

I also focus on citizenship status (born or naturalized) and immigration generation—that is, whether a person immigrated as an adult (first-generation), as a child (1.5-generation), is the native-born child of immigrants (second-generation), etc. Given the larger societal contexts of meaning of legal work surrounding criminal immigration proceedings, I find that U.S. citizenship is a highly valued social identity among lawyers and judges because it helps them to rationalize their continued participation in the program. Based on prior literature on the importance of within group variation of Latino/as, citizenship/generational status also holds importance in the Operation Streamline context with clear distinctions between the groups of 1.5- and 2nd-generation respondents and respondents who naturalized/migrated themselves later in life and third-generation-plus respondents (Chapter 6).

Gender is also a relevant social identity in this study. Throughout interviews with attorneys and judges involved in Operation Streamline, many women attorneys in particular explained how this social identity impacted their daily work with clients as well as how they think about their own work. From emulating maternal roles to having to convince *machismo* defendants that they are "a real lawyer," Latinas in particular shared how behavioral expectations within their work-related role identity were deeply impacted by their gender social identity (Chapter 7).

In sum, work-related roles and the behavioral expectations that govern how lawyers and judges act in the courtroom end up in competition with a Latino/a racial/ethnic social identity where Latino/a legal professionals are not showing the theoretically expected loyalty, preference, and favoritism toward those in their same social identity group. This also occurs for citizenship/generational status and gender social identities. As such, competition between social and role identities requires distinct identity management processes. In short, mechanisms for dealing with work-related role strain—such as withdrawal, commitment, psychological compartmentalization, and bargaining—are examples of identity management strategies between competing social and role identities.

Identity Work

In order to theorize additional processes of identity management, I turn to the work of David Snow and his colleagues Leon Anderson and Doug McAdam, adding processual and negotiated symbolic interaction to the structural. Snow and Anderson (1987, 1993) examined the various ways people "make" their role identities through processes of role identity construction and avowal. They examine patterns of distancing, embracement, and fictive story telling. Distancing refers to verbally detaching from certain roles, attachments, or institutions. For example, an attorney might say they are nothing like their clients, even if they are the same race/ethnicity. Embracement is the opposite, happening when people verbally affirm and accept given roles, associations, or ideologies. A different attorney might say, for example, they actually do think they are similar to their clients. Fictive story telling refers to explaining one's own past, present, or future through embellishment or fantasizing. For example, attorneys might tell romanticized stories about how or why they chose that profession. I argue these mechanisms may be used not only to make roles, as Snow and Anderson suggest, but also to deal with role strain and with competing social and role identities.

I also propose that the identity processes Snow and McAdam (2000) observe can be marshaled to deal with the strains that affect Operation Streamline attorneys and judges. These are amplification, consolidation, extension, and transformation. Amplification refers to the strengthening of an existing identity to support action. A judge might, for example, explain that this is "what all judges do" to amplify why their work-related role dictates their behavior. Consolidation means combining two prior identities that appeared incompatible into a new identity that supports action. This could be, for example, an attorney highlighting how "real justice" and "formal law" are indeed compatible. Extension indicates expanding an existing identity to be congruent with action. An attorney who goes above and beyond their traditional work-related role by doing extra work for clients is extending their role identity. Transformation suggests the distinct conversion or alteration of existing identity into a new, different identity in order to support action. An attorney who quits the law to become a policy advocate transforms their lawyerly work-related role into an activist role.

Ethnographically observable instances of identity management as well as lawyers' and judges' own descriptions of their identities and behaviors in interviews demonstrate that Operation Streamline attorneys and judges practice amplification, consolidation, extension, and transformation as well as processes of distancing, embracement, fictive story telling. Because a Latino/a social identity is frequently shared with the "defendants" or "border-crossers" that lawyers and judges deal with in their everyday work, it is less valued. Chapter 6 shows that citizenship/generational status in the Operation Streamline setting is more valued. In holding the work-related role identity of "lawyer," or of "judge," these Latino/a individuals most likely seek to distinguish themselves from the roles of "defendant" or "border-crossers," whereas a shared social identity of "Latino/a" minimizes this distinction.

Contrastingly, however, some lawyers and judges who share the Latino/a social identity with defendants instead emphasize how highly valued this social identity is in their ability to build rapport and work with defendants. Latino/a attorneys in particular sometimes use their shared social identity to build rapport as a management strategy to decrease work-related role strain by emphasizing they can better effect substantive justice by understanding border-crossers and explaining the situation to them better. This situationality is explored in Chapter 8.

The process of dealing with this identity competition between a work-related role identity as a lawyer or judge and a social identity as a Latino/a and U.S. citizen is fraught with both micro level and macro level concerns. The conceptualization of *competing identity management*, described below and developed throughout, helps specify different varieties of identity management strategies—or the need for less management altogether—as well as an exploration of under what circumstances certain competing identities are emphasized or de-emphasized.

Cultural Theories of Racial/Ethnic and National/Citizenship Identity

In addition to the social psychological literature on identity, the sociology of culture provides theoretical insights into identity processes as well. Stephen Cornell and Douglas Hartman (1998) suggest that racial/ethnic identity is based on the interaction among the historic, economic, political, and cultural circumstances a given racial/ethnic group faces and the actions of the individual group members engaging in identity construction within these constraints. For example, "Hispanic" on the U.S. Census is only an ethnic category that can also be any race, but there are many arguments about the racialization of this group in recent history (Omi and Winant 1986; Bonilla-Silva 1997; Itzigsohn and Dore-Cabral 2000; Cobas et al. 2009; Roth 2009, 2014). Cornell and Hartman develop a constructionist approach to racial/ethnic identity on two axes: "thick versus thin" and "assigned versus asserted." A person with a thick racial/ethnic identity finds it organizes their life in many ways; a thin racial/ethnic identity has lesser impact. An assigned racial/ethnic identity relies on external forces, such as others' perception of one's race or ethnicity, while a more asserted identity relies on the person who holds it to claim it. While other researchers of racial/ethnic identity broadly and of Latino/a identity specifically use other terms or ideas to understand identity management, I found that Cornell and Hartman's two axes ("thick versus thin" and "assigned versus asserted") most clearly mapped onto the variation within legal professionals for this study.

Among the lawyers and judges I spoke with in Operation Streamline, a constructionist view of racial/ethnic identity adds to the social identity of

"Latino/a" because we can examine to what degree lawyers or judges think of their racial/ethnic identity as thick or thin or as assigned or asserted. Those who have thicker racial/ethnic identities, such as those who identify deeply with their Latino/a heritage, experience greater competition between their social identity and their role identity than those with thinner racial/ethnic identities. Those who see their racial/ethnic identity as asserted, such as a Latino/a who claims that label proudly, felt greater control over how this social identity impacts their work-related behavior and thus felt less work-related role strain than those who were "assigned" the racial/ethnic identity of Latino/a. In this way, Cornell and Hartman provide an additional lens through which to view lawyers' and judges' actions as meaningful parts of their own social identity construction via identity management strategies.

Another cultural theory of identity used in this book comes from what Andreas Glaeser (2000) calls negotiated or non-negotiated identifications. The process of developing negotiated identifications occurs through making connections with spaces, times, other people, beliefs, ideas, morals, and values as they relate to existing categorical social identities such as nationality. Glaeser argues that these negotiated identifications are the building blocks of identity and, when put together, an idea of the self is built. Negotiated identifications are also subject to change over time, which allows people to dynamically give meaning to the world around them.

Despite the suggestion of individual autonomy in these negotiated identifications, there also exists non-negotiated identifications that "are typically inscribed in policies, rules, regulations, and of course the law, but also in customs and traditions" (Glaeser 2000:92). Non-negotiated identifications tend to be less dynamic, as they are tied to larger social and structural pillars. Glaeser's approach thus enriches our understanding of opportunity and constraint in identity processes.

This theoretical model also focuses squarely on observing the patterns of negotiated identifications to particular spaces, time, people, etc. As such, I argue these negotiated identification are form of identity management that can also be observed in this case of attorneys and judges in Operation Streamline. This study will integrate Glaeser's approach by observing how lawyers and judges use the identity management strategy of negotiated identifications to manage their own competing social and role identities. The non-negotiated associations with the law were consistent across all attorneys and judges, but negotiated identifications varied based on their racial/ethnic social identities of Latino/a and non-Latino/a and their citizenship/generational status. For example, some lawyers and judges (Latino/a or non-Latino/a) may make strong negotiated identifications with certain places, time, other people, beliefs, ideas, morals, values, etc. By looking for the different negotiated identifications that lawyers and judges make, I further develop a sense of how these legal professionals manage their various identities and which identities hold more salience in certain circumstances.

Impression Management

Bringing together culture and social psychology, Goffman (1959) suggests that as people take on different roles, they struggle to manage the impressions of themselves that they are displaying to others. Goffman focused on role identities, but I would extend his logic to social identities such as race/ethnicity or citizenship/generational status as well. Like actors in a play, we behave in particular ways to emphasize particular identities to our given "audiences." Goffman's idea of social behavior as interaction ritual (1967) then provides observable evidence of identity processes. Social rules of conduct create the structural constraints in situations that partially determine behavior. For example, if one were to "act" like a lawyer, they would wear a suit, carry a briefcase, use legal jargon in their speech, etc. Thus, impression management can be thought of as an identity management strategy especially related not only to roles, situationality, and job performance, but also to social identities.

In Goffman's perspective, inequality comes into play through symmetrical and asymmetrical relationships between individuals who demonstrate deference—respect, obligation, or duty that an inferior owes to a superior—and demeanor—a behavioral signal that suggests whether or not one is owed deference. Thus, deference and demeanor are also identity management strategies entwined to situationality. This ties directly to Stryker's identity theory and structural symbolic interactionism in that Goffman suggests that the social structure and setting encourages particular behavior based on roles, though again, there is no reason to assume this strategy does not also apply to social identities.

To study the degree to which lawyers or judges' competing social and role identities affect their identity management strategies in the case of Operation Streamline, I examine individual lawyers and judges' identity management strategies using impression management and deference and demeanor. For example, a Latino lawyer who became a naturalized citizen of the United States might emphasize his citizenship status to differentiate himself from a client and also downplay his Mexican heritage which he shares with a client. Thus, in addition to other identity management strategies, I examine participants' use of impression management.

Developing *Competing Identity Management*

The controversy and critical history surrounding Operation Streamline creates an extra level of scrutiny both in the realm of professional, work-related role identity as well as calling up relevant social identities of race/ethnicity, citizenship/generational status, and gender for attorneys and judges involved. Thus, there are difficulties for these attorneys and judges in managing their various competing identities. All attorneys and judges involved in Operation Streamline feel some work-related role strain. This strain is based on the constant assertion by activists/media/legal scholars that Operation Streamline denies *substantive justice* to defendants and therefore attorneys and judges should refuse to apply *formal justice* while completing their assigned cases. This strain requires identity management strategies. The social identity of being Latino/a for attorneys and judges (all of whom were citizens themselves, but of varying generation status and gender) increased work-related role strain as described in Chapter 3 but also led to competition between their professional roles and their social identities, as explored in Chapter 4. My conceptual framework integrates the work of Stryker, Tajfel, Snow with Anderson and McAdam, Cornell and Hartman, Glaeser, and Goffman to explain the conditions under which work-related role strain and competing social and role identities arise and their resultant identity management strategies. Investigation of the identity management strategies the attorneys and judges employ at the micro level to work through these strained and competing identities in order to remain involved in Operation Streamline are also impacted by macro level systems of structural inequality based on racism, nationalism, and patriarchy.

The conceptualization of *competing identity management* uses a very basic definition of identity: One's various conceptions and expressions of self. This is sufficiently broad to incorporate the various types of identities explicated above—most centrally social and role identities. Using this definition, I argue that Operation Streamline legal professionals experience identity strains and competitions, express their unease, and manage their various identities invoked by being involved in the program in different ways because of larger social forces from being inside the criminal justice and immigration systems.

First, most attorneys and judges involved in Operation Streamline, regardless of social identities, evidenced some work-related role strain. They have all been educated, indoctrinated, and socialized into the legal profession with its various behavioral expectations and many aspects of Operation Streamline might be inconsistent with some of these common work-related role expectations for attorneys and judges. I analyze this work-related role strain through the inconsistent poles of formal justice versus substantive justice in Chapter 3. The many questions about due process, constitutionality, Rule 11, etc. that activists, media, and legal scholars have directed at Operation Streamline are likely to make lawyers feel the need to justify their involvement by arguing that these proceedings meet appropriate work-related role behavior regarding both formal and substantive justice.

Using instances of role making and playing; psychological compartmentalization (Stryker 1980); identity extension (Snow and Anderson 1987); fictive story telling (Snow and McAdam 2000); and negotiated identifications (Glaeser 2000), I expect all attorneys and judges to engage in identity management strategies that justify their participation in Operation Streamline based on its formal justice pole and not the substantive justice reservations they may have about these proceedings.

I also find that Latino/a attorneys and judges demonstrate greater identity strain than their non-Latino/a counterparts, detailed in Chapter 4. Issues of race, ethnicity, and immigration are all intricately intertwined (Waters and Eschbach 1995; Massey, Durand, and Malone 2002; Lee and Bean 2004; Calavita 2007). This is especially true near the México-U.S. border and in Operation Streamline, where 99% of the defendants are Latino/a. Many activists have focused their objection to Operation Streamline on its racial/ethnic dimensions and the historically racist project that is immigration control in the United States (Menjívar and Abrego 2012; Molina 2014; Golash-Boza 2015). Thus, controversial proceedings such as Operation Streamline in Tucson, which in its application focuses on a specific racial/ethnic group, are bound to produce racial/ethnic tensions, especially in a state like Arizona with a racially charged climate. The highly racially charged environment in Arizona has been particularly evident since 2010 with the enactment of several state laws against immigrants (such as S.B. 1070) and banning the teaching of Mexican American Studies in the Tucson Unified School District in H.B. 2281 (Anderson and Finch 2014). Attorneys' and judges' work-related role identities are defined in opposition to defendants, as well, who in Operation Streamline are chosen based on language, which can serve as a proxy for racial/ethnic identity (Anderson and Finch 2014, 2017). Thus, attorneys who share a racial/ethnic identity with their border-crosser defendants feel extra work-related role strain and increased scrutiny in their work-role identity and social identity management because they often feel more pulled to the substantive justice pole of their work-related role identity.

Given their competing identities highlighted by the contentious nature of Operation Streamline, I find that Latino/a legal professionals experience more work-related role strain based on their racial/ethnic *social identity,* whereas non-Latino/a attorneys and judges do not need to downplay their own social identities to avoid work-related role strain. This may result in tactics of downplaying social identity cues, such as variation in how they demonstrate racial/ethnic categorical membership. For example, a judge might highlight his American citizenship over his Mexican heritage when explaining why he carries out the law as it is written (formal justice) or over the seemingly unfair outcomes that defendants face (substantive justice).

The conceptualization of *competing identity management,* then, suggests that Latino/a attorneys and judges will use more and different types of identity management strategies to deal with work-related role strain and resultant social and role identity competition than non-Latino/a attorneys and judges. This is because Latino/as have to negotiate both standard work-related role strain and the competition between the role's formal justice pole and their categorical identity calling out for substantive justice for their defendants with whom they share a racial/ethnic social identity. The details of these additional identity management strategies for Latino/a legal professionals involved in Operation Streamline are reviewed in Chapter 4.

However, there are also variations in identity management strategies *within* this group, based on other social identity categories, such as citizenship/generational status and gender. Thus, some Latino/a legal professionals will downplay their racial/ethnic social identity and emphasize their more valued social identity as U.S. citizen. This brings forth different (or often just fewer) identity management strategies. As detailed in Chapter 6, those who are naturalized citizens who migrated themselves later in life (as opposed to born citizens) are more likely to explicitly differentiate themselves from defendants because they were so recently non-citizens. They seek to distance themselves from their clients. This differentiation takes the form of a thin and assigned racial/ethnic social identity for recent migrants. However, overall, born citizens in the 1.5- and 2nd-generation experience more sympathy for defendants and exhibit more work-related role strain than first-generation immigrants. They need only to look to their parents to understand the immigration experience and thus often have thick and asserted Latino/a social identity. Third-generation-plus Latino/as in this study feel the least connection to defendants and experience the least amount of work-related role strain because they identify more strongly as long-time Americans who do not necessarily feel an affinity with Latino/a defendants that would call for a vigorous defense of substantive justice. Thus, third-generation-plus Latino/as also frequently had thin and assigned Latino/a social identities.

As we see in Chapter 8, however, Latino/a legal professionals sometimes mobilize their similarities to defendants to build rapport with them, even if they downplay them in other contexts. The conceptualization of *competing identity management* helps to specify the conditions under which these different strategies are employed to manage strain within role as well as competing social and role identities. Beyond just *why* and *how* these attorneys and judges demonstrate their identity management, *competing identity management* also examines when these different management strategies become more and less relevant, expanding Stryker's ideas of situationality to include what respondents do with different audiences (for themselves and in situations involving different audiences/interlocutors or types of challenges) to manage work-related role strain as well as managing the competition of social and role identities.

Given the amount of activism around Operation Streamline, I find that attorneys and judges manage their identities differently when they interact with activist groups than in other situations. Latino/a attorneys and judges experience more strain and pressure from these outside groups (including the media and legal scholars) than their non-Latino/a counterparts. These Latino/a legal professionals also then use different identity management strategies when they interact with clients as they try to build rapport and trust with this group.

I also find that Spanish language usage is an indicator of social identity and in-group preference in addition to the other types of identity management strategies. For example, those Latino/a legal professionals who use

Spanish more frequently are more likely to have "thick" Latino/a identities (Cornell and Hartman 1998). Language usage can be a cultural indicator of racial/ethnic categories—that is, people use nondominant languages to highlight their racial/ethnic identity (Dressler, Oths, and Gravlee 2005). Spanish language usage has also long been used by researchers as an indicator of acculturation (Vega and Gil 1998; Anderson and Finch 2014, 2017). Studies of Latino/as show that Spanish language preference accounts for the majority of variance in most acculturation measures (Escobar and Vega 2000). "English-Only" laws, which for example, bar teachers from using other languages in the classroom, reflect structural racism, which demonstrate the link between language usage and racial/ethnic groups (Santoro 1999; Macedo 2000). In the heightened racial/ethnic context of Arizona, for example, Arizonans voted English the official language of the state in 2006. In this context, non-Latino/as racialize Latino/a Arizonans because of their Spanish language usage, meaning they assign social identity merely through language preference (Anderson and Finch 2014, 2017).

The remainder of this book examines Operation Streamline empirically as a case of *competing identity management* in order to better understand the variability of and conditions influencing identity management strategies at the micro level based on macro level systems of structural inequality. Invoking the iterative quality of strategic narrative analysis and grounded theory building within a spelled out theoretical terrain—identity management as reviewed in this chapter—I demonstrate the patterns of strategies used and the conditional influences of current systems of structural racism, nationalism, and patriarchy.

With a basic theoretical background that is then informed by empirical evidence, full development of the conceptualization of *competing identity management* helps to specify the competition between social identities and role identities. This allows me to build theoretical propositions in the Conclusion about the conditions under which particular identity management strategies are adopted and further conceptualize what those strategies are. This in turn paves the way for future work to test, further generalize, and expand the conceptualization of *competing identity management*.

References

Anderson, Kathryn Freeman, and Jessie K. Finch. 2017. "The Role of Racial Microaggressions, Stress, and Acculturation in Understanding Latino Health Outcomes in the U.S.A." *Race and Social Problems* 9(3):218–33. https://doi.org/10.1007/s12552-017-9212-2.

Anderson, Kathryn Freeman, and Jessie K. Finch. 2014. "Racially Charged Legislation and Latino/A Health Disparities: The Case of Arizona's S.B. 1070." *Sociological Spectrum* 34(6):526–48. https://doi.org/10.1080/02732173.2014.947452.

Bonilla-Silva, Eduardo. 1997. "Rethinking Racism: Toward a Structural Interpretation." *American Sociological Review* 62(3):465–80. https://doi.org/10.2307/2657316.

Bonilla-Silva, Eduardo. 2014. *Racism Without Racists: Color-Blind Racism and the Persistence of Racial Inequality in the United States*. Fourth Edition. New York, NY: Rowman and Littlefield Publishers.

Calavita, Kitty. 2007. "Immigration Law, Race, and Identity." *Annual Review of Law and Social Science* 3(1):1–20. https://doi.org/10.1146/annurev.lawsocsci.3.081806.112745.

Cobas, José A., Jorge Duany, and Joe R. Feagin. 2009. *How the United States Racializes Latinos: White Hegemony and Its Consequences*. Boulder, CO: Paradigm Publishers.

Cornell, Stephen, and Douglas Hartman. 1998. *Ethnicity and Race: Making Identities in a Changing World*. Thousand Oaks, CA: Pine Forge Press.

Dressler, William W., Kathryn S. Oths, and Clarence C. Gravlee. 2005. "Race and Ethnicity in Public Health Research: Models to Explain Health Disparities." *Annual Review of Anthropology* 34:231–52. https://doi.org/10.1146/annurev.anthro.34.081804.120505.

Escobar, Javier I., and William A. Vega. 2000. "Mental Health and Immigration's AAAs: Where Are We and Where Do We Go from Here?" *Journal of Nervous and Mental Disease* 188(11):736–40. https://doi.org/10.1097/00005053-200011000-00003.

Glaeser, Andreas. 2000. *Divided in Unity: Identity, Germany, and the Berlin Police*. Chicago, IL: University of Chicago Press.

Goffman, Erving. 1959. *The Presentation of Self in Everyday Life*. Garden City, NY: Doubleday.

Goffman, Erving. 1967. *Interaction Ritual: Essays on Face-To-Face Behavior*. Garden City, NY: Doubleday.

Golash-Boza, Tanya Maria. 2015. *Immigration Nation: Raids, Detentions, and Deportations in Post-9/11 America*. Boulder, CO: Paradigm Press.

Hogg, Michael A., and Kipling D. Williams. 2000. "From I to We: Social Identity and the Collective Self." *Group Dynamics: Theory, Research, and Practice* 4(1): 81–97. https://doi.org/10.1037/1089-2699.4.1.81.

Hogg, Michael A., Dominic Abrams, Sabine Oteen, and Steve Hinkle. 2004. "The Social Identity Perspective: Intergroup Relations, Self-Conception, and Small Groups." *Small Group Research* 35:246–76. https://doi.org/10.1177/1046496404263424.

Itzigsohn, Jose, and Carlos Dore-Cabral. 2000. "Competing Identities? Race, Ethnicity and Panethnicity Among Dominicans in the United States." *Sociological Forum* 15(2)225–47. https://www.jstor.org/stable/684815.

Jackson, Pamela Braboy, Peggy A. Thoits, and Howard F. Taylor. 1995. "Composition of the Workplace and Psychological Well-Being: the Effects of Tokenism on America's Black Elite." *Social Forces* 74(2):543–57. https://doi.org/10.1093/sf/74.2.543.

Lee, Jennifer, and Frank D. Bean. 2004. "America's Changing Color Lines: Immigration, Race/Ethnicity, and Multiracial Identification." *Annual Review of Sociology* 30(1):221–42. https://doi.org/10.1146/annurev.soc.30.012703.110519.

Macedo, Donaldo. 2000. "The Colonialism of the English Only Movement." *Educational Researcher* 29(3):5–24. https://doi.org/10.3102/0013189x029003015.

Massey, Douglas S., Jorge Durand, and Nolan J. Malone. 2002. *Beyond Smoke and Mirrors: Mexican Immigration in an Era of Economic Integration*. New York, NY: Russell Sage Foundation.

McCall, George J., and J. L. Simmons. 1978. *Identities and Interactions: An Examination of Human Associations in Everyday Life.* New York, NY: Free Press.

Menjívar, Cecilia and Leisy J. AbregoLegal Violence: Immigration Law and the Lives of Central American Immigrants." *American Journal of Sociology* 117(5):1380–421. https://doi.org/10.1086/663575.

Merton, Robert K. 1957. "The Role-Set: Problems in Sociological Theory." *The British Journal of Sociology* 8(2):106–20. https://doi.org/10.2307/587363.

Molina, Natalia. 2014. *How Race Is Made in America: Immigration, Citizenship, and the Historical Power of Racial Scripts.* Los Angeles, CA: University of California Press.

Omi, Michael, and Howard Winant. 1986. *Racial Formation in the United States: From the 1960s to the 1990s.* New York, NY: Routledge and Kegan Paul.

Owens, Timothy J. 2003. "Self and Identity" Pp. 205–32 in *The Handbook of Social Psychology,* Delamater, John D., Ed. New York, NY: Kluwer/Plenum.

Roth, Wendy D. 2009. "'Latino/a Before the World': The Transnational Extension of Panethnicity." *Ethnic and Racial Studies* 32(6):927–47. https://doi.org/10.1080/01419870802245042.

Santoro, Wayne. 1999. "Conventional Politics Takes Center Stage: The Latino Struggle Against English-Only Laws." *Social Forces* 77(3):887–909. https://doi.org/10.2307/3005965.

Snow, David A., and Leon Anderson. 1987. "Identity Work Among the Homeless: The Verbal Construction and Avowal of Personal Identities." *American Journal of Sociology* 92:1336–71. https://www.jstor.org/stable/2779840.

Snow, David A., and Doug McAdam. 2000. "Identity Work Processes in the Context of Social Movements: Clarifying the Identity/Movement Nexus" Pp. 41–67 in *Self, Identity, and Social Movements,* Stryker, Sheldon, Owens, Timothy J., and White, Robert W., Eds. Minneapolis, MN: University of Minnesota Press.

Snow, David A., and Leon Anderson. 1993. *Down on Their Luck: A Study of Homeless Street People.* Berkeley, CA: University of California Press.

Stryker, Sheldon, and Anne Statham Macke. 1978. "Status Inconsistency and Role Conflict." *Annual Review of Sociology* 4: 57–90. https://doi.org/10.1146/annurev.so.04.080178.000421.

Stryker, Sheldon, and Peter J. Burke. 2000. "The Past, Present, and Future of an Identity Theory." *Social Psychology Quarterly* 63(4):284–97. https://doi.org/10.2307/2695840.

Stryker, Sheldon, and Richard T. Serpe. 1994. "Identity Salience and Psychological Centrality: Equivalent, Overlapping, or Complementary Concepts?" *Social Psychology Quarterly* 57(1):16–35. https://doi.org/10.2307/2786972.

Stryker, Sheldon. 1980. *Symbolic Interactionism: A Social Structural Version.* Menlo Park, CA: Benjamin/Cummings Publishing Company.

Stryker, Sheldon. 1987. "The Vitalization of Symbolic Interactionism" *Social Psychology Quarterly,* 50(1):83–94. https://doi.org/10.2307/2786893.

Tajfel, Henri. 1970. "Aspects of National and Ethnic Loyalty." *Social Science Information* 9(3):119–144. https://doi.org/10.1177/053901847000900305.

Tajfel, Henri. 1981. *Human Groups and Social Categories: Studies in Social Psychology.* Cambridge, UK: Cambridge University Press.

Tajfel, Henri. 1982. *Social Identity and Intergroup Relations.* Cambridge, UK: Cambridge University Press.

Tajfel, Henri, and R.J. Turner. 1986. "Social Identity Theory of Intergroup Behavior" Pp. 7–24 in *Psychology of Intergroup Relations*, Worchel, Stephen, and Austin, William, Eds. Chicago, IL: Nelson-Hall.

Thoits, Peggy A. 1983. "Multiple Identities and Psychological Well-Being: A Reformulation and Test of the Social Isolation Hypothesis." *American Sociological Review* 48(2):174–87. https://doi.org/10.2307/2095103.

Thoits, Peggy A. 1986. "Multiple Identities: Examining Gender and Marital Status Differences in Distress." *American Sociological Review* 51(2):259–72. https://doi.org/10.2307/2095520.

Vega, William, and Andres G. Gil. 1998. *Drug Use and Ethnicity in Early Adolescence*. New York, NY: Plenum Press.

Waters, Mary C., and Karl Eschbach. 1995. "Immigration and Ethnic and Racial Inequality in the United States." *Annual Review of Sociology* 21(1):419–46. http://dx.doi.org/10.1146/annurev.so.21.080195.002223.

Weber, Max. 1978. *Economy and Society: An Outline of Interpretive Sociology*. Roth, Guenther and Wittich, Claus, Eds. Berkeley, CA: University of California Press.

3 "YOU MIGHT THINK IT'S UNJUST, BUT IT'S PERFECTLY LEGAL"

WORK-RELATED ROLE STRAIN FOR LEGAL PROFESSIONALS

Mickey has been a defense attorney working on Operation Streamline in Arizona since its inception in 2008. He works on the Criminal Justice Act panel (CJA) and represents "indigent" clients who cannot afford their own attorneys. He has a friendly but disheveled presence, with suit jackets that seem just a bit too small for his blockish frame. Identifying as a white man, he has a history of primarily working as a defense attorney in misdemeanor city and county courts. He says, "I keep up with the controversy" about Operation Streamline, "but I don't think there's anything unethical." He goes on:

> One of the things I dislike about it is that I find these activists irritating. They might—I mean it's fine if you might think it's unjust, but it's perfectly legal. They say we're unethical because we're doing it. There's nothing unethical in what we're doing. It's not unethical to represent or defend somebody who's charged with a crime even if you don't agree with the law. It's not unethical to represent them just because they're not getting a good deal. I just think these groups are wrong headed.

Summarizing his position, Mickey said, "I agree with their sentiments, but I'm not going to stop doing it." In agreeing that the program can be seen as unjust, or that he might not agree with the law, while agreeing to continue doing the work, Mickey shows the exact nuanced identity management needed for any attorney to navigate the work-related role strain brought about by involvement in Operation Streamline.

As this chapter will lay out, there are racialized patterns at work in the exploration of identity management strategies around work-related role and social identity for the case of Operation Streamline. While some attorneys and judges would expressly deny any personal experience of racialized differences in their work, interviews with over 50 legal professionals showed larger-level patterns that demonstrated Latino/as and non-Latino/as experience their work differently, particularly when it comes to role strain. Latino/a legal professionals, because of the inherent racialized processes around the U.S. immigration and criminal justice systems (Browne-Marshall 2013; Golash-Boza 2015) felt more conflict between the formal and substantive justice poles of their work as legal

DOI: 10.4324/9781003272410-4

professionals in Operation Streamline. That is to say, it was harder for Latino/a legal professionals to feel good about their work in Operation Streamline.

I define work-related role strain as instances of respondents problematizing Operation Streamline—such as explaining that they do not personally like Operation Streamline, or they think it is an ineffective program—despite continuing to participate. In this chapter, I present analysis that shows Latino/a attorneys and judges more often describe work-related role strain than non-Latino/a attorneys and judges. This work-related role strain variation between Latino/a and non-Latino/a attorneys and judges who participate in Operation Streamline proceedings also results in competing social and role identities. This strain and competition results in a variation of identity management strategies based on legal professionals' race/ethnicity. This demonstration of work-related role strain that results in increased competition between social and role identities, which leads Latino/a attorneys and judges specifically to more frequently use identity management strategies compared to non-Latino/as, and, in some cases, to use different identity management strategies altogether. In his now-classic work *Racism Without Racists,* Bonilla-Silva (2014) describes how structural racism in the United States broadly is upheld through U.S. institutions even if individuals involved in those institutions do not think they are contributing to racial/ethnic inequality. The differences between Latino/a and non-Latino/a legal professionals show how structural racism plays out in immigration and criminal cases, which ties micro level individual behaviors to larger macro level systems of social inequality.

I first explain the two poles of work-related role strain experienced by almost all attorneys and judges in Operation Streamline—"substantive justice" versus "formal justice." I then present data pertaining to the increased demonstration of strain specifically for Latino/a attorneys and judges. I go on to describe the identity management strategy of identity consolidation that is used by a majority of all respondents but used slightly more by Latino/a attorneys and judges. In terms of work-related role identity management strategies, Latino/a attorneys and judges are also more likely than non-Latino/a attorneys and judges to use the management strategies of role making/identity extension, psychological compartmentalization, and fictive story telling while non-Latino/as use role playing more often.

The "Substantive Justice" Pole of Work-Related Role Strain

Substantive justice involves interpreting the law using extra-legal norms and values. That is, substantive justice asks whether the operation and impact of the law is consistent with society's—or even the attorney's own—ethics, morality, politics, and other socially constructed concerns. There is an assumption that attorneys should serve true justice to meet their work-related role obligations, not just formal justice. That is, they are not just "going through the motions" but are instead sincerely "fighting the good fight." Legal scholars as far back as Max Weber (1978) in *Economy and Society* have highlighted substantive justice as a focus for legal professionals. Despite the oft-cited jokes of unscrupulous lawyers, the idea of substantive justice highlights the expectation that lawyers should be trying to serve the common good.

When describing their work and work-related role in Operation Streamline, many attorneys and judges, both Latino/a and non-Latino/a, suggested they had substantive justice concerns about their daily job: *are the laws they are following in Operation Streamline actually just?* This concern is what causes many of the Operation Streamline legal professionals to experience work-related role strain.

Connor, a Latino CJA attorney, couched his concerns in terms of an incident he had witnessed during one of his first Operation Streamline proceedings. Connor noticed another defense attorney, César, was shaking and taking deep breaths. Connor was not the only one who noticed and the judge in the courtroom asked César, "Is everything okay?" As Connor recalled, César answered, "No, ma'am, everything's not okay. You know, there's about 75 people walking out of here in chains who really didn't do anything wrong. And so that distresses me." Connor reflected:

> I remember that distinctly. When he said that, I was like, 'Yeah, that's kind of how I feel, too,' you know? You got a bunch of people here in chains. They just want to come here and work. They have families, they're poor, and for probably largely political purposes, they're swept up into this terrible proceeding. Eric Holder or whoever else won't put a stop to it, you know?

A number of research participants felt that illegal entry should not be considered a criminal offense punishable by jail time, as César suggested. Many attorneys and judges understood that Operation Streamline defendants were economic migrants, coming to the United States because of the need to work and support themselves and/or their families (Massey 2013). Indeed, the fact that crossing a border is often motivated by economic inequality rooted in larger United States imperialism—and not violent or criminal intent—causes many defense attorneys to wonder, in the words of one Latina CJA attorney Carlita, if the United States is "wasting their time and taxpayer money" on criminalizing these migrants.

Participants focus on other standards less related to strict issues of law. Some were upset about the arbitrary nature of the program; it seemed to them "just not fair" that some migrants are released by Border Patrol while others went through Operation Streamline or other court proceedings. The ways in which the U.S. Border Patrol chose who is and who is not going into Operation Streamline was not exactly clear to the attorneys or judges working in Operation Streamline, though it was supposedly outlined in the Border Patrol's "Consequence Delivery System." Upon request for this information from the prosecuting attorneys, all of my asks were denied or sent onto other government employees and subsequently ignored. The fact that some migrants were criminalized, and others were not—for the exact same behavior based on seeming luck—was another way that legal professionals I interview used external norms of "right and wrong" and "fairness" to criticize the lack of substantive justice in Operation Streamline.

Valentina, a Latina federal public defender (FPD), describes the program as "disgusting" not only on it being arbitrary, but also on it being "absolutely racist." Some of the attorneys, and certainly many more activists and media portrayals, suggest that the program is an example of racial/ethnic inequality in the U.S. criminal justice system as well as the immigration system. Indeed, prior literature on race, law, and immigration has discussed the underlying systemic racism as it has both influenced and been influenced by racial/ethnic hierarchy in the United States. (Browne-Marshall 2013; Golash-Boza 2015). Molina (2014), for example, suggests that historical forces around racialization projects in the mid-century also created "immigration regimes" that have influenced the racial/ethnic categorization of Mexicans in particular. Other work has shown this is not specific to Mexicans, but other Latino/a people such as Central Americans who are also subject to increased racialization based on immigration polices rooted in white nativism (Rodriguez and Menjívar 2009). This literature suggests that the Illegal Immigration Reform and Immigration Responsibility Act of 1996 (IIRIRA) may as well have been called "The Latino Exclusion Act." This reference to the 1882 Chinese Exclusion Act highlights the racialized nature of this immigration policy's true aim as well as the historic underpinnings of racialized "I" in general (Chacón 2009). IIRIRA also laid the groundwork for the mass criminalization of migrants that is seen in Operation Streamline, linking the systemically racist immigration and criminal justice systems (Abrego et al. 2017; Martínez, Slack, and Martínez-Schuldt 2018). Though not many attorneys made these direct racist claims for themselves, social science and legal literatures certainly support this lack of substantive justice based on systemic racism in Operation Streamline.

Given issues around racism, arbitrary enforcement of the law, and the questioning of immigration offenses needing to even be criminalized, the lack of substantive justice these attorneys and judges describe creates work-related role strain for respondents when compared to the necessary formal justice they are required to carry out. This links with prior literature on the toll that workers face in daily carrying out labor that upholds structures of power and inequality in the United States (Press 2021). At the micro level, these substantive justice issues create work-related role strain, but at the macro level, they uphold the structural racism inherent in the U.S. crimmigration system.

The "Formal Justice" Pole of Work-Related Role Strain

Formal justice has to do with following legal rules in a status-neutral way—the letter of the law. Whether a law is "good" or "just" is not a part of formal justice (Weber 1978). Instead, the focus is on procedure and making sure all proper legal precedents are followed and that constitutionality is upheld. Many attorneys and judges in Operation Streamline used the idea of following already set procedures correctly (a fulfillment of this formal justice work-related role obligation) to justify their participation in Operation Streamline. To some extent, as Salvadór, a Latino CJA attorney, acknowledged, the program meets any standards of formal justice: "You know, Streamline has basically been approved by the Ninth Circuit at least twice." Indeed, in rulings from 2009, 2011, and 2013, the general structure of Operation Streamline was upheld (*U.S. v. Roblero-Solis, 2009; U.S. v. Escamilla-Rojas, 2011; U.S. v. Arqueta-Ramos, 2013*). Because the Ninth-Circuit Court has formally stipulated that the current *en masse* proceeding for Operation Streamline will be allowed to continue with only minor adjustments, these Ninth Circuit cases have never gone on to a higher court for formal legal review. As such, the program has been assessed and permitted by the highest appellate court to which it has been subjected. This is a strong indication that it has met a "formal justice" standard in the current legal system and legal professionals relied on this information heavily to rationalize their continued participation.

At the same time, some attorneys, more often Latino/as, suggested that they doubted Operation Streamline's constitutionality. Salvadór, for example, continued on from his point about the Ninth Circuit, saying that as an attorney he was "basically forced" to accept Operation Streamline because of the appellate court's approval. He argues that Operation Streamline is just "something that has to be done because it's the system in place." To further show formal compliance with laws, he argued that state courts, for example, "basically have similar processes but not as many people." As such, in terms of formal justice he says "unless you fight it in terms of constitutional grounds or whatever" there is little to be done to stop the proceedings from the view of formal justice. While the U.S. Supreme Court has not actually reviewed the constitutionality of Operation Streamline, Salvadór said:

> So now, you just kind of do your work—as lawyers, you work within the procedure set up by the Supreme Court, the state Supreme Court, Congress, and the legislatures. That's what we're forced to do and fight with what they're giving us within the system that exists.

Salvadór was not among the attorneys who directly suggested that Operation Streamline violates substantive justice. He had a very formal justice orientation, suggesting it is not part of his work-related role to have opinions on the substantive justice or question the system, only to carry out his work within the existing system. He also claims he is being "forced" to do this work, though as a CJA attorney, he is technically contracting with the government voluntarily to take on Operations Streamline case work.

Soledad, a Latina CJA attorney, openly said she did not "really like" the Operation Streamline process but "someone should tell [the activists] it's not a terrible process. I know it's not a great process. But it's a legal process," emphasizing that it does not break any known laws and it's been approved by appellate courts. In other words, attorneys and judges justify their participation because Operation Streamline represents "the rules" as formally enunciated by legislation and validated by courts and, as lawyers and judges, it is their job to follow the rules, as formal justice would demand.

Increased Work-Related Role Strain for Latino/a Legal Professionals

Virtually, all of the attorneys and judges I interviewed, both Latino/a and non-Latino/a, had some reservations about Operation Streamline's level of justice, at least when they began participating in the procedure. For example, Judge Ochoa, a Latino respondent, said "whenever they make something like Streamline up, it's not actually based in good policy" when I asked him if Operation Streamline was a successful program that should be expanded. Overall, 95% of respondents experienced work-related role strain based on not being able to enact the work-related role obligations of both substantive justice and formal justice.

Only 3 out of 52 respondents described Operation Streamline as a successful program that should be expanded and exhibited no qualms about being involved in the program. In the clearest example of supporting the program, Barney, a white CJA attorney suggested:

> There are a lot of things that the good folks who want to end Operation Streamline just don't get. So, while I understand their heart, I just think that they're trying to put a death nail into Operation Streamline and, quite frankly, I think they should increase it.

On the other end of the spectrum, Valentina, a Latina FPD was the most outspoken attorney who objects to Operation Streamline. She said:

> How can we say that [Operation Streamline] isn't violative of the constitution when we are specifically impacting a specific population of foreign nationals? It may not be a violation of due process because there's a neutrality in the law, but in its application, it's illegal. [I]t's an evolution of racism, but no one will call it racist, because on its face, the law is [gesture indicating gives air quotes] 'race neutral.' So, I mean, it's just disgusting.

I characterize Valentina's response as the pinnacle of work-related role strain, or "a felt difficulty in fulfilling role obligations" (Stryker 1980:76). Doing their job as an attorney or judge involved in Operation Streamline and feeling like Operation Streamline is inherently flawed presented a particular problem for Latino/a participants, while non-Latino/a participants had an easier time shrugging it off. This provides support for the links between micro level identity management of these individual legal professionals and the larger, macro level systems of social inequality, particularly around race/ethnicity. A shared racial/ethnic social identity with defendants who are being oppressed affects attorney's and judges' ability to work as effectively (that is, with less role strain) within the structurally racist I system.

In my analysis, a distinct pattern emerged where Latino/as expressed more distress and anxiety about being involved in Operation Streamline via an emphasis on the substantive justice "pole" of their legal professional identity. That is, Latino/as were more likely to say that Operation Streamline provided little if any substantive justice for Operation Streamline defendants despite the legal, formal justice of the program, having been approved by the Ninth Circuit appellate court. This is not to say that all Latino/a attorneys and judges felt more work-related role strain. Nor is this to say that none of the non-Latino/a attorneys and judges felt work-related role strain or felt connected to and concerned about defendants. However, on average, the Latino/a attorney interviews showed higher coding for instances of work-related role strain, supporting the conceptualization of *competing identity management*. In my qualitative coding scheme for work-related role strain, 90% of Latino/a respondents mentioned work-related role strain in their interviews while only 43% of non-Latino/a respondents did so. This higher instance of work-related role strain in Latino/a attorneys and judges is based on structural racism and thus also leads to increased competition between their work-related role identities as legal professionals and their social identity of race/ethnicity as Latino/as.

Identity Consolidation among Non-Latino/a Respondents

Mickey's statement that Operation Streamline is "perfectly legal" suggests he managed his work-related role strain in part through identity consolidation (Snow and McAdam 2000). This means that he blends two or more of his identities in order to justify action. Mickey admits to disliking Operation Streamline but says he has no qualms about his own participation. He demonstrates strain through comparing "unjust" feelings (substantive justice) and "legal" definitions (formal justice) and then explains why he stays involved though *consolidating those poles* through his work-related role identity of a defense attorney. He describes the procedure as substantively "just" by comparison to other formal procedures:

> I've done a lot of work in misdemeanor courts, in a regular civil court, and these people [in Operation Streamline] are getting more attorney time, more attorney attention than a lot of people who go through Tucson city court. Occasionally, I've seen lawyers that I didn't think were doing a good job but most of them are really thorough, so it's fine, and [Operation Streamline] is completely legal.

Mickey's statement about "more attorney time" seems to ignore that each attorney's time and attention is divided among 10–15 defendants each day in Operation Streamline, but still, he demonstrations his formal-legal sense of following legal procedure by comparing Operation Streamline to other court settings. By saying the process is "legal" and in some ways provides more substantive justice than other programs, he is consolidating these two "poles" in order to minimize his work-related role strain.

The work-related role strain of formal versus substantive concerns often came up when I would ask attorneys and judges about their interactions with the activist groups. Mickey was not the only non-Latino/a attorney to say that he generally agreed with activists; but also Ethan, a non-Latino/a FPD, for example, said of Operation Streamline

> Personally, I agree with the activists. We have an unfair system, but as a public defender, I can't not defend someone because I disagree with the law—I have to save that for a different setting. This is the system we have right now and in Operation Streamline, I have to focus only on my client in this courtroom and my job as his attorney. *Roblero* [the 2009 Ninth-Circuit Appeal] said this is legal and how we have to do it, so I am going to do it.

Like Mickey, Ethan has perfected the defense of Operation Streamline through a formal "legal" justification of their work in Operation Streamline, citing the appellate court endorsement of the program. Rather than defining substantive justice according to participation in a particular system, he defines it by his own work-related role—in this case, as a public defender.

Non-Latino/a attorneys who highlight both substantive and formal justice as standards for evaluating Operation Streamline often did so in a short period of time, expressing what would seem like contradictory feelings about the program while justifying their continued participation. Participants quickly followed this demonstration of work-related role strain with an identity management strategy.

Identity Consolidation among Latino/a Respondents

Latino/a attorneys, like non-Latino/a attorneys, evidenced identity consolidation—the blending of identities in order to justify action (Snow and McAdam 2000)—but felt the need to do so more explicitly. For example, in my courtroom observations, I saw many attorneys and judges talk to activist groups or individuals at the courthouse and take lots of their time to describe details of the law as it is written and the proceedings to these audiences. Some attorneys themselves even brought in groups from schools or brought their family members to observe the proceeding.

For example, Solomón, a Latino CJA attorney, brought his teenage niece to observe the proceeding as a way of "showing her the true face of the

U.S. legal system." He described warning her that Operation Streamline defendants would be in chains and seemed aware she would be upset by the visit. He said he had described the proceeding to her as "an important part of the U.S. legal system" that was different from what she might see on TV. In my fieldnotes, I have written "emphasizes legality and approval of Ninth Circuit" (Fieldnotes April 16, 2014). This justification of the program extends to a justification of his involvement via the identity management strategy of identity consolidation.

Another attorney had similar sentiments as she explained the ins and outs of the proceeding to me:

> [Judges] don't really like it, but they do it because that's their job. The lawyers in there, they don't like it. I know I don't really like it, but they do it because it's their job. And that's the unfortunate thing. It's not perfect, but it's, it's, it's being cleared up and cleaned up. Because we're a system of laws. And the people who are working there are the people who want to help, who want to help the defendants. Not everybody there is in it just for the money. But they really want to help. And, and, attacking them is, is just disheartening. It's, it's just, it's counterproductive and, and kind of stupid.

Soledad, a Latina CJA attorney, recognizes the substantive justice issues around Operation Streamline but uses formal justice principles to explain her continued participation. However, her attempts are not totally successful, as it is significant that she could not seem to manage to say, "I do it because it's my job." Instead, she externalizes the process from herself to other attorneys and judges and stutters quite a bit in her rationalization.

Identity consolidation happens when attorneys and judges must justify their continued participation despite having a strong personal dislike of the laws being enforced or the process by which they are carried out. While identity consolidation was a common strategy among both Latino/a attorneys and non-Latino/a attorneys, Latino/a attorneys and judges tended to use this strategy just slightly more often than non-Latino/a attorneys and judges, with 55% of all Latino/a respondents using identity consolidation and only 48% of non-Latino/a respondents using it to explain their seemingly contradictory behavior.

Going through the Motions versus Role Making

Another way Latino/a and non-Latino/a attorneys and judges differed was in their use of the various identity management strategies directly related to their legal professional role identity. Use of previously defined role identity strategies (Stryker 1980; Snow and Anderson 1987; Snow and McAdam 2000) also had clear racial/ethnic patterns in this case, linking micro level identity work with and macro level structural racism. Latino/a attorneys and judges were more likely to use strategies of role making/identity extension instead of just role playing. For example, non-Latino/a attorneys and judges more often just "went through the motions" of their work-related role in Operation Streamline, playing it out as directed. Latino/a attorneys and judges did more identity management work in order to make their daily work during Operation Streamline fit into their conceptions of the work-related role of "attorney" or "judge." I coded this expansion of what Logan, a non-Latino/a CJA attorney called "just the typical program" as role making/identity extension. The discrepancy in using these two different identity management strategies of role making/identity extension versus role playing is due to the salience of the Latino/a social identity for Latino/a respondents involved in Operation Streamline. Role playing—a more basic identity management strategy—was used by 52% of non-Latino/a respondents and only 32% of Latino/a respondents. Role making/identity extension—a more intensive identity management strategy—was almost reversed, with 55% of Latino/a respondents and only 24% of non-Latino/a respondents. This distinct variation highlights how racial/ethnic social identities play out in the daily identity management of legal professionals based on the current social structural inequality that Operation Streamline represents—criminalizing migrants, particularly based on race.

Barney, a non-Latino/a CJA attorney, has a very set, role playing routine that he follows with each client in the Operation Streamline morning sessions. He described it thus:

> I can give my little speech to people, my little presentation, if you will, in about ten minutes. The first five or seven minutes is sort of, hey, how are you; how are you feeling; are those [chains] comfortable; tell me how that is, you know what I'm saying? Are you comfortable? Try to make a little rapport with them. So that's five to seven minutes. Then I gather needed information for five or six minutes. I find out whether or not their parents were born in the United States, whether they were born in the United States, whether they had legal status to be here in the United States, if they have any claim for the right to be here. Then they sign [the pleas agreement]. The end. So, it takes me about 20 to 25 minutes per client and that's what I do.

Down to exact timings of each section, Barney knows the exact role he is playing and sees no need to expand or extend his work. Reynold, another non-Latino/a CJA respondent, described his similar procedure as "going through the motions." He says that the process is "truly is a relatively simple thing in terms of the legal aspects," and that criticism of defendants being "railroaded or churned through" is inaccurate. He suggests he goes through the same process in Operation Streamline as he would if he were to visit those clients in a detention facility and all defense attorneys know the exact, role playing process to follow.

By contrast, Latino/a attorneys were more likely to role make—that is, expand the typical agenda and show extra care toward Operation Streamline defendants by doing things the job does not necessarily require from a formal legal perspective. They do this extra work to ease work-related role strain as well as the identity competition brought on by their racial/ethnic social identity. For Latino/a attorneys, the most common "extra" was calling their clients' families. Only 13% of non-Latino/a attorneys mentioned this practice, while 48% of Latino/a attorneys did.

Salvadór, a Latino CJA attorney, said he asked all clients, "[W]here were you going? What were you going to do? Have you been to the court before? Is there somebody there I can call?" If they said they had someone he could call, he always called, either on the spot if the person was in the United States or back at his office if the number was in or México. These calls, while optional, are able to give clients and their families peace of mind, knowing where their loved one currently is, as they likely had not heard from them since they left home. Salvadór had the impression some of his colleagues had taken up the practice because of seeing him make calls in the morning session, even though as he noted, the job did not require it:

> It's not something we have to do, but you can see—when you call and they're able to listen. You can't hand them the phone because of the marshals, but it puts them at ease to know their family knows they're OK.

Estelle, a Latina CJA attorney, told me that she calls clients' families on her lunch break—which is time she cannot bill to the court—but then she is able to tell defendants in the afternoon session that their families know they are in custody.

Another Latina CJA attorney, Bridget, said she has even gone as far as to reclaim client's possessions from Border Patrol, often in order to get phone numbers that a client did not have memorized. She explains this ordeal:

> You have to write a letter and make an appointment and show up [at the Border Patrol Station] and wait. They dig it out and then hand you the stuff and, you know, and then they won't take the stuff back after you've touched it. Then it's your job to pack it up and ship it by UPS to México, which I've done—I've spent, like, 40-50 bucks doing this, and I don't get paid for any of the time, you know what I mean? That's not billable.

She goes on to say she'd be "bankrupt" if she did this for every client, but that these extra steps help remind her that "I am still human, they are still human, we can go through this system, but still be kind." Attorneys who made these additional kinds of efforts are *extending* their attorney identity and making the work-related role more palatable in the face of a system they may not agree with. They are activating substantive justice work and highlighting it as beyond the formal justice, or "billable" work they have to do as a way to justify their continued participation and ease their own conscience.

This role making/identity extension expanded to observable courtroom behavior as well as attorney's descriptions of their work in interviews. Operation Streamline has a practice I found shocking at first; if an attorney had another proceeding to participate in at the same time as Operation Streamline proceedings, another attorney can fill in for him or her as a "stand-in." This was a clear indication of how scripted and rote the proceedings are; in my observations of 64 hearings, I saw lawyers perform this stand-in maneuver eight times. What struck me was that six of those times the departing attorney was non-Latino/a—a highly disproportionate number, given how Latino/a attorneys outnumbered their counterparts. While sometimes these conflicts were unavoidable based on court scheduling, many Latino/a attorneys told me specifically in interviews they avoid scheduling meetings on the day they have Operation Streamline, which demonstrates more commitment to the substantive justice part of their work in the program. Thus, the pattern reflects non-Latino/a attorneys' preference for role playing over role making/identity extension, as they did not see it as important enough that they be personally present for their clients.

Latino/a Legal Professional's Use of Psychological Compartmentalization

One role identity management strategy that only Latino/a attorneys and judges used was psychological compartmentalization. Nineteen percent of the Latino/a attorneys and judges used this identity management strategy as a way of "boxing off" or "splitting up" their work at Operation Streamline in order to cope or create emotional boundaries from the work-related role strain they experienced. The strongest example directly used the term "compartmentalize." When I asked César, a Latino CJA attorney, if he felt that work affected his personal life unduly, he said,

> No. No, I don't have any trouble. I know how to compartmentalize. You just think about the task at hand. And that's the way I do everything in my life. And I think men aren't as emotional as women. Women are more touchy-feely, really care, you know. I care, but not to the point where it affects me. I mean I have no control. I look at it this way, if it's something I did wrong that's causing, you know, harm to someone, that's something I'd worry about. But nothing I do here causes harm to anybody. I'm helping them. I'm the only one helping them. I mean, I can't control that they're going to get 180 days, you know, but I do hear some really sad stories and I can't do anything about it, you know, so I just let that go.

César emphasizes the importance of staying within his work-related role as an attorney and focusing on "the task at hand." He sees himself carrying out formal duties and not "causing any harm." He also describes this as related to gender (see Chapter 7) but explains he has no control over what happens beyond his direct interaction with clients, so he will not think about his work-related role affecting his other identities beyond that scenario. Psychological compartmentalization, then, is an identity management strategy used for dealing with work-related role strain (what a legal professional can or cannot control) as well as competing social and role identities (none of the non-Latino/a respondents used this strategy).

Fictive Story Telling

Another identity management strategy that Latino/as used exclusively was fictive story telling. As developed by Snow and Anderson (1987, 1993), one use of fictive story telling occurs when respondents use embellishment or hyperbole to explain how they got to where they are, or how they landed in their current identity. This kind of fictive story telling is an identity management strategy that was used exclusively by Latino/a respondents (though, only 13%) for dealing with work-related role strain as well as competing social and role identities they face in Operation Streamline. Once again, this demonstrates the additional identity management required of those who have non-situationally valued social identities (those oppressed by current systems of structural inequality).

My first interview question to respondents asked them to tell me about how they ended up working in criminal defense and ultimately in Operation Streamline. Latino/as were more likely to go into great detail about how they became attorneys and judges, whereas many of the non-Latino/a respondents explained more matter-of-factly how they ended up in law school. In fact, many non-Latino/a attorneys used phrases like "flipped a coin" or "nothing else to do" when describing their career path. In contrast, many Latino/a respondents described their activist-oriented past, their desire to help people, and other more thoughtful causes for entering their career, particularly as the related to substantive justice and the desire to improve the legal system for all people.

In some of these career history "flashbacks," there were examples of vivid, hyperbolic story telling, which was then coded as fictive story telling *a la* Snow and Anderson (1987). Fictive story telling is an identity management strategy used to emphasize the importance of the current role a respondent holds, which helps to minimizes role strain. A particularly telling racialized, as well as classed, example from Micah, a Latino CJA attorney:

> In Hispanic culture, the guy who wears the tie is somebody. Okay? So, one day—and so I knew lawyers wore ties, just for starters. But one day, I remember this so vividly, my dad worked for [an office], and I remember us being on vacation. We were at Disneyland and all the kids wanted to stay. And so, my dad called, and I remember him begging his boss to

let us stay an extra three days, over the phone. And I said to myself, I am never, ever going to be put in that situation. So, I figured a lawyer is the kind of guy that doesn't beg for vacation time, and of course, wears a tie. [He motioned toward the tie on his own chest.]

For Micah, a tie symbolizes power and autonomy. His story about why he became a lawyer is an identity management strategy that provides a description of how he has come into his work-related role, but tellingly, it is prefaced with his social identity as part of a shared idea of status in Hispanic culture.

Summary

In line with the conceptualization of *competing identity management*, the salient social identity of race/ethnicity for Latino/a attorneys and judges created race/ethnicity-based patterns in variation of how attorneys and judges manage both experiences of work-related role strain and competition between their social and their work-related role identities in Operation Streamline. Indeed, as expected, Latino/a attorneys and judges (90%) expressed more work-related role strain about being involved in Operation Streamline than non-Latino/as (43%) based on their shared social identities with defendants. These Latino/a legal professionals are pulled more heavily toward the substantive justice pole of their work-related role identity, which causes them to engage in different identity management work than do non-Latino/as when justifying their participation in Operation Streamline.

In addition to Latino/a respondents expressing more work-related role strain, there were also systematically patterned behaviors in terms of identity management strategies when examined between Latino/a and non-Latino/a respondents. To deal with work-related role strain, Latino/as were more likely to use the identity management strategy of identity consolidation. Latino/a work-related role identity management work also focused on role making/identity extension, psychological compartmentalization, and fictive story telling, while non-Latino/a attorneys and judges were more likely to engage in the identity management strategy of role playing. Table 3.1 provides a summary of the identity management strategies discussed in this chapter as they break down by racial/ethnic group.

Overall, the higher levels of work-related role strain for Latino/as and these differential usages of identity management strategies based on racial/ethnic social identity support the conceptualization of *competing identity management* because Latino/as were more likely to experience competition between their racial/ethnic social identity and their work-related role identity as attorneys or judges. This links the larger macro level issues of structural racism in the context of Operation Streamline to the micro level ways legal professionals deal with their own work. However, the story is not as simple as just racial/ethnic social identity, as will be explored via variation within the group of Latino/a attorneys and judges in Chapters 6 and 7.

Table 3.1 Role Identity Management Strategies by Racial/Ethnic Group

Strategy	Definition	Example	Group using strategy more	% Latino/a using strategy (N = 31)	% Non-Latino/a using strategy (N = 21)
Dealing with role strain					
Identity Consolidation	Recognizing the substantive justice issues around Operation Streamline while using formal-legal justice and a desire to help defendants to explain their continued participation	"You might think it's unjust, but it's perfectly legal [...] It's not unethical to represent or defend somebody who's charged with a crime."	Latino/as	55	48
Role identity management strategies					
Role Playing	Simply going through the motions of your daily work in Operation Streamline	"It truly is a relatively simple thing in terms of the legal aspects."	Non-Latino/as	32	52
Role Making/Identity Extension	Trying to expand the typical program of daily work in Operation Streamline to diminish role strain	Calling defendants' families	Latino/as	55	24
Psychological Compartmentalization	Separating work at Operation Streamline in order to cope with role strain	"I know how to compartmentalize. You just think about the task at hand."	Latino/as	19	0
Fictive Story Telling	Use of embellishment or hyperbole to explain how respondents got to where they are	"And I said to myself, I am never, ever going to be put in that situation"	Latino/as	13	0

References

Abrego, Leisy, Mat Coleman, Daniel Martínez, Cecilia Menjívar, and Jeremy Slack. 2017. "Making Immigrants into Criminals: Legal Processes of Criminalization in the Post-IIRIRA Era." *Journal on Migration and Human Security* 5(3):694–715. https://doi.org/10.1177/233150241700500308.

Bonilla-Silva, Eduardo. 2014. *Racism Without Racists: Color-Blind Racism and the Persistence of Racial Inequality in the United States.* Fourth Edition. New York, NY: Rowman and Littlefield Publishers.

Browne-Marshall, Gloria J. 2013. *Race, Law, and American Society: 1607-Present.* New York, NY: Routledge.

Chacón, Jennifer M. 2009. "Managing Migration Through Crime." *Columbia Law Review Sidebar* 109:135–48. http://dx.doi.org/10.2139/ssrn.2033931.

Golash-Boza, Tanya Maria. 2015. *Immigration Nation: Raids, Detentions, and Deportations in Post-9/11 America.* Boulder, CO: Paradigm Press.

Martínez, Daniel E., Jeremy Slack, and Ricardo Martínez-Schuldt. 2018. "The Rise of Mass Deportation in the United States" Pp. 173–201 in *the Handbook of Race, Ethnicity, Crime, and Justice*, Ramiro, Martínez Jr, Hollis, Megan E., and Stowell, Jacob I., Eds. Hoboken, NJ: Willey Blackwell.

Massey, Douglas S. 2013. "America's Immigration Policy Fiasco: Learning from Past Mistakes." *Daedalus* 142(3):5–15. http://www.jstor.org/stable/43297247.

Molina, Natalia. 2014. *How Race Is Made in America: Immigration, Citizenship, and the Historical Power of Racial Scripts.* Los Angeles, CA: University of California Press.

Press, Eyal. 2021. *Dirty Work: Essential Jobs and the Hidden Toll of Inequality in America.* New York, NY: Farrar, Straus, and Giroux.

Rodriguez, Nestor P., and Cecilia Menjívar. 2009. "Central American Immigrants and Racialization in A Post-Civil Rights Era" Pp. 183–99 in *How the United States Racializes Latinos: White Hegemony and Its Consequences*, Cobas, José A., Duany, Jorge, and Feagin, Joe R., Eds. Boulder, CO: Paradigm Publishers.

Snow, David A., and Leon Anderson. 1987. "Identity Work Among the Homeless: The Verbal Construction and Avowal of Personal Identities." *American Journal of Sociology* 92:1336–71. https://www.jstor.org/stable/2779840.

Snow, David A., and Doug McAdam. 2000. "Identity Work Processes in the Context of Social Movements: Clarifying the Identity/Movement Nexus" Pp. 41–67 in *Self, Identity, and Social Movements*, Stryker, Sheldon, Owens, Timothy J., and White, Robert W., Eds. Minneapolis, MN: University of Minnesota Press.

Snow, David A., and Leon Anderson. 1993. *Down on Their Luck: A Study of Homeless Street People.* Berkeley, CA: University of California Press.

Stryker, Sheldon. 1980. *Symbolic Interactionism: A Social Structural Version.* Menlo Park, CA: Benjamin/Cummings Publishing Company.

Weber, Max. 1978. *Economy and Society: An Outline of Interpretive Sociology.* Roth, Guenther and Claus Wittich, Eds. Berkeley, CA: University of California Press.

4 "HONESTLY, I AM JUST LIKE THEM"
THE IMPACT OF RACIAL/ ETHNIC SOCIAL IDENTITY

Carlita, a Latina Criminal Justice Act (CJA) panel attorney, made physical contact with her clients more than any other attorney I observed. She would often help her clients up by extending her hand out, assist them with adjusting their headset or their chains, and she always shook every single client's hand whenever they left the courtroom after their case was heard. This behavior that I observed in the court sessions was explained by her in her interview:

> My personal motivation is, given that they are going to be prosecuted and processed this way, you know, I try to do what I can to make it as humane a process as possible for them on an individual level. Obviously, I know that doesn't address the real issue behind it—the fact that the government has decided to prosecute them—but I try to make sure they have water, I always shake their hand, I try to attend to their needs when I am with them because I don't think anyone else does that for them.

Carlita explained the reason she wanted to show such care to each of her migrant clients was that her dad migrated in the 1950's to the United States and she felt both a shared connection to them and an obligation to help them. This highlights how both racial/ethnic social identity and citizenship/ generational status (further explored in Chapter 6) directly impact the work of legal professionals like Carlita as she thinks of how her own family background changes her work with clients.

Beyond Carlita, I took tallies of physical contact between attorneys and their clients for four months during my field work. This included gestures such as shaking the client's hand or removing their headset for them because they were in chains. There were also some more intimate gestures, physical comforts such as a hand on the back or shoulder or a light squeeze of the forearm as they spoke. Often, given the placement and weight of the chains and the fact that belts had been removed, some attorneys even helped clients to adjust their pants as they stood before the judge.

DOI: 10.4324/9781003272410-5

In a demonstration of physical distance from clients, which can symbolically represent social-structural identity distance, non-Latino/a attorneys were less likely to touch their clients than Latino/a attorneys. While I saw 21 of the 36 Latino/a attorneys (58%) who I observed more than once during this period touch a client at least three times in a single-courtroom session, only 7 out of the observed 19 non-Latino/a attorneys (37%) did so more than three times. Some attorneys missed several of their regularly scheduled days during this period, which is why I did not observe all 45 of my defense attorney respondents' touching pattern. However, the overall pattern was quite clear—nearly two-thirds of the Latino/a attorneys (especially Latinas, see Chapter 7) regularly engaged in physical contact while only about a third of the non-Latino/a attorneys did so.

Hand sanitizer use in the courtroom showed similar patterns. Long before COVID-19, alcohol-based sanitizer was ubiquitous in the courtroom; on one day I counted 14 small bottles, one on each of the small tables at which the defense attorneys, the government prosecutor, the U.S. Marshals, and one of the translators sat, and 3 large ones on the judge's stand, about 32 oz. each. The acrid smell of alcohol was pervasive in the courtroom, every day.

Much like tallying physical contact between attorneys and their clients, the tallies of hand sanitizer use in the courtroom showed a racial/ethnic pattern as well. I found that fully 15 of the 19 non-Latino/a attorneys (79% of those observed) used hand sanitizer in the courtroom, while only 23 of 36 Latino/a attorneys did so (64% of those observed). All translators who handled the headsets not only wore latex gloves, but they also sanitized the headsets with some kind of wipes when they received them back.

The use of gloves and sanitizer is, of course, for hygienic purposes but, so-called cleanliness has long been symbolically associated with "unclean" racial/ethnic distinctions. Activists who attended Operation Streamline, for example, would often say that the hand sanitizer use made them feel uncomfortable. A volunteer for a local migrant rights group who I had seen at several hearings once mentioned to me that she thought the attorneys used the sanitizer "to wash their hands clean of this terrible program." The presence of so much hand sanitizer and the practice of these attorneys were also noted in the media as "echoing a long history of anti-immigrant disease hysteria" (Cohen 2015). Thus, I argue differential touching and use of hand sanitizer by race/ethnicity of legal professionals underscores macro level structural racism present in criminal immigration settings (Chacón 2009; Golash-Boza 2015). That there would be a racial/ethnic breakdown in touching and the use of this hand sanitizer certainly emphasizes the importance of racial/ethnic social identity management in the courtroom.

As seen in these touching and hand-sanitizer tallies, issues of racial/ethnic social identity pattern how legal professionals perform their work in Operation Streamline. Social identity theory holds that members of social groups/categories will engage in identity management via demonstrating their group membership and by showing preference for those in their group. However, in the case of Operation Streamline, shared social identities, such as race/ethnicity, are sometimes incongruent with the work-related role identity of being a legal professional. That is, Latino/a attorneys and judges should show in-group preference to Latino/a Operation Streamline defendants, but their work-related role identity competes with this demand of their social identity. Because Latino/a respondents showed more work-related role strain than non-Latino/a respondents (90% versus 43%), it is relevant to explore how this strain in turn influences competition between social and role identities. This chapter shows that work-related role strain and competing social and role identities result in systematic variation in the use of identity management strategies between Latino/a and non-Latino/a attorneys and judges in terms of how they demonstrate their categorical group membership. This links macro level structural racism of criminalized immigration proceedings with micro level legal professional's identity behaviors, where non-Latino/a attorneys and judges have to do overall less identity work to justify their continued participation in Operation Streamline.

For example, I find that only Latino/a attorneys and judges feel competition between their race/ethnicity and their work-related role based on the identity management strategy of in-group similarities. Because immigration law in the United States from its inception has privileged "free white persons" (1790's H.R. 40 Naturalization Bill), it is not surprising that non-Latino/as do not feel this same identity competition. Indeed, some of the white attorneys in particular recognized that their status as "gringos" (white, non-Hispanic Americans) might be problematic for their clients. These non-Latino/a attorneys and judges used the identity management strategy of overt demonstration of out-group difference to deal with these daily interactions with clients.

Other non-Latino/a attorneys and judges did not overtly demonstrate out-group difference but instead used the identity management strategy of socially distancing themselves from defendants, or what social identity theorists would call out-group negativity. Still other non-Latino/a attorneys and judges had no recognition of social identities as relevant at all, which I describe as a distinct identity management strategy linked to white privilege. This lack of awareness of any racial/ethnic tension in their legal work sometimes hindered their job performance, particularly in terms of connecting with clients or recognizing issues of substantive justice.

In-Group Similarities among Latino/a Respondents

As expected, Latino/a attorneys and judges were able to describe in-group similarities based on race/ethnicity between themselves and their Latino/a defendants, a connection that non-Latino/a attorneys and judges cannot explicitly demonstrate. In-group similarities were coded as when attorneys or judges suggested they could really understand defendants' actions because of a shared personal background (either via migration history, cultural and social references, racial/ethnic identity, or a shared upbringing). In a striking example of announcing her in-group similarities, Imelda, a Latina CJA attorney, says:

> I mean, I know why Operation Streamline is so hard. It's because I would probably do the same thing as my clients if I were any of them and leave México. Honestly, I am just like them. Hearing their stories and not thinking of my parents, I just can't help by think about my own family. And, and I just—it's heartbreaking.

Clearly, her family background and shared national heritage leads Imelda to demonstrate her own similarities to her clients, both in terms of shared history and also in terms of potential behaviors.

Not all Latino/a attorneys and judges demonstrated in-group similarities based on race/ethnicity; about three-quarters (77% of Latino/a respondents) did. Non-Latino/a attorneys obviously could not highlight a shared race/ethnicity, but they could have acknowledged they are descended from immigrants to this country, but none did. Some non-Latino/as acknowledged that they might do the same thing as their defendants if they were in the same circumstances—showing some level of empathy—but they never personalized it to their own racial/ethnic identity or their own citizenship/generational status, even those who were migrants themselves from countries in the global North. A more nuanced review of how various Latino/a respondents dealt with their differing social identities of citizenship/generational status is explicated in Chapter 6.

Out-Group Differences among Non-Latino/a Respondents

Overall, Latino/a attorneys and judges tended to emphasize their shared racial/ethnic identity with defendants when discussing client interactions, while some non-Latino/a attorneys and judges demonstrated their recognition that they did *not* share this categorical membership with defendants. Non-Latino/a attorneys and judges were more likely to describe their out-group difference from defendants either directly (i.e., "I'm just some gringo") or through describing the culture shock these migrant defendants must have coming to the United States compared to these defendants' home conditions. Non-Latino/a attorneys' frequent talk about individuals from México and Latin America living in extreme poverty with no recognition of systemic causes demonstrated a lack of shared social identity and instead showed strong out-group differences. Finally, some respondents did not even think about the social identity of race/ethnicity as a factor in Operation Streamline. Lewis (2004) suggests that "part of the privilege associated with whiteness is, in fact, the ability not to think about race at all, not to take any notice whatsoever of its role in daily life" (641). As such, failing to even consider race/ethnicity in Operation Streamline is a unique version of out-group differences via the concept of white privilege.

Gringos

Barney has been a CJA attorney within Operation Streamline for seven years. He said of his clients that "they have to be thinking, 'This white boy is my lawyer?'" Barney's Spanish is not great by his own admission, but he seeks to validate his clients' feelings by addressing them in Spanish:

> '*Soy gringo. Tengo orejas gringo, boca gringo, y mente gringo, so por favor si usted no me entiendes cien por ciento, déjame un ratito y voy a cambiar mi proceso.*' What I mean is, 'I'm a white guy. I've got white ears. I've got a white mouth. I've got a white brain. So, if you don't understand me 100 percent just stop me and we'll do it another way, okay?' So, I tell them right up that I'm a white guy. I try to break the ice with it. It's the first thing I say with them.

The term *gringo* has numerous interpretations, but in this case, it generally connotes a non-Hispanic—usually white—American. It has a longer history of referring to foreigners or even those who speak Spanish with a strange accent or dialect (Varela 1996). While it is not always used as a derogatory term, there is some negative valence in terms of lacking certain cultural understanding.

Another white CJA attorney, Mickey, not only had a better handle on Spanish than Barney, perhaps suggesting more of a commitment to being understood by his clients, but he also used the term gringo to show a similar identity management approach with his clients:

> I think—you know, I have to kind of do something extra to show that I'm not the government, you know? Making sure they know like, 'Oh, I'm a gringo walking in here but I'm your attorney and I work for you, not for them' and that kind of thing. So, some of those obvious barriers to break down and then I can build up their trust.

This straightforward description is an acknowledgement of the known differences between racial/ethnic social identities, especially with an affiliation to the U.S. government. That is, Mickey as a white man is intrinsically associated with the U.S. government by his clients who are being punished in Operation Streamline through prosecution of border-crossing. This links micro level identity work ("making sure they know [...] I work for you") with macro level structural racism because a white attorney would be assumed by clients to *not* work for them, but to work for "the system." Overall, 24% of non-Latino/a attorneys and judges used this identity management strategy.

Describing Social-Structural Identity Distance

Other non-Latino/a attorneys demonstrated their out-group difference but did not describe acknowledging it to clients. They explained that their racial/ethnic social identity distanced them from their clients. While not necessarily directly addressing issues of racial/ethnic identity, they alluded to broader, macro level group differences. Though "social distancing" is an identity management strategy for role identities (Snow and Anderson 1987), I coded non-overt discussion to non-Latino/a out-group differences as social-structural identity distancing from Operation Streamline defendants. This identity management strategy is consistent with social identity theory in that one would expect members of different groups to distance themselves from one another.

Oliver exemplified a non-Latino/a CJA attorney's distancing of himself from his clients based on social location when he said:

> This client was from the mountains in Chiapas somewhere, and he kept saying he came because his wife is sick. [When I asked what was wrong] he said, '*Es una bruja.*' And I was like, 'What's that?' you know? I had to go ask someone else, it's like, she's possessed, like a witch [laughs]. He was going to come and save up enough money to go back to Chiapas and pay the witch doctor to go and do an exorcism for her.

> Then I realized how much of a different world these guys who are from the hills in México, heck, anywhere in México, what a different world this must be for them. That's pretty insane.

> So, yeah, there's a really interesting sort of clash of cultures so to speak being, you know, in a very straight-laced bureaucratic legal courtroom and then thinking your wife is possessed [laughs]. She's probably just mentally ill, you know what I mean? She probably just needs some sort of medication or mood changer or something like that, you know. Some Xanax or something.

Oliver laughed again, thinking about the client whose wife was possessed. He brought up this anecdote in response to a question about particularly challenging cases. Oliver's language covertly calls out the differences between himself and his clients as an identity management strategy. He knows he will never have that same shared cultural understanding and instead laughingly imposes a Western-medical perspective onto his client.

Of course, it is uncommon to attribute undesirable behavior to demonic possession in the United States, at least among Oliver's socioeconomic class. But Oliver extended this sense of difference to all of his clients, even the most urban, when he said that "heck, anywhere in México" is extremely different from Tucson. Non-Latino/as often described the conditions in México or other sending countries in very hyperbolic terms, demonstrating a lack of personal experience in the region or a tendency to negatively stereotype. For example, Tiffany, a white CJA attorney, described México as "people living in garbage dumps and in cardboard boxes," when in reality México has a variety of classes and regions just like any other country. Basing her assumptions in low-class encounters with some of her Operation Streamline clients is a problematic example of social-structural identity distancing. Like Oliver, though, she tried to demonstrate compassion for clients by recognizing the trying circumstances they were seeking to leave, but these statements also demonstrate a privileged sense of social location.

In another example of social-structural identity distancing, Sheldon, a white CJA attorney, said:

> I talk to people, some of them were turned out of their house and lived off of garbage cans since they were like eight years old, never had a day of school, have no idea how to write their name, that cannot look at person in the eye because they're—they're gutter people. That's who comes through Streamline, gutter people.

Most Operation Streamline defendants are indeed very poor compared to the attorneys who work with them in Operation Streamline, and the overall standard of wealth or material comfort in México may often be lower than in the United States. Sheldon rightly says that "some" of his clients are desperately poor and may have grown up rummaging for food and without any formal schooling, but it is likely not the case for every single client, as he later generalizes. Thus, the oversimplification demonstrates the social-structural identity distance he feels and which he deploys to manage his identity while participating in Operation Streamline. Generally, those who used this social-structural identity distancing strategy—those who saw their clients as "gutter people," who were overly superstitious, or perennially homeless—were more likely to avoid physical contact with clients based on my tallies of touch—highlighting their perceived social-structural identity distance. The mostly middle- and upper-class non-Latino/a attorneys use both class and racial/ethnic hierarchies to "other" their Operation Streamline clients and demonstrate how different they are from one another.

Failing to Recognize Racial/Ethnic Social Identity

Some non-Latino/as suggested that racial/ethnic identities had absolutely no bearing on their relationship with their clients or in Operation Streamline at all when I asked them about it directly. The four non-Latino/a respondents who used this identity management strategy all identify as white. One CJA attorney, Gavin, was the most extreme example. When I asked him if race and ethnicity had ever affected him in his work-related role as a lawyer in

Operation Streamline, he expressed surprise: "Like how—like in like what way? How would that—because I'm a white guy and I'm going around and I'm representing Mexicans? I don't understand." He seemed potentially offended and generally bewildered by my question.

After I had read Gavin the vignette from my interview guide that high-lights the attorney's racial/ethnic social identity (See Appendix B), I asked him about how race/ethnicity may impact his daily work. He did not seem to understand the question. Our dialogue continued:

AUTHOR: Well, in the vignette, for example, the race of the attorney causes
    the client to be upset—
GAVIN: Well, well, I didn't even catch it. Where was it?
AUTHOR: Oh, the client says to his lawyer that 'You're just a Mexican guy
    on a power trip.' So, it's sort of subtle.
GAVIN: Oh, I didn't—you know what ran through my head is, I'm not
    Mexican so this guy [the client] is nuts. That's what ran through my
    head. But I'm like, whatever. I've never had that issue. Yeah, I don't
    think that, well—I don't know. I—I don't know.

When I explained to him that some activists, media coverage, or legal schol-arship mention issues of systemic racism as a factor in their criticisms of Operation Streamline, he did not seem to know about this critique. I told him I also considered race/ethnicity relevant to my research, and he said he had never had any experience of his race mattering at work in general or in Operation Streamline specifically. He went on about the vignette:

Yeah. What did I—I didn't even know that they were saying that or
using it that way? Because I don't—I didn't even notice that. I hadn't
even thought about it. I think part of it might be just because I come—
I don't know, maybe. I don't know. I'll—I feel comfortable in just about
any environment.

His stuttering and halting in talking about the race of the characters in the vignette demonstrate the palpable discomfort he felt at this point in the interview. In a textbook example of white privilege (Rothenberg 2015), Gavin had not even thought of the racialized nature of the court or about his own work. He also expresses his comfort in any situation, emphasizing that it has not ever been a problem for him while completely ignoring the fact that it might be something Operation Streamline defendants may expe-rience. In saying he is "comfortable in any environment," Gavin may also be expressing a sort of colorblind optimism that race should not impact his work. His response is in line with prior work on the lack of recognition that whites have a race (Lewis 2004) and their subsequent failure to understand how it would impact given social situations.

Table 4.1 Social Identity Management Strategies by Racial/Ethnic Group

Strategy	Definition	Example	Group using strategy more	% Latino/a using strategy (N = 31)	% Non-Latino/a using strategy (N = 21)
Demonstration of in-group similarities	Understanding defendants' actions because of a shared personal background (either via migration history, cultural and social references, or shared upbringing)	"Honestly, I am just like them."	Only Latino/as share social identities with defendants	77	–
Overt demonstration of out-group differences	Obvious recognition of one's non-Latino/a social identity	"*Soy gringo* [...] I'm a white guy. I've got white ears. I've got a white mouth. I've got a white brain."	Non-Latino/as do not share social identities with defendants	–	24
Social-structural distancing/out-group negativity	Non-overt discussion to non-Latino/as out-group differences, specifically those that had a negative valence	"Then I realized how much of a different world [...] this must be for them."	Non-Latino/as do not share social identities with defendants	–	33
Social-structural distancing via white privilege	Privileged lack of awareness around racial/ethnic social identities	"I hadn't even thought about it."	Non-Latino/as do not share social identities with defendants	–	19

Summary

In terms of social identity management strategies, a majority of Latino/
as described in-group similarity to Operation Streamline defendants,
while many non-Latino/as demonstrated their out-group differences from
these defendants. Some of these out-group differences for non-Latino/as
were explicit—explaining how their social location was so different from
Operation Streamline defendants—while others were more covert or some
completely lacking in recognition of race/ethnicity as impacting their work
in any way. The differences displayed in these two groups demonstrate that
racial/ethnic social identities impact legal professionals' work based on who
is privileged and who is oppressed by current systems of structural inequality. At the micro level, lawyers and judges who are Latino/a are more likely to
experience higher levels of work-related role strain resulting in competition
between their social and role identities. That is, Latino/a legal professionals'
racial/ethnic social identity complicates their work in Operation Streamline.
Table 4.1 provides a summary of the identity management strategies discussed
in this chapter as they break down by racial/ethnic group. These strategies by
different racial/ethnic groups demonstrate the salience of racial/ethnic social
identities in immigration-related work (Chacón 2009; Golash-Boza 2015)
and in the criminal justice system at large (Browne-Marshall 2013).

References

Browne-Marshall, Gloria J. 2013. *Race, Law, and American Society: 1607-Present.*
New York, NY: Routledge.
Chacón, Jennifer M. 2009. "Managing Migration Through Crime." *Columbia Law
Review Sidebar* 109:135–48. http://dx.doi.org/10.2139/ssrn.2033931.
Cohen, Dan. 2015. "From Nogales, Arizona to Ofer Prison: Witnessing Racism in
the American and Israeli Borderlands" *Mondoweiss.* Retrieved January 15, 2022.
http://mondoweiss.net/2015/03/witnessing-american-borderlands.
Golash-Boza, Tanya Maria. 2015. *Immigration Nation: Raids, Detentions, and
Deportations in Post-9/11 America.* Boulder, CO: Paradigm Press.
Lewis, Amanda E. 2004. "What Group? "Studying Whites and Whiteness in the
Era of" Color-Blindness." *Sociological Theory* 22: 623–46. https://doi.org/10.1111/
j.0735-2751.2004.00237.x.
Rothenberg, Paula S. 2015. *White Privilege: Essential Readings on the Other Side of
Racism, 5th Edition.* New York, NY: Worth Publishers.
Snow, David A., and Leon Anderson. 1987. "Identity Work Among the Homeless:
The Verbal Construction and Avowal of Personal Identities." *American Journal
of Sociology* 92:1336–71. https://www.jstor.org/stable/2779840.
Varela, Beatriz. 1996. "Ethnic Nicknames of Spanish Origin" Pp. 139–156 in *Spanish
Loanwords in the English Language: A Tendency Towards Hegemony Reversal,*
Rodríguez González, Félix, Ed. Berlin, Germany: Mouton De Gruyter.

5 "IF THERE WAS AN INFLUX OF WHITE CANADIAN PEOPLE COMING ACROSS THE BORDER, THEY WOULD TREAT THEM BETTER"
NEGOTIATING IDENTIFICATIONS

Orlando, a Latino Criminal Justice Act (CJA) panel attorney, told me that Operation Streamline would come out on "the wrong side of history, like the Holocaust or something." Another Latino CJA attorney, Craig, compared the entire practice of criminalizing migrants to Hitler's Germany but suggested that felony prosecutions were a more serious problem than Operation Streamline:

> [Streamline] is unconstitutional, but [all programs that arrest border-crossers are] unconstitutional, which takes me back to this premise: for people opposing Streamline, I would cite a parallel of Hitler's Germany. So, Streamline is unconstitutional, but the consequences are pretty light when you compare them to the felonies. Would you have been objecting to [Jews in Germany] being deported rather than being sent to the death camps? No, you'd be focusing on the worse consequence. Deporting's pretty bad, you know, you're leaving your homeland, you're leaving your house, your business, you've got to go build a house somewhere else, but you know what? You're alive. We ought to be protesting [felony convictions of border-crossers].

Craig might have concluded this reference with the idea that he is the metaphorical equivalent of a low-level Nazi officer, but instead, he dismissed activists' critical focus on Operation Streamline and diverted blame to others. He excused himself by trying to shift the focus away from the problems of Operation Streamline to the broader immigration system and "worse consequences" than his own participation in it. This is an example of negotiated identifications with certain beliefs/ideas/values as an identity management strategy. This type of strategy was used almost twice as often by Latino/a legal professionals compared to non-Latino/as when they justified their continued work in Operation Streamline.

DOI: 10.4324/9781003272410-6

Valentina, a Latina federal public defender (FPD), compared Operation Streamline with the Japanese Internment Camps that U.S. Government created during World War II. She said:

> We need to communicate with the [Obama] administration, with our Congress people, and say, 'No, we're not going to allow you to water down [immigrants'] rights.' Would we allow another Japanese Internment? I don't know if you listen to NPR, but they were talking on Arizona Spotlight. They were talking about a guy who was interned at the Japanese Internment Camp here on the Catalina Mountains because he violated the curfew law. And I—I don't see this as being any different.

Valentina profoundly objects to Operation Streamline, more than most legal professionals who participated in this research, perhaps because she does Operation Streamline as a required part of her job as a FPD—as opposed to CJA attorneys who volunteer to work in Operation Streamline. Her position as a FPD may be why she is particularly negative and sees herself as a witness instead of complicit in Operation Streamline:

> We have an obligation to bear witness, because in 20 years, or 30 years, or who knows, because now things take so little time, when we go back and we look at this, I don't want to say, what happened? Because it'll be gone in memory. So, I see myself as a witness.

These references to Hitler or Japanese Internment were used by Latino/a attorneys and judges to compare the problematic nature of Operation Streamline to other more egregious human rights abuses at twice the rate of non-Latino/a legal professionals. Negotiated identifications, as defined by Glaeser (2000), deal with how individuals use references to time, place, people, or beliefs/ideas/values as a way of emphasizing their own identities. These negotiated identifications are used as identity management strategies that vary based on racial/ethnic social identity, linking macro level racialization in immigration and criminal justice systems to micro level identity management of legal professionals. Here, I focus on three aspects of how the social identity of Latino/as versus non-Latino/as affects temporal identifications in two different areas (time with clients, and changes to Operation Streamline over time); spatial identifications (México versus Canada); and beliefs/ideas/values identifications in discourse via metaphors and references.

The use of negotiated identifications with time, place, and beliefs/ideas/values showed a racialized pattern. In terms of time, Latino/as were more likely to say they had insufficient time with clients and use identity management strategies of negotiated identifications with different times in the history of Operation Streamline to justify their continued participation in Operation Streamline. Latino/as were also more likely to engage in identity management strategies via negotiated identification with place by problematizing Operation Streamline with a hypothetical comparison to the Canadian border, while non-Latino/as did the exact opposite. Finally, Latino/as were also more likely to engage in identity management strategies via negotiated identification with beliefs/ideas/values via metaphors. These metaphors compared Operation Streamline defendants to animals and Operation Streamline attorneys to cogs in a machine in addition to the above references about Operation Streamline being similar to other human rights abuses, such as the Holocaust and Japanese Internment Camps.

Time with Clients

Several Latino/a participants and some non-Latino/a participants felt strongly that they had insufficient time with clients. A total of 35% of Latino/a attorneys suggested they sometimes had to rush or often did not have enough time to tell clients everything they wanted to convey in the morning sessions. Contrastingly, only 10% of non-Latino/a attorneys made similar complaints. In this vein, Latino/as were more likely to say they would show up right at 9:00 AM to assure they had as much time as possible with clients and they were more likely to describe staying until the last possible moment before noon to work with clients. These negative attitudes toward the amount of time spent with clients in Operation Streamline were usually prefaced with attorneys saying they got the "basics" out, but that there could have been more elaboration. Thus, I argue negotiated identification around insufficient time with clients is an identity management strategy. In particular, legal professionals are dealing with one of the issues that activists target in decrying Operation Streamline—that the proceeding is rushed.

While there was variation within each group, one of the main factors that also affected time-use with clients was the amount of training the attorney had had in immigration law. Interestingly, though not surprising in terms of other racialized patterns, Latino/as (16%) were more likely than non-Latino/as (5%) to have had a background in immigration law as well as in criminal defense. Having both an immigration and criminal defense background made legal professionals feel more pressed for time with clients because they felt they had more material to cover. Orlando, a Latino/a attorney who had been serving in Operation Streamline as a CJA attorney since 2011, explains the conundrum he faced because of this background:

> Sometimes, what I frankly don't have time to relay, is the immigration possibilities down the road, to be able to express it fully in a way in which they understand, and they also understand the impact, the consequence of [this Operation Streamline] kind of thing. Not that they have many options, you know—at the end of the day they tell us, you know, the immigration part of it, you don't really have to advise them on it.

Orlando feels that he should advise clients about when and if they would ever be able to return to the country in a safe and legal way, especially with the Operation Streamline conviction they were "agreeing" to that day being on their criminal record. Legal literature on this aspect of Operation Streamline has also critiqued the long-term consequences of an Operation Streamline conviction (Sarabia 2012; Martínez and Slack 2013). Orlando said that while some clients understand that they may be subject to a ten-year bar, or even a lifetime bar, given enough time, he might explain the impact of that fully to those who do not understand. But, given the amount of time he has with clients, he says he has to strike a "balance" in order "to advise some clients of certain points that will help them, and other clients not advising them on points that are not going to help them." As such, he has to prioritize relevant legal information given the time limitations he faces.

Attorneys who said they had insufficient time with clients enacted a negotiated identification, as defined by Glaeser (2000), as an identity management strategy. They explain their own understanding of time as different from others in the same social context. This identity management strategy is also specifically patterned by racial/ethnic social identity, linking micro and macro level factors of structural racism. Attorneys who were not concerned about the time spent with clients (90% of non-Latino/as) generally said that if they ever needed more time—and they rarely did—the continuance process served as a "pressure release valve" (Max, non-Latino, FPD). Jordan, a non-Latino CJA attorney, said:

> I think we get plenty of time. And I think to the extent that we wouldn't, that there's plenty of forgiveness as far as if you need more time. Prosecutors and judges are willing to continue these cases and stuff like that. You know, we have from 9:00 in the morning until noon to meet with them. I've never run out of time. The fact is you just run out of stuff to talk about. You've fully done your diligence on the case and that's it. As sad as it is, that's it. So as far as the process itself, no, I don't think I would change anything.

Other attorneys and judges also discussed the similarities of timing with non–Operation Streamline cases, specifically those called "flip-flops," which is a term that generally refers to plea bargains used in the federal court. These flip-flop proceedings are similar in content to Operation Streamline but take place over about a week and usually include at least two visits to court for defendants and additional time for clients to consider the plea bargain. As justification for the proposition that Operation Streamline provides sufficient time, more non-Latino/as (48%) compared Operation Streamline to flip-flops than Latino/as (16%). Harry is a non-Latino CJA attorney who demonstrated almost no work-related role strain. He explains his reaction to activists by asserting that Operation Streamline is "the same" as every other case he takes:

They've sent me these emails from time to time—about how I can end Operation Streamline, but—This is all I do, Streamline and flip-flops. [The setting doesn't] affect the way I do the proceeding. [Operation Streamline] is pretty much the same work as flip-flops. It's just that it has a name and so it gets targeted [by activists]. The flip-flop calendar is just like Streamline but [defendants] get a week of time served in after they initial them. When you get assigned a flip-flop, then you go out to the prison to talk to the person. But I give the same exact talk to them in the prison. You have the same time, too, and then you have a similar hearing like Operation Streamline. But it seems to me not to be that different from flip-flops.

Not only does Harry not "think about it much," a telling sign of lacking any social identity management strategies, but also he does not draw a distinction between his Operation Streamline clients and flip-flop clients in terms of the time he spends talking to them, even though they have more time to process the facts of their case. In fact, attorneys have minimal time constraints when visiting clients in flip-flop cases. Harry later said he has had so many clients he can barely remember any of them, so he was sure he spent the same amount of time with them all.

Overall, then Latino/as were more concerned about having insufficient time with clients in the morning consultation session of Operation Streamline than non-Latino/as. These Latino/a respondents demonstrated the identity management strategy of negotiated time identification because they had thought more about these temporal issues, wanted to see the amount of time spent with clients changed or expanded, and were more concerned about the immigration repercussions of insufficient time than non-Latino/as. This links to the idea of Latino/a respondents experiencing more work-related role strain as well as competing role and social identities through their continued participation in Operation Streamline.

Changes to Operation Streamline Over Time

Many respondents see Operation Streamline as "better" than its predecessor in Tucson—known as "the petty calendar system"—and believe that the program has improved over time in terms of how defendants are treated. Many participants cite this over-time improvement as a reason they feel comfortable participating in Operation Streamline as it existed prior to the COVID-19 pandemic halting the program. Oscar, a Latino FPD, felt that critics of Operation Streamline fail to recognize its intent or how it fits into the progress of history. He said:

Streamline came along [and it is] really an awful lot better than [the previous system of all] flip-flops. But it's sort of become the poster child of everything that's wrong with everything. You know, it's—it's funny, but okay. People don't know that Streamline is just the latest procedural iteration of enforcement of 1325 and 1326. I mean, it's not something that's really all that different than what was going on before, other than it's slightly more organized and set aside from the other courtrooms. And honestly, it's actually better in terms of time spent with clients. I mean, these flip-flops were going through in large numbers before, too.

This represents another identity management strategy related to temporal identification made by respondents who compare Operation Streamline to the "petty calendar" that existed before the program's implementation in 2008, as well as sharing how Operation Streamline has changed over time. Respondents described Operation Streamline as "the lesser of two evils" (Austin, non-Latino, CJA) in comparison to how clients were treated before the program existed. A total of 48% of Latino/a respondents—double the 24% of non-Latino/a respondents—compared Operation Streamline to the "petty calendar" that existed before 2008, emphasizing that they had more time (and privacy) with clients than they had before.

Under the petty calendar system before Operation Streamline, the court would assign defendants a time on the court calendar—such as 9:15. Clients would then meet their public defender for the first time usually just 10 or 15 minutes before the first hearing. Attorney participants told me how they would meet with three to five defendants at once in a holding cell; there would be a screen in between and no confidentiality. There were usually not sufficient seats for the lawyers and all of the clients in the cells to sit. Clients who were taller than 5″4′ would have to squat or lean over in order to see through the screen to be able to talk to their lawyer. A group hearing would follow; everyone pled guilty. As Héctor, a Latino CJA attorney who has worked with Operation Streamline since its inception, told me:

> Sometimes they would get 60 [or] more days in jail after having such a cursory review of their case with their attorneys. So, my point of reference was *that* [his emphasis] travesty. And I said, well, this [Operation Streamline] is a hell of a lot better.

Héctor emphasized that, while Operation Streamline does not offer strict confidentiality, clients get direct, one-on-one contact with a lawyer unlike in the "petty calendar" system. He described the interaction as "much more professional," calling it a "more quality experience" for defendants. Héctor acknowledged that Operation Streamline realizes a prosecutorial goal in terms of larger numbers of convictions, but he felt that, on balance, Operation Streamline had improved the way defendants were treated:

> Now, in the afternoon session, you know, the numbers are roughly double what we used to have in the morning and, you know, I understood that that was the prosecution initiative at the time but, for me, I was less worried about the distressing optics of the afternoon session. I was just

more concerned and happier to be there participating in something where defendants got a quality experience with their lawyer in the morning.

For Héctor, his involvement in Operation Streamline is justified because it is better than the system it replaced. Thus, he is using the identity management strategy of negotiated identification with a time before Operation Streamline to justify his continued participation.

Another Latino/a FPD, Oscar, describes the time before Operation Streamline similarly to Héctor:

> There was always a petty calendar, and there was always a 1325/1326 procedure before Streamline. And it—I mean, look, originally, these kinds of flip-flops were an awful lot worse than Streamline. You would have ten minutes, maybe, to meet with three or four people—and you would be meeting with them in the courtroom, giving them a plea to sign and marching them up to the judge right then. No confidentiality, hardly and time, and that was—that was deemed okay back then. Nobody complained about that.

Though he differs from Héctor in terms of the numbers of defendants being processed at each time, Oscar also confirms that FPDs were working on 1325 and 1326 cases before Operation Streamline and under worse conditions. The negotiated identification with a time before Operation Streamline as done by these Latino/a attorneys and judges suggests an identity management strategy that allows them to better justify their continued involvement with Operation Streamline because it was better than what came before.

Similarly, respondents see the 2013 shift away from prosecuting first-time border-crossers to focusing on prosecuting "criminal aliens"—people with a criminal record in the United States—in a positive light. For ease and clarity, I have dubbed this switch to focusing on criminal aliens "Streamline 2.0."

Many Operation Streamline attorneys and judges justified their participation in Operation Streamline based on the "criminal alien" focus of Streamline 2.0. Some non-Latino/as also discussed this change, but there was more emphasis on the "good deal" that clients received when Latino/as discussed this change. Thus, instances of negotiated identification with Streamline 2.0 were coded as an identity management strategy and were found to be used more frequently by Latino/as at 45% compared to only 14% of non-Latino/as.

When I asked Vivian, a Latina CJA attorney, about her "likes and dislikes" in her job, she had this to say regarding the legal benefits her clients are now receiving in Streamline 2.0:

> As far as liking the program, I mean, obviously I don't think anybody wants people to go to prison for immigration offenses. But now—which is different than when Streamline first started—there are those clients

who are really benefiting. I have people who are going through the felony system who have less severe backgrounds than some of the people who are coming through Streamline now. So, on one end, they're getting a benefit and I do like that part about it. But it's always hard to see somebody with no real criminal history have another prior after Streamline.

Despite describing her own distaste for the program, Vivian also gives the added description of how Operation Streamline may now actually be a "better deal" for clients than going through the regular system—at least if they were to be charged with the felony offense. This justification represents a specific identity management strategy of negotiated identification with the times before Streamline 2.0.

Esteban, who is a Latino CJA attorney, talked about this advantage as well. As he said, Operation Streamline's maximum sentences are shorter than a felony conviction might hold, "so it's a big benefit to some of these individuals and they're more than happy to accept the 180 days." He mentions some Operation Streamline clients who have prior felony convictions who would be subject to felony charges and sentences of 2, 10, or 20 years in prison if their border-crossings were tried outside of Operation Streamline. He also pointed out that with the lack of felony convictions that come from Operation Streamline, defendants can later apply for citizenship through, for example, citizen children, although the Operation Streamline plea does shut that avenue for usually at least ten years (Sarabia 2012; Martínez and Slack 2013). Esteban's attention to these far-reaching consequences suggests he is particularly understanding of the situation his clients are in and recognizes the issue at hand: "I mean, it's hard. I understand. I understand why they try this way. But I try to tell them what they are doing and that's all I can do."

The fact that more Latino/as than non-Latino/as emphasize that there has been progress in terms of the law's treatment of their clients suggests that they have needed to find more reasons to justify their involvement in Operation Streamline. Because they are feeling more strain of being involved in Operation Streamline than their non-Latino/a colleagues, Latino/a legal professionals use more identity management strategies given their non-situationally valued race/ethnicity in our current systems of structural inequality. Using negotiated identifications with different themes of time demonstrates their extra identity management work.

Place: Oh, Canada

Another negotiated identification used by respondents had to do not with time, but with place. There were many claims regarding distinctions—or lack thereof—between policies governing the Canada-U.S. border and the México-U.S. border. This often came up when I would ask about the relevance of race/ethnicity to the Operation Streamline process. While both Latino/a legal professionals and non-Latino/a legal professionals made this

Canada-México comparison, they did so to opposite effect. Latino/as would argue that Canadians would likely be treated better than the primarily Mexican defendants in Operation Streamline and non-Latino/as would claim they would be treated the same, failing to recognize the racialized nature of immigration in the U.S. Context (Chacón 2009; Golash-Boza 2015).

Six out of seven references to Canada by non-Latino/as were brought up in the race/ethnicity portion of the interviews to claim that the program would treat white Canadian nationals the same way it was treating Brown Mexican nationals. Magistrate Judge Angle, non-Latino, in responding to the idea that activists have highlighted the racialized component of Operation Streamline, gave the following response:

> That to me is the most ignorant kind of statement I can imagine. I mean there just aren't a lot of German or Italian illegal aliens trying to get into the U.S. illegally. I would submit to you that if there was a problem with immigration in Canada, there would be the same kind of response and it would be white people that would be coming in. They would absolutely just transfer Streamline to those courts if that were the case.

The judge went on to describe the focus on keeping Mexicans out as an economic issue, rather than one having to do with race or ethnicity. He argued it was primarily about keeping American jobs for Americans, but not about racial/ethnic exclusion. Of course, the literature on immigration (Rodriguez and Menjívar 2009; Molina 2014; Abrego et al. 2017) shows that structural racism and systemic economic inequality are highly correlated, but the Judge here refuses to think race is a factor in any way, shape, or form. He uses the Canadian counterpoint to highlight what he thinks would be the hypothetical similar treatment of white migrants trying to enter the United States without documentation.

Barney—who was one of the three attorneys out of all respondents who supported and defended Operation Streamline and wanted to expand the program—argued that Operation Streamline should be in place at the Canadian border specifically. He also said race/ethnic identity should have no place in interior enforcement throughout the 50 states as well. As a white CJA attorney, he argued, "I think every single person arrested—caught [illegally] in the country—should go through Operation Streamline, wherever they are, no matter their race." He then proceeded—in a mock Canadian accent using what some consider a Canadian slur—to impersonate a Canadian who had entered the country illegally, saying "You know what I'm talking about, eh? You know us illegal hosers?" He then concluded:

> There should be this kind of Streamline process to get all people who are here illegally out of the country. They shouldn't be here, you know. We don't have an immigration problem. We just have an unwillingness to buck up our immigration process.

Interestingly, however, Barney named two other cities in Arizona as well as Florida, Georgia, and Texas—all states where Latino/a immigrants predominate—as examples of places where Operation Streamline should be expanded, rather than states that border Canada such as Michigan, Washington, or Maine. This is a clear example of structural racism playing out in micro level identity strategies as legal professionals attempt to rationalize their continued participation in this program.

In contrast to the above non-Latino/a uses of negotiated identifications with the Canadian border, Latino/a attorneys and judges all but called the program racist when they made specific references to Canada. For example, when I asked Imelda, a Latina CJA attorney, about racial/ethnic tensions around Operation Streamline, she said:

> I guess we don't have much to compare it to is the problem. There's not a bunch of whites—a group of white people coming across. Maybe in Canada if there was a mass exit or influx of Canadian people coming across the border unfettered, maybe we'd have something to compare it to. But I guess we just don't. And, umm, I don't want to say it's racial, but it's a bit inhumane why they would keep them in this warehouse for two days, no shower. [pause] And in court, um, you know, it doesn't look great to have all these dark-skinned clients chained. I guess, I don't want to say racial, just because you don't have anything to compare it to, but it is inhumane. My thinking, though, would be that if there was an influx of white Canadian people coming across the border, they would treat them better. Yah, I definitely think they would, so maybe that is a racial tension.

Imelda shrinks from outright saying that Operation Streamline is a part of structural racism, but she does admit there would likely be better treatment for defendants if they were white. She has to follow her own analogy to its logical conclusion in order to really describe the process as racialized. Others were more direct, such as Hugo, a Latino CJA attorney, who said, "I don't know that any Canadian in his right mind would want to come into this country, but if he did, he sure wouldn't be sent through something as awful as Streamline."

Though only 10% of Latino/a respondents used the identity management strategy of negotiated identification with Canada, they all did so to describe Operation Streamline negatively in comparison to how Canadian people—who they identified as primarily white—would be treated in an immigration proceeding. In contrast, 33% of non-Latino/as used this identity management strategy and all but one respondent did so to suggest a positive comparison—that is, white Canadian migrants and current Operation Streamline migrants would be treated the same. As such, Latino/a legal professionals who compared the program to Canada specifically said Canadians would be treated better, while non-Latino/as did the opposite, saying Canadians would be treated the same. This denial of the structural racism present in Operation Streamline goes against the majority of social scientific and legal literature on the program specifically (Boyce and Launius 2013; De La Rosa 2019; Finch and Stryker 2020; Finch 2021; Sarabia and Perales 2021) and on the trend of increasing criminalization of migrants (Chacón 2009; Rodriguez and Menjívar 2009; Menjívar and Abrego 2012).

Beliefs/Ideas/Values through Common Metaphors

Sometimes work-related role strain and competing role and social identity management were dealt with through negotiated identifications that were linked to commonly shared beliefs/ideas/values. In the case of Operation Streamline, commonly used metaphors represent shared ideas. In my coding scheme, I found several common metaphors used to describe Operation Streamline, legal professionals' roles in Operation Streamline, and Operation Streamline defendants. These metaphors include comparing the program to other human rights abuses, comparing the defendants to animals, and comparing legal professionals to pawns or low-level cogs. Latino/a respondents were often more empathetic to clients and activists in their interviews, as demonstrated by their increased work-related role strain compared to non-Latino/a legal professionals (90% versus 43%). In order to deal with this work-related role strain and the subsequent competition of their racial/ethnic social identity with their legal professional role identity, one identity management strategy Latino/a respondents (45%) used more often than non-Latino/a respondents (24%) was using these common metaphors in their descriptions of the Operation Streamline process and their perspectives on themselves and clients. This discourse is an example of negotiated identifications with certain beliefs/ideas/values, that is, shared metaphors. In this section, I describe the identity management strategy of negotiated identifications with certain beliefs/ideas/values that became apparent through the use of common metaphors and references.

Vivid metaphors, which were more frequently used by Latino/a respondents, serve as an identity management strategy that provides strong testament to the work-related role strain and social and role identity competition experienced by Latino/a attorneys and judges. Prior literature on immigration-related media coverage specifically has shown that "everyday metaphor [...] weaves the patterns of social relations into natural language expression" (Santa Ana 2002:19–20). That is to say, the language we use conveys the racialized socialization of our broader system. Linking the macro level structural racism of both immigration and criminal justice systems in the United States, many attorneys and judges used these metaphors as a micro level identity management strategy.

Particularly for Latino/a legal professionals, animal metaphors describing Operation Streamline defendants came up with quite some frequency. Comparing defendants to animals conveys a shared belief/idea/value that defendants are being disrespected. Estelle, a Latina CJA attorney, said that trying to help a client was like trying to "save one fish in a huge oil spill."

Julio, a Latino CJA attorney, compared Operation Streamline to a "cattle call" because it processes so many people at once. Sabrina, a Latina CJA attorney, felt that the high quantity of people made Operation Streamline feel "like leading sheep to the slaughterhouse." Andrew, another Latino CJA attorney, said that the top thing he would change about Operation Streamline is to "stop treating them [clients] like animals." The barriers to allowing clients to attend to their personal hygiene—in addition to the lack of access to a showering and changing clothes, he also referred to the denial of dental hygiene—struck him as a sign of disrespect for defendants.

Another set of metaphors related to attorneys' sense of powerlessness within their own role as legal professionals. Three Latino/a CJA attorneys— Soledad, Oscar, and Santana—all described themselves as a "cog" in, respectively, a "machine," a "system," and a "wheel." Santana also said she felt like the government's "pawn." This pattern of a sense of lacking control (being a cog) and the inhumane way defendants were treated (like animals) was not only evidenced in interviews but also was supported by behavioral observations. That is, Latino/a attorneys had markedly different client inter-actions in court proceedings. Specifically, as noted previously, they had more physical interactions with clients and used less hand sanitizer after working with clients, which also demonstrates their more human nature by touching clients and not treating them as unclean, despite their access to means of personal hygiene.

The use of these metaphors by Latino/a respondents at nearly double the rate of Latino/a legal professionals demonstrates a specific identity man-agement strategy that highlights their work-related role strain and their social and role identity competition. Latino/a legal professionals have more vivid language to problematize the work that they are doing in Operation Streamline. Racialized metaphors around immigration are not new (Santa Ana 2002; Zavisca 2016), but the ways in which Latino/a legal professionals problematize their own work and the treatment of their clients in Operation Streamline demonstrate the continued impact of structural racism in the immigration and criminal justice systems. Shared negotiated identifications with these same beliefs/ideas/values—with metaphors where Operation Streamline defendants are treated inhumanely (literally like animals), and attorneys are not a part of serving substantive justice (just legal pawns or cogs in a formal justice system)—show the additional identity management that Latino/a legal professionals encounter when thinking about why they continue to participate in this problematic program.

Summary

Latino/a legal professionals displayed specific patterns in negotiated iden-tifications with times, place, and beliefs/ideas/values compared to their non-Latino/a counterparts. Table 5.1 provides a summary of the iden-tity management strategies discussed in this chapter as they break down

Table 5.1 Negotiated Identifications by Racial/Ethnic Group

Strategy	Definition	Example	Group using strategy more	% Latino/a using strategy (N = 31)	% Non-Latino/a using strategy (N = 21)
Time: Insufficient Time with Clients	Negative attitudes toward the amount of time attorneys spent with clients in Operation Streamline	"Sometimes the problem is you just don't have enough time to lay out the entire scenario"	Latino/as more likely to say insufficient time	**35**	10
Time: Operation Streamline as Better than Pre–Operation Streamline Days	Comparing Operation Streamline to the "petty calendar" that existed before Operation Streamline's implementation in 2008 and deeming it better	"So, my point of reference was that travesty. And I said, well, this is a hell of a lot better."	Latino/as more likely to use as justification	**48**	24
Time: Streamline 2.0 as an Improvement	Comparing Operation Streamline at the start (2008) to Operation Streamline since changes made in 2013 and deeming it an improvement	"But now, which is different than when Streamline first started, there are those clients who are really benefiting."	Latino/as more likely to use as justification	**45**	14

(Continued)

Table 5.1 Negotiated Identifications by Racial/Ethnic Group *(Continued)*

Strategy	Definition	Example	Group using strategy more	% Latino/a using strategy (N = 31)	% Non-Latino/a using strategy (N = 21)
Place: Oh, Canada	Latino/as use comparison to explain that Canadians would be treated better than Mexicans	"My thinking, though, would be that if there was an influx of white Canadian people coming across the border, they would treat them better." —Latino/a	Latino/as more likely to problematize	10	**33**
	Non-Latino/as make opposite case	"I would submit to you that if there was a problem with immigration in Canada, there would be the same kind of response and it would be white people that would be coming in" —Non-Latino/a	Non-Latino/as more likely to use as justification		
Beliefs/Ideas/ Values: Common Metaphors and References	Animal metaphors	"It's like a cattle call"	Latino/as	**45**	24
	Cog metaphors	"I'm a very low-level cog in the system"			
	References to other human rights abuses	Holocaust; Japanese Internment			

by racial/ethnic group. In terms of using time-based justifications, 35% of Latino/as found the time they spent with clients to be insufficient compared with only 10% of non-Latino/as. Additionally, half of the Latino/a respondents justified their participation in Operation Streamline by comparing it to pre–Operation Streamline or early Operation Streamline proceedings, while only a quarter or less of non-Latino/as did so. A total of 33% of non-Latino/as suggested that if Operation Streamline were to happen on the Canada-U.S. border, there would be no difference in how defendants were treated based on race. On the other hand, the 10% of Latino/a respondents who compared the Mexican and Canadian borders suggested it would absolutely be different based on the race/ethnicity of border-crossers. Finally, negotiated identifications with beliefs/ideas/values via metaphors that compared defendants to animals and themselves to cogs—as well as references about Operation Streamline being similar to other human rights abuses such as the Holocaust and Japanese Internment Camps—were twice as likely to be used by Latino/a respondents. Micro level identity management strategies differed based on racial/ethnic social identity because of larger macro issues around structural inequality that are represented by Operation Streamline.

References

Abrego, Leisy, Mat Coleman, Daniel Martínez, Cecilia Menjívar, and Jeremy Slack. 2017. "Making Immigrants into Criminals: Legal Processes of Criminalization in the Post-IIRIRA Era." *Journal on Migration and Human Security* 5(3):694–715. https://doi.org/10.1177/233150241700500308.

Boyce, Geoffrey, and Sarah Launius. 2013. "Warehousing the Poor: How Federal Prosecution Initiatives Like "Operation Streamline" Hurt Immigrants, Drive Mass Incarceration and Damage U.S. Communities." Retrieved January 15, 2022. https://dspace.hampshire.edu/bitstream/10009/935/1/popdev_differentakes_082.pdf.

Chacón, Jennifer M. 2009. "Managing Migration Through Crime." *Columbia Law Review Sidebar* 109:135–48. http://dx.doi.org/10.2139/ssrn.2033931.

De La Rosa, Bill. 2019. "Criminalization, Social Exclusion, and Punishment: The United States Prosecution of Migrants Under Operation Streamline." MSC Criminology and Criminal Justice, 2018-19, Dissertation Submission. https://www.law.ox.ac.uk/sites/files/oxlaw/bill_de_la_rosa_msc_dissertation.pdf.

Finch, Jessie K. 2021. "Racialized Habitus in Criminal Immigration Defense Attorneys." Pp. 165–84 in *The Logic of Racial Practice: Explorations in the Habituation of Racism*, Bahler, Brock, Ed. Lanham, MD: Lexington Books.

Finch, Jessie K., and Robin Stryker. 2020. "Competing Identity Standards and Managing Identity Verification." Pp. 119–48 in *Identity and Symbolic Interaction: Deepening Foundations; Building Bridges*, Serpe, Richard T., Stryker, Robin, and Powell, Brian, Eds. New York, NY: Springer.

Glaeser, Andreas. 2000. *Divided in Unity: Identity, Germany, and the Berlin Police.* Chicago, IL: University of Chicago Press.

Golash-Boza, Tanya Maria. 2015. *Immigration Nation: Raids, Detentions, and Deportations in Post-9/11 America.* Boulder, CO: Paradigm Press.

Martínez, Daniel E., and Jeremy Slack. 2013. "What Part of 'Illegal' Don't You Understand? The Social Consequences of Criminalizing Unauthorized Mexican Migrants in the United States." *Social and Legal Studies* 22(4):535–51. https://doi.org/10.1177/0964663913484638.

Menjívar, Cecilia, and Leisy J Abrego. 2012. "Legal Violence: Immigration Law and the Lives of Central American Immigrants." *American Journal of Sociology* 117(5):1380–421. https://doi.org/10.1086/663575.

Molina, Natalia. 2014. *How Race Is Made in America: Immigration, Citizenship, and the Historical Power of Racial Scripts*. Los Angeles, CA: University of California Press.

Rodriguez, Nestor P., and Cecilia Menjívar. 2009. "Central American Immigrants and Racialization in A Post-Civil Rights Era." Pp. 183–99 in *How the United States Racializes Latinos: White Hegemony and Its Consequences*, Cobas, José A., Duany, Jorge, and Feagin, Joe R., Eds. Boulder, CO: Paradigm Publishers.

Santa Ana, Otto. 2002. *Brown Tide Rising: Metaphors of Latinos in Contemporary American Public Discourse*. Austin, TX: University of Texas Press.

Sarabia, Heidy, and Maria Perales. 2021. "Operation Streamline: Producing Legal Violence, Racialized Illegality, and Perpetual Exclusion" Pp. 403–415 in *Race and Ethnicity in the U.S.: The Sociological Mindful Approach*, Brooks, Jacqueline, Sarabia, Heidy, and Ida, Aya Kimura, Eds. San Diego, CA: Cognella Academic Publishing.

Sarabia, Heidy. 2012. "Perpetual Illegality: Results of Border Enforcement and Policies for Mexican Undocumented Migrants in the United States." *Analyses of Social Issues and Public Policy* 12(1):49–67. https://doi.org/10.1111/j.1530-2415.2011.01256.x.

Zavisca, Jane. 2016. "Metaphorical Imagery in News Reporting on Migrant Deaths." Pp. 167–89 in *Migrant Deaths in the Arizona Desert: La Vida No Vale Nada*, Rubio-Goldsmith, Raquel, Fernández, Celestino, Finch, Jessie K., and Masterson-Algar, Araceli, Eds. Tucson, AZ: University of Arizona Press.

6 "I'M AN AMERICAN. THE PROBLEM IS THIS: YOU THINK I'M A MEXICAN"

CITIZENSHIP/GENERATIONAL STATUS

> You know, it's like I'm a different type of Mexican, and people often think that everybody's life is the same.
> —Mateo, Latino, Criminal Justice Act (CJA) panel attorney

> If it's someone who's lived here a long time—like a DREAMer—I'll say, 'You're just like me. You're a *pocho* like me.'
> —Emiliano, Latino, CJA attorney

Mateo's great-grandparents immigrated to the United States decades ago, but his grandparents and parents were born U.S. citizens, as was he, making him a third-generation American. Emiliano's parents immigrated to the United States, and he was born in shortly afterward, making him a second-generation American. These two men, and their quotes above, typified the variations I generally found between Latino/a attorneys and judges in terms of how their sense of racial/ethnic identity varied given their different citizenship/generational status.

Emiliano described the Spanish term "*pocho*" as meaning "a sellout"— slang for someone of Mexican ancestry who was raised and perhaps even born in the United States, but who lacks knowledge of Mexican culture and/ or the Spanish language. His formulation of thinking about clients as "like me" clearly suggests a feeling of connection he has to these border-crossers. His reference to DREAMers also highlights the importance of citizenship/ generational status as a social identity. DREAMers are a social category created from the "Development, Relief, and Education for Alien Minors (DREAM) Act." While this act has yet to pass through U.S. Congress, Barack Obama's "Deferred Action for Childhood Arrivals (DACA)" policy (enacted through Presidential Memorandum) is also linked to DREAMers (Abrego 2018; Cornejo and Kam 2021). Generally, those who qualify for DACA—and those who often get called DREAMers—are primarily Latino/a youth who are not legal U.S. residents, who were brought to the United States before the age of 16, who have lived in the United States for five or more years, and who have attended or graduated from U.S. schools.

DOI: 10.4324/9781003272410-7

Mateo on the other hand is trying to distance himself from stereotypes that he might be assigned and distinguish himself as "a different type of Mexican." This social-structural distancing from racial/ethnic assumptions in general—and from his clients in particular—demonstrates he does not think the folks he works regularly with in Operation Streamline are, as Emiliano suggests, "like me."

While there were certainly racial/ethnic patterns of distinction between Latino/a and non-Latino/a attorneys and judges as discussed in prior chapters, there was also variation *within* the group of Latino/a legal professionals. In this chapter, I discuss the first social identity that resulted in variation of identity management strategies within the Latino/a attorneys and judges: citizenship/generational status.

Given that Operation Streamline is focused on citizenship as a legal qualifier, Latino/a attorneys' and judges' identity management strategies varied based on their own personal relationship to citizenship, including their generational background. Though all the attorneys and judges who practiced in Operation Streamline were U.S. citizens, there was quite a bit of diversity in their generational status. This diversity influenced how respondents thought about the salience of their racial/ethnic identity as well as influencing their experiences of work-related role strain, social and role identity competition, and use of identity management strategies.

Latino/a attorneys and judges who came to the United States as young children or whose parents immigrated to the United States (defined here as 1.5- and 2nd-generation) had "thicker" racial/ethnic social identities and were more likely to experience work-related role strain and increased social and role identity competition. I argue this thicker identity for 1.5- and 2nd-generation migrants, like Emiliano, is due to a close social proximity to migrants via their parents, but also a shared sense of the United States as their home and a strongly Americanized social identity. This understanding of the migrant experience combined with a solid U.S. upbringing increases 1.5- and 2nd-generation respondents' racial/ethnic social identity, levels of strain, subsequent competition between social and role identities, and use of identity management strategies.

Contrastingly, those who immigrated themselves later in life to become naturalized citizens as well as those whose nearest migrant ancestor was beyond their grandparents (third-generation-plus) had thinner racial/ethnic identities and experienced less work-related role strain. Respondents who were naturalized/migrated themselves later in life are intentionally trying to distance themselves from their defendants and thus felt less strain and competition from their social and role identity. That is to say, immigrating later in life is associated with more conscious thinking about wanting to give up a Mexican identity in favor of being seen as more American. While one might expect recent immigrants to identify with migrant defendants more closely, instead, naturalized respondents see themselves as having come "the right way" (meaning legally) and hence distinguish themselves strongly from people going through Operation Streamline. Similarly, those in the third-generation-plus do not have personal experience with either their own or a parent's immigration and have always identified with the United States. This group also distanced themselves from defendants because they wanted to be seen as fully American. Thus, in line with the conceptualization of *competing identity management*, respondents who were not 1.5- or 2nd-generation (and who were naturalized/migrated themselves later in life and those from the third-generation-plus) demonstrated fewer incidents of work-related role strain and competition between their social and role identities due to this thin identity. These two groups—the 1.5/2 group and the 1/3+ group—systematically varied in their use of identity management strategies.

The variation in identity management strategies between these two groups of Latino/a respondents (the 1.5/2 group and the 1/3+ group) bore a striking resemblance to the patterns seen between Latino/as and non-Latino/as. This further supports the conceptualization of *competing identity management* because those with the strongest or "thickest" sense of a non-situationally valued racial/ethnic social identity (Latino/a) have to do more work to manage their work-related role strain as well as their competing social and role identities. The systemic patterns in using identity management strategies were the same for the 1.5/2 group and Latino/a legal professionals overall in all strategies except for negotiated identifications with the time since Streamline 2.0 began.

Citizenship/Generational Status's Effect on Racial/Ethnic Social Identity

Among Latino/a attorneys and judges, there were a variety of factors that contributed to how their social identity of race/ethnicity impacted their work. Though salience is often a term associated with role identities, I argue here that Latino/a respondents vary in the salience of their racial/ethnic social identity, which would in term affect work-related role strain, competition between social and role identities and use of identity management strategies. In order to further specify what is meant by the salience of the racial/ethnic social identity, I turn to the social constructionist point of view on racial/ethnic identities. Cornell and Hartmann (1998) use two axes to describe variation in racial/ethnic identity: "thick versus thin" (how much one's racial/ethnic identity organizes one's life) and "assigned versus asserted" (to what degree do external versus internal forces create and maintain racial/ethnic identity). Thus, we can think of Latino/a respondents as having variation in the salience of their social identity in terms of thick/asserted identities and thin/assigned identities.

Based on the relevance of citizenship in criminal immigration proceedings, this social identity of citizenship/generational status has some influence on legal professionals' other social identities, such as race/ethnicity. My findings suggest that citizenships/generational status influences the salience of racial/ethnic social identity via Cornell and Hartmann's two axes to create either thicker/asserted social identities or thinner/assigned social identities in Latino/a attorneys and judges. This then influences their work-related

Table 6.1 Latino/a Respondents by Citizenship/Generational Status

Naturalized/migrated themselves later in life	4 (13%)
1.5-generation	7 (23%)
2nd-generation	12 (39%)
3rd-generation-plus	8 (26%)
	31 (100%)

role strain, sense of competition between identities, and resultant identity management strategies.

There was a great deal of variation in immigrant history among the attorneys and judges involved in Operation Streamline. Table 6.1 shows the distribution of Latino/a respondents according to their citizenship/generational status.

The third-generation-plus group included CJA attorneys like Dean who called themselves "American-Mexicans," referring to the fact his ancestors lived on land annexed during the Treaty of Guadalupe-Hidalgo in 1848. As Dean said, this made them among "the first Americans" because their families had never migrated into the United States. Another common phrase for this used by two respondents in this category was "my family didn't cross the border, the border crossed them." The naturalized group included migrants who had attended law school in México or other foreign countries and some Operation Streamline attorneys who had become U.S. citizens within the preceding ten years. Most of the 1.5-generation had come to the United States at an age under 10.

In combining groups based on their identity management strategies, 100% of the 1.5/2 group expressed some form of work-related role strain; 84% in the 1/3+ group did, which, while still a majority, is a smaller one. The 1.5/2 group generally showed thicker and asserted racial/ethnic identities. This created a stronger sense of competition between a salient racial/ethnic social identity and their work-related role, which made them more likely to sympathize with defendants and denounce Operation Streamline. In contrast, the 1/3+ group was more likely to display thinner and assigned racial/ethnic social identities. This impacted their work in Operation Streamline in that the 1/3+ group was not especially concerned with issues of substantive justice and displayed less work-related role strain. This demonstrates decreased competition between a less salient racial/ethnic social identity and work-related role, resulting in identity management strategies where they were less sympathetic toward clients and more likely to engage in social-structural identity distancing activities between themselves and their migrant defendants.

A summary of the differences between these two groups (the 1.5/2 group and the 1/3+ group) is provided in Table 6.2 with full discussion in the

Table 6.2 Association of Social Identity Salience with Citizenship/Generational Status

Demonstration of salience	Definition	Example	Group using strategy more	% Naturalized (N = 4)	% 1.5-gen. (N = 7)	% 2nd-gen. (N = 12)	% 3rd-gen.-plus (N = 8)
Thick identities	One's racial/ethnic identity strongly organizes one's life	"My dad came in the 50's to this country. And he would always remind us [...] that we were Mexican, that we were immigrants here. So that is really present in all I do."	1.5- and 2nd-generation Latino/as	25	71	67	25
Asserted identities	Internal forces create and maintain racial/ethnic identity	Volunteer full immigration history	1.5- and 2nd-generation Latino/as	25	71	75	23
Thin identities	One's racial/ethnic identity weakly organizes one's life	"I'm a Mexican, too, but I don't listen to Indian music; I don't dance to that type of music. I don't even know it. You know, it's like I'm a different type of Mexican."	Naturalized and 3rd-generation-plus Latino/as	50	29	33	63
Assigned identities	External forces create and maintain racial/ethnic identity	"Yah, people say, 'Well, how can you do that?' like to me, as a judge, sentence these people to time. I look at them and I say, 'I'm an American. The problem is this: you think I'm a Mexican.'"	Naturalized and 3rd-generation-plus Latino/as	50	29	25	50

following sections. Each generational group was tallied individually, but the similarities between naturalized/migrated themselves later in life and third-generation-plus respondents and 1.5- and 2nd-generation respondents are clear from the percentages provided.

Thick and Asserted Identities among 1.5- and 2nd-Generation Migrants

Latino/a respondents in the 1.5/2 group were more likely to demonstrate thick and asserted social identities than those in the 1/3+ group. That is, for 1.5- and 2nd-generation migrants, racial/ethnic identity more heavily organized their lives, and they asserted their connection to this social identity, embracing their Latino/a identity. They thought about their racial/ethnic identity as important to them, as well as influential in their lives and work. For example, I found that respondents in this group immediately volunteered their full immigration history when I asked if they were from Tucson originally. This demonstrates an internal assertion of social identity. Most Latino/a legal professionals in the 1.5/2 group linked their social identity of citizenship/generational status with their social identity of racial/ethnic identity. For example, Soledad, a Latina CJA attorney says:

> Both my parents are immigrants. I had some sense about responsibility because of that. How they didn't get a lot of benefits, but they were here, and we were lucky they were here. I am a proud Chicana. I have a very long history of immigration activism in the law. And that, that's why I'm really sort of surprised that I'm here in this situation being challenged because of my work related to immigration.

Immediately volunteering one's citizenship/generational status unprompted demonstrates a high degree of assertion—that is, internal forces are being used to create and maintain one's racial/ethnic identity. Additionally, volunteering the identity of "proud Chicana" while giving her immigration history links these two social identities of citizenship/generational status and race/ethnicity.

Others described the "thickness" of their racial/ethnicity as being tied to their citizenship/generational status—that is, the degree to which being a Latino/a links to immigration and influences/organizes one's life—including in their work in Operation Streamline. Carlita, a Latina CJA attorney, gave a particularly clear demonstration of thick social identity salience when I asked her whether racial/ethnic issues arise often in her work:

> I was just thinking you know, my dad died about a year ago, but he used to always pray for the immigrants who were coming across the border. My dad came in the 50s to this country. And he would always remind us of how important our heritage was—that we were Mexican, that we

were immigrants here. So that is really present in all I do. He was very proud of what I do, my dad, because these people need our help. I was lucky to be born here, so I feel compelled to help them.

Not only does Carlita explain that her racial/ethnic and immigration heritage organize her life (they are "present in all I do"), but it also influences how she interacts with clients (compassionately), and it affects how she thinks of the work she is doing (helping immigrants). This demonstration of social identity salience via a thick social identity of both citizenship/generational status and racial/ethnic identity affected the work of Latino/a legal professionals who were in the 1.5/2 group.

Pochos *and DREAMers*

Emiliano was not the only respondent to use the term *pocho*. He and others in the 1.5/2 group directly related his status as a Mexican raised in the United States to his sympathy for his clients, saying he would tell them outright he understood:

> I tell clients, you were raised here since a young age and sending you back to México is the real punishment, not the jail time. And I understand that. And I wish there was some way we could figure out how to make it not happen. And, so, let's go through and try and figure out how—if there's anything that we can do.

Relating to a client's citizenship/generational status is also a way to connect to certain clients who share this mixed nationality background and have a preference for living in the United States. For these respondents, *pocho* is a shared variation of a citizenship/generational status social identity that they can use to relate to clients even though the term *pocho* is typically used to mean something negative—like a traitor. Judge Darrell, who is Latina, also identified herself as a *pocha* when she said, "I am a lucky *pocha* compared to the folks going through Operation Streamline."

It was common for respondents across the citizenship/generational status groups, and including non-Latino/a respondents, to discuss the so-called DREAMers in their interviews. However, members of the 1.5/2 group were much more likely to bring up this category unprompted and describe them as particularly troubling cases that created work-related role strain and role and social identity competition. César, a Latino CJA attorney, explains:

> The other ones that are sad are the young people who were brought here by their parents. It's through no fault of their own, but now they have no home. They're like a man with no country. We don't let them stay here and they don't know anything about living in México at all. They're just kids and now they've got a really rough life ahead of them.

He mentioned another case that had troubled him particularly—a young man who had been raised by an older sister because their parents worked long hours—and how the older sister was in a gang. Because of her illicit dealings, the young man also got deported at 18 to a country he had never known. César explained how the young DREAMer had done "literally nothing wrong" but because of his citizenship/generational status, he was forced to suffer for his family members' choices and so he no longer qualified for DACA or other immigration programs.

Overall, the 1.5/2 group demonstrated a special affinity for their clients compared to the 1/3+ group, being more likely to personally identify with clients and see them as similar to them. Julio, a Latino CJA attorney, for example, describes this close link:

> When I first did Streamline, I really didn't like seeing the sea of humanity chained together. These people are like my family. They're like my people. I would have almost any of these people that are in Streamline as my neighbor. And if I had a flat tire, I'm sure they'd come over and help me. I feel terrible that this is the rotten system we have in place for these people who could be my distant cousins or something.

Julio clearly considers the system lacking in substantive justice and describes competition between his identity as a Latino/a and how he feels about participating in the larger, structurally inequitable system around Operation Streamline.

Thin and Assigned Identities among Naturalized Migrants and the Third-Generation-Plus

Contrasting the thick and asserted identity of the 1.5/2 group, the 1/3+ group does not especially associate their work or their lives with their racial/ethnic social identity that they share with defendants because they highlight a different citizenship/generational status. Naturalized citizens (who chose to migrate themselves later in life) and third-generation-plus respondents had a thin sense of racial/ethnic identity—meaning they did not use it to define themselves or their work. The 1/3+ group often discussed how their social identity less heavily organized their lives—thinness—and how they were merely assigned a connection to defendants by those who are not directly involved in Operation Streamline (such as activists, courtroom observers, and the media). Overall, the 1/3+ respondents were less distressed about issues of substantive justice, showing less work-related role strain, less competition between their social and role identity, and different uses of identity management strategies.

In contrast to embracing an immigrant or Mexican identity, 1/3+ Latino/a attorneys and judges did not think their race/ethnicity was especially relevant to their work and as such felt less work-related role strain and less identity competition. They often distinguished themselves a great deal from their defendants, who they did assign a salient Latino/a immigrant identity. In contrast to these legal professionals *asserting* their own racial/ethnic identity, external forces or circumstances tended to *assign* a racial/ethnic identity upon them. The 1/3+ group would discuss the mistaken assumptions of others that they would have a special connection with Operation Streamline defendants who share one social identity (race/ethnicity) but not another (citizenship/generational status). Judge Ochoa, Latino, emphasized his citizenship/generational status as an American when explaining the critiques that he receives about Operation Streamline:

> Yah, people say, 'Well, how can you do that?' like to me, as a judge, sentence these people to time. I look at them and I say, 'I'm an American. The problem is this: You think I'm a Mexican.' There are people who look at you and say, 'Wait a minute, you should care about Mexicans,' and it's like 'Wait a minute, No.' This is not class, this is not ethnic, it doesn't matter. This is justice.

Judge Ochoa explained to me he was a fourth-generation, "American-Mexican." He distinguishes himself from Operation Streamline defendants on the basis of this status and objects to the idea that being a Latino should have any bearing on the work he does in Operation Streamline. This refusal to identify with defendants is a demonstration of an assigned identity by those who are not directly involved in Operation Streamline (such as activists, courtroom observers, and the media), as opposed to him asserting that identity himself.

Mateo, a CJA attorney, made similar remarks. He is a migrant himself who attended law school in México, but he has been a naturalized U.S. citizen for many years. When I asked whether there was any sort of racial/ethnic tensions in his work for Operation Streamline, he said there absolutely was not. As such, he rebuffs not only the relevance of his recent immigrant identity but also demonstrates his thin racial/ethnic identity as only assigned by others. When I pressed him on the topic, he said:

> That's—there's a tendency to group—when somebody invites me to a dinner even with Hispanic groups of people, what we get is a group of young people dancing like Indians, or like dancing to indigenous style music, you know? I told my friend the other day, you know, I'm a Mexican, too, but I don't listen to Indian music; I don't dance to that type of music. I don't even know it.

Perhaps Mateo was politely and indirectly accusing me of stereotyping him—of being similar to someone who asserts a strongly Mexican or mixed-indigenous culture. Or perhaps he was merely saying that Operation Streamline is not part of the larger structural inequities associated with immigration and criminal justice systems because it is simply based on nationality. It began to seem like the latter when he went on to say:

> So, some people see everything like it's racist, and *La Raza* and they say, 'We are like this, we like tacos and this type of music.' But it's not true because there's lots of Mexicans like me that live in a different world. I didn't even notice about all of this stuff. I don't see any racist aspect.

Mateo went on to argue that Operation Streamline could not be "racist" because of the multitude of people working in the system who are Latino, though he acknowledged that there might be isolated cases of racism:

> How many Hispanic judges do we have? In Justice Court we have a bunch of Latinos. We have Hispanic judges in City Court, as well. The attorneys, most of them, are Hispanic. Most of the people working there are Hispanic, you know. I'm sure that, you know, sometimes you get people who are racist or whatever, but it's not the majority. It's an isolated type of personality problem.

He did not directly consider the possibility that the *system* is racist. Similar to non-Latino/a legal professionals who practice a colorblind version of criminal justice, he fails to see any structural issues and instead focuses on individual prejudices. Indeed, he even accused activists of being unreasonable and backward:

> You go to a meeting, and you see these people playing and dancing like 200 years ago and this costume from 200 years ago. Who cares? Like Grijalva, Raúl Grijalva [one of Tucson's congressmen, a second-generation Mexican immigrant], acting like we're still in the Mexican Revolution of 1910, 1915. You don't belong to that war. He thinks everything is racist, everything is *La Raza* [the people/Hispanics/ Latino/as]. It's like their little world. And I disagree with that. And I'm not even that conservative. I'm just saying, you know, we're not all the same as these immigrants coming through Streamline.

Mateo denies that he is similar to Operation Streamline defendants and in doing so denies the assigned racial/ethnic connection he has with them put onto him by outside groups. He creates a boundary between himself and those with thick Latino/a identities as well, referencing a politician who strongly asserts his racial/ethnic social identity. While it might seem counter-intuitive that a recent immigrant would demonstrate a thin racial/ethnic identity, his desire to be seen as a citizen is more salient. Mateo also emphasized the socioeconomic class difference between himself and his clients, the vast majority of whom are from poorer families than his own.

Dean, a Latino CJA attorney, made remarks fairly similar to Mateo's, despite being fourth-generation. His grandparents were all born in the United States and his ancestors had become American citizens because they lived on land that became part of the United States in the middle nineteenth century. He said he does not identify with clients because for "American-Mexicans" like him, with as long a history in the United States as his family's, they focus more on their citizenship/generational status than their race/ethnicity:

> It's like Irish Americans and Italian Americans—we've become Americanized. We don't identify with [Operation Streamline defendants]. I don't know about the other [attorneys], but I would think most of them who just grew up in Tucson and were just another American— the third-generation, the fourth-generation—I don't think they identify with these clients. I don't identify myself with those people. I don't identify myself with Mexicans. I mean, that's a whole different culture. I could never identify with them. So, it's a totally different life—but it had no impact on me or people of my generation or the one before. Streamline is just a totally different group of individuals.

Dean proposes Latino/a immigrants of later generations are assimilating in the same manner as the Italians or Irish decades before them, suggesting a thin racial/ethnic identity that is far less relevant than his salient citizenship/generational status. Not only does Dean fail to identify with "those people," he assumes other Latino/as also do not identify with them and that Operation Streamline defendants are a "totally different group" compared to the Latino/a legal professionals working in Operation Streamline.

Sergio, a CJA attorney who naturalized as an adult after growing up in Latin America, also emphasized that his family had "come the right way, waited our turn, not one of these Operation Streamline things." He created a strong boundary between himself and his clients who, implicitly, then, are doing it "the wrong way." He discussed not feeling any particular connection to them through his shared citizenship/generational status because the way they have come into the country was not approved, as opposed to how his family came into the country. As such, he had very little work-related role strain and thought that Operation Streamline "isn't some terrible program."

The 1/3+ group confirmed the initial expectations of *competing identity management* that naturalized and third-generation plus respondents have a thinner/assigned racial/ethnic identity, which results in less work-related role strain, less competition between social and role identities, and management strategies where they often differentiated themselves from the defendants they represent. By disavowing their shared racial/ethnic social identity with Operation Streamline defendants, Latino/a legal professionals from the 1/3+ group instead emphasize their different citizenship/generational status in order to mitigate work-related role strain and role and social identity competition.

Differences in Identity Management Strategies by Citizenship/Generational Status

Respondents of the third-generation-plus had a thinner/assigned sense of Latino/a social identity—that is, less thick and asserted identities—that decreased respondent work-related role strain and subsequent competition between social and role identities. This then resulted in identity management strategies of distancing themselves from recent-immigration experiences and Operation Streamline defendants. This attitude is in contrast to the 1.5- and 2nd-generation Latino/as who have a more immediate connection to the struggle of migrants while still being fully Americanized. Those with thick and asserted identities feel compelled to explain the importance of the help they are offering defendants or the work they have done with other immigration assistance in the community. This increased work-related role strain for the 1.5/2 group then leads to more competition between social and role identities and subsequent variation in identity management strategies.

Table 6.3 summarizes the variation in the use of identity management strategies by citizenship/generational status. As it shows, the pattern of group differences between the 1.5/2 group and the 1/3+ group was similar to the differences seen between Latino/a and non-Latino/a respondents. The only distinction has to do with the tendency to emphasize that Streamline 2.0 is better than the original Operation Streamline. It is also the case that role playing was essentially equally common in the two citizenship/generational status groups, although the tiny difference went in the same direction as between the Latino/a and non-Latino/a groups. Given the small numbers, it is hard to make significant conclusions based on these patterns, but it is relatively clear that the distinction between Latino/a and non-Latino/a respondents is largely the same as the difference between respondents in the 1.5/2 group and the 1/3+ group. Even though 1/3+ group respondents experience some of the same anti-immigrant and anti-Latino/a sentiment that the 1.5/2 group experience from activists or those who are not directly involved in Operation Streamline, citizenship/generational status seems to be a more salient identity for them than their thin, assigned racial/ethnic identities.

In addition to these patterns of identity management strategies, a re-analysis of the "tallies of touch" data also shows a clear pattern that the citizenship/generational status of Latino/a attorneys mattered in their physical contact with clients. As reported in Chapter 4, Latino/a attorneys were more likely to touch clients and less likely to use hand sanitizer. Within the group of Latino/a attorneys, though, there were similar

Table 6.3 Identity Management Strategies by Citizenship/Generational Status

Strategy	Definition	Group using strategy more	% 1.5- and 2nd-gen. using strategy (N = 19)	% Naturalized and 3rd-gen.-plus using strategy (N = 12)
		Dealing with role strain		
Identity consolidation	Recognizing the substantive justice issues around Operation Streamline while using formal-legal justice and a desire to help defendants to explain their continued participation	1.5- and 2nd-generation Latino/as	74	25
		Influences of social identity		
Demonstration of in-group similarities	Understanding defendants' actions because of a shared personal background (either via migration history, cultural and social references, or shared upbringing)	1.5- and 2nd-generation Latino/as	79	75
		Negotiated identifications		
Time: insufficient time with clients	Negative attitudes toward the amount of time spent attorneys with clients in Operation Streamline	1.5- and 2nd-generation Latino/as more likely to say insufficient time	58	0
Time: Operation Streamline as better than pre-Operation Streamline days	Comparing Operation Streamline to the "petty calendar" that existed before Operation Streamline's implementation in 2008 and deeming it better	1.5- and 2nd-generation Latino/as more likely to use as justification	53	42
Time: Streamline 2.0 as an improvement	Comparing Operation Streamline at the start (2008) to Operation Streamline since changes made in 2013 and deeming it an improvement	Naturalized and 3rd-generation-plus Latino/as	37	58

(Continued)

Table 6.3 Identity Management Strategies by Citizenship/Generational Status *(Continued)*

Strategy	Definition	Group using strategy more	% 1.5- and 2nd-gen. using strategy (N = 19)	% Naturalized and 3rd-gen.-plus using strategy (N = 12)
Place: Oh, Canada	Latino/as use comparison to explain that Canadians would be treated better than Mexicans	1.5- and 2nd-generation Latino/as more likely to problematize	5	17
	Non-Latino/as make opposite case	Naturalized and 3rd-generation-plus Latino/as more likely to use as justification		
Beliefs/ideas/values: common metaphors and references	Animal metaphors	1.5- and 2nd-generation Latino/as	53	33
	Cog metaphors			
	References to other Human rights abuses			
Role identity management strategies				
Role playing	Simply going through the motions of your daily work in Operation Streamline	Naturalized and 3rd-generation-plus Latino/as	32	33
Role making/identity extension	Trying to expand the typical program of daily work in Operation Streamline to diminish role strain	1.5- and 2nd-generation Latino/as	58	50
Psychological compartmentalization	Separating work at Operation Streamline in order to cope with role strain	1.5- and 2nd-generation Latino/as	21	17
Fictive story telling	Use of embellishment or hyperbole to explain how respondents got to where they are	1.5- and 2nd-generation Latino/as	16	8

distinctions based on citizenship/generational status with respect to touch. That is to say, 1.5/2 Latino/as (those with thicker/asserted identities) were doing more of the physical contact with clients, at 63%, comparted to the 1/3+ Latino/as (who have thinner/assigned identities) who made up only 46% of the tallies. Hand sanitizer use showed the same pattern, but very narrowly (54% versus 51%). Approximately half of the Latino/a attorneys used hand sanitizer after physical contact with clients regardless of their citizenship/generational status.

Summary

Many scholars have called for increased research on variation within the panethnic cluster of "Latinos" (Ochoa 2004; Jiménez 2010; Martínez and Gonzalez 2021) based on other characteristics such as immigration status, language usage, class, and gender. Findings about this larger "Latino" group are often over-generalized by not only the public, but also by scholars who often lack sufficient data to make distinctions on various other demographic factors within the category of Latino/a. Given the qualitative nature of this research, I am especially well positioned to explore variation within the social identity category of Latino/as.

This chapter addresses the differences within the group of Latino/a attorneys and judges based on the social identity of citizenship/generational status. First, the theory of social construction of identity describes the variation in salience of racial/ethnic social identities for Latino/a respondents in terms of thick and thin identities and assigned and asserted identities. Findings show that citizenship/generational status among Latino/a respondents influences racial/ethnic social identity salience. Two groups emerge: (1) those respondents who are 1.5- and 2nd-generation Latino/as who tend to have thicker racial/ethnic identities that they themselves assert and (2) those respondents who are naturalized/migrated themselves later in life or who are third-generation-plus who tend to have thinner racial/ethnic identities that are assigned by others.

Variations in citizenship/generational status impact how thick/asserted or thin/assigned a respondent's racial/ethnic social identity is, which affects their subsequent level of work-related role strain and identity competition. Overall, 100% of 1.5- and 2nd-generation Latino/as experienced work-related role strain, whereas only 84% of naturalized/migrated themselves later in life and third-generation-plus respondents did so. This increased experience of strain for 1.5- and 2nd-generation Latino/as in turn affects the level of competition between their social and role identities and affects their identity management strategies. Naturalized/migrated themselves later in life and third-generation-plus Latino/a respondents more closely resembled non-Latino/as in their use of identity management strategies, while 1.5- and 2nd-generation Latino/as mirrored the overall Latino/a patterns explicated in Chapter 4. This supports the conceptualization of *competing identity management because* Latino/as who had a more salient racial/ethnic identity experienced more work-related role strain and had to engage in higher levels of identity management strategies than those who experienced less work-related role strain.

References

Abrego, Leisy J. 2018. "Renewed Optimism and Spatial Mobility: Legal Consciousness of Latino Deferred Action for Childhood Arrivals Recipients and their Families in Los Angeles." *Ethnicities* 18(2):192–207. https://doi.org/10.1177/1468796817752563.

Cornejo, Monica, and Jennifer A. Kam. 2021. "Exploring the Ascribed and Avowed Identities of Deferred Action for Childhood Arrivals (DACA) Recipients in Early Adulthood." *Cultural Diversity and Ethnic Minority Psychology* 27(3):460–70. https://doi.org/10.1037/cdp0000378.

Cornell, Stephen, and Douglas Hartmann. 1998. *Ethnicity and Race: Making Identities in a Changing World*. Thousand Oaks, CA: Pine Forge Press.

Jiménez, Tomás R. 2010. *Replenished Ethnicity: Mexican Americans, Immigration, and Identity*. Berkeley, CA: University of California Press.

Martínez, Daniel E., and Kelsey E. Gonzalez. 2021. "Panethnicity as a Reactive Identity: Primary Panethnic Identification among Latino-Hispanics in the United States." *Ethnic and Racial Studies* 44(4):595–617. https://doi.org/10.1080/01419870.2020.1752392.

Ochoa, Gilda L. 2004. *Becoming Neighbors in a Mexican American Community: Power, Conflict, and Solidarity*. Austin, TX: University of Texas Press.

7 "I'LL TRY TO GET YOU A BOY LAWYER"

GENDER DIFFERENCES

Estelle and Bridget were in rushed side conversations with their respective clients before Judge Ochoa when I heard Bridget expressing audible frustration through a loud sigh. They were both trying to get his attention in order to get him to slow down, but he was calling rounds of defendants forward without giving attorneys any chance to record asylum claims, medical issues, judicial recommendations, or other special circumstances. Bridget said, "He's just ignoring the ladies!" While the smile on her face suggested she was joking, it certainly contained a kernel of truth. Many attorneys of both genders complained to me about Judge Ochoa's speed, but other research in the sociology of gender does show that women often have to make special efforts to assert themselves in professional conduct (Babcock and Laschever 2003; Martin and Jurik 2006).

In justice professions (Siemsen 2004; Helfgott et al. 2018; Batton and Wright 2019) as well as in the broader immigration system (Pessar 2005; Ochoa-O'Leary 2008; Donato and Gabaccia 2015; Boyd 2021), the social identity of gender can impact many outcomes. Through iterative use of grounded theory and experience in the field, clear patterns emerged with respect to the impact of research participants' gender social identities as well as for defendants involved in Operation Streamline. Within the Latino/a legal professionals in particular, Latina attorneys and judges were more likely to demonstrate work-related role strain and describe competition between their social and role identities than Latino attorneys and judges (100% versus 86%).

Women attorneys and judges were also more likely to sympathize with their migrant defendants than their men counterparts overall, resulting in extra identity management and increased work-related role strain. Latinas specifically—due to the interactions between social identities of race/ethnicity and gender—were more likely to engage in conscientious impression management, *a la* Goffman (1967), and had to work extra hard to establish authority and credibility with clients due to their gender. Latina attorneys were also more likely to have an activist background and describe their work-related role as attorneys with an intention of serving others and improving their life conditions, which increased their level of work-related role strain.

DOI: 10.4324/9781003272410-8

Complicating our understanding of these patterns in this particular study, however, is the fact that the non-Latino/a respondents were all men except for two white women respondents. However, I could compare the Latino men to the non-Latino men, and I found that men attorneys and judges—regardless of race/ethnicity—displayed benevolent sexism that increased work-related role strain. Generally speaking, all men attorneys expressed greater concern for the women defendants in Operation Streamline than for the men.

In this chapter, I first discuss how gender as a social identity was relevant in court proceedings and interviews with attorneys and judges. First, I look at men's benevolent sexism; then, I examine gendered patterns with respect to respondents' comments about emotional issues. I also look at statements in which Latina respondents suggested they have to engage in extra identity management in order to assert their authority with clients. Finally, I examine work-related role strain among attorneys who had activist backgrounds and altruistic motivations—most of whom were Latina.

The Influence of Gender

Throughout the course of my empirical investigations, the social identity of gender was a relevant influence in the daily lives and work of attorneys and judges in Operation Streamline. Given the patriarchal nature of both the U.S. legal system and the U.S. immigration system (Golash-Boza, Duenas, and Xiong 2019), many respondents emphasized the significance of gender and it also served to pattern the behavior of both men- and women-identifying attorneys and judges. None of the legal professionals who were interviewed identified outside of the man-woman binary. There were both gender-focused responses from interviews with Latina attorneys, as well as gendered patterns in courtroom observations. In observations, women attorneys were more likely to sit with other women attorneys, both in the hallway before the proceedings began as well as during the proceedings in the courtroom. Also, I noted more interaction between women attorneys who relied on other women for support, such as the example with Estelle and Bridget and Judge Ochoa.

The conceptualization of *competing identity management* argues that competing social identities impact work-related role strain, competition between social and role identities, and use of identity management strategies. These various social identities are dependent on current systems of structural inequality, so in addition to the issues of race/ethnicity and citizenship/generational status, structural concerns around intersectionality and patriarchy created variation based on the social identity of gender, particularly for Latina legal professionals. As such, gender social identity impacted work-related role strain, interacted with other social identities of race/ethnicity, and changed respondents' identity management strategies.

Benevolent sexism (Glick and Fiske 1997, 2011) was a very common theme that came up, particularly for men-identifying legal professionals. Men of all races/ethnicities had a very different response toward the women defend-ants in Operation Streamline compared to the men. This often occurred through men attorneys or judges wanting to protect the women defendants and suggesting that legal processes should be changed for women specifi-cally. This occurred both because of protective patriarchy and idealization, which is all too common among legal professionals (Salerno and Phalen 2019; Rachlinski and Wistrich 2021). When men legal professionals thought about Operation Streamline as more problematic for women defendants, this resulted in higher levels of work-related role strain—that is, worrying about substantive justice issues in Operation Streamline specifically as it pertained to women defendants.

Women legal professionals whom I interviewed also discussed emotional issues more frequently in their work-related roles than men respondents. They discussed how they had more sympathy with all their clients in gen-eral but also for women clients who were mothers in particular because of a tendency to overidentify with these clients. I also provide evidence of women respondents, especially judges, acting more sympathetically toward all Operation Streamline defendants based on their association with a mothering role identity. Additionally, many women respondents, specifically Latinas, suggested that they have to engage in extra identity management to assert their authority with clients, usually men. This took the form of impression management as an identity management strategy and other role extensions, such as calling forth the gendered role of "mom" as another identity management strategy. Finally, Latina respondents were also more likely to experience work-related role strain about being involved in Operation Streamline because of activist backgrounds and altruistic motivations. This discussion of "jaded" views on the legal system based on an activist background occurred almost exclusively among Latina attor-neys, providing an interesting look at the interaction of racial/ethnic and gender social identities.

Benevolent Sexism from Men Attorneys and Judges

Benevolent sexism is part of ambivalent sexism theory developed by Glick and Fiske (1997) and is defined as "subjectively positive attitudes toward women in traditional roles: protective paternalism, idealization of women, and desire for intimate relations" (119). I found that in the case of Operation Streamline, many men attorneys and judges demonstrate protective pater-nalism and idealization of the women defendants in Operation Streamline. I observed that men attorneys were more likely to offer a hand to help their women clients up to the stand than their men clients and would con-fer with them more thoroughly if they had difficulty answering a judge's questions. This is just one example of how benevolent sexism organizes many Operation Streamline interactions. This kind of benevolent sexism was associated with higher levels of work-related role strain because men respondents were more concerned about the substantive justice concerns and other problematic aspects of Operation Streamline as they applied to women defendants. As such, the social identity of gender is brought in Operation Streamline because of existing structural inequities of patriarchy in legal and immigration systems.

Judge Mott is not Latino, and he shows little evidence of work-related role strain. However, he is the only Operation Streamline judge who processes all of the women defendants first at every proceeding. He framed this as a practical concern, saying he knows they are transported separately from the men, and that doing the women first lets the women's transport leave the court sooner. However, he also noted, "with the women, they are kept separately [from men], but I am not sure how much they can avoid being in close proximity to others being held, so I want them to get out as soon as possible." His assumption is that the men in Operation Streamline—who are defendants in federal court for the exact same border-crossing infraction as the women—would automatically present a threat or danger to the women defendants. And while women are indeed more likely to be victims of violence or sexual assault at the hands of men than vice versa, it is telling that he is more concerned about the Operation Streamline process for women defendants. Showing the relevance of the gender social identity, he says he hopes to make the process "quicker and less dehumanizing" for these women in particular. In speaking with Judge Mott, the only indication he gave that Operation Streamline was "dehumanizing" was in reference to women defendants. As such, it was the gender of a defendant that gave him any pause toward the substantive justice or any indication that he held work-related role strain.

Sergio, a Latino Crrminal Justice Act (CJA) panel attorney, also expressed particular concern about women defendants, saying that men defendants in Operation Streamline sometimes sexually harass the women defendants and that the marshals do not always recognize it. Sergio says he has asked marshals to move men who were harassing women defendants, or that he has himself moved women who are subject to harassment in the court seating. While Sergio naturalized as an adult and displays little work-related role strain in general, he felt strongly about the treatment of women in Operation Streamline:

> These women, they're already coming from cultures where they're taught to be deferential and now, they're going to have to sit here and speak up to a professional, especially if they get a male lawyer and they have to speak up and speak for themselves. It's a very scary thing. They're coming from a very deferential point of view. And then to be having that kind of, 'Hey, *chula* [beautiful]' stuff coming at them, I don't like that at all.

Sergio's reference to *machismo* in Latin American culture further demonstrates benevolent sexism in the form of protective paternalism. While these cultural issues are indeed relevant to Operation Streamline proceedings, his response is to protect women clients, not change the broader system that has placed them there. In fact, he more closely monitors his *own* behavior and describes working with women clients as more problematic, which I argue is a demonstration of work-related role strain. He noted that the physical aspects of dealing with women clients made him uncomfortable:

> I talk to these tiny, tiny women from the interior of México that obviously are darker skinned and more Indian features than Spanish features, or from Guatemala or whatever, I mean, they barely make it up to here on me [motions to sternum], you know. And I'm sitting there trying to say, 'I'm here for you and, you know, I'm here to listen to you.' They're looking down and they're ashamed, and the power structure is just—it's not only heartbreaking but it's just—it's just like, you know, I feel like I'm shouting at them. And when I ask them to speak up, you know, I feel like I'm scolding them.

He concluded, "The guys, it's going to be a little more fluid and an easier situation. But I always just feel that that experience for the women is really, really tough and it makes it tough on me." Women clients were the only aspect of the program that created work-related role strain for Sergio, demonstrating his protective paternalism and the relevance of structural gender inequality in Operation Streamline.

Hugo, a Latino CJA attorney, goes even further than Sergio and Judge Mott. Whereas Sergio expresses concern about harassment and Judge Mott expresses concern about women defendants in Operation Streamline mixing with men, Hugo calls flat out for special treatment for women defendants:

> I don't think it's fair to treat women the same as other border-crossers. To me, the way I look at it is women are in a way, way more vulnerable position. I did a case where these women were material witnesses and they were not able to talk about what happened to them and I was somehow, in interviewing them, I learned that they had been kidnapped and raped repeatedly for weeks before they actually made it into this country and became material witnesses and the government didn't know about it. The government didn't know about what their experience was. It was just through this weird set of questions that I asked them that the whole thing came up.

Hugo is a second-generation U.S. citizen, and he had previously expressed his certainty that the United States would never treat Canadian border-crossers the way it treats Latino/a border-crossers and so he demonstrated broad work-related role strain. But he was particularly concerned, based on his conversations with defendants, about the treatment of women at the border. He recognized that many Latin American governments do not protect women from rape by *coyotes* (border-crossing guides) saying, "there should be some means to keep them from being harmed the way they are by these *coyotes*." While full legal reform of the immigration system is the more broadly obvious way to reverse the vulnerability of such women, he stopped short of embracing such an idea, saying that illegal border-crossers should be "you know, taken out of the country, punished, sure." But he did not think that Operation Streamline should process women at all.

Hugo thus displays a defining trait of benevolent sexism: "subjective affection as a form of prejudice" (Glick and Fiske 2011:533). The sympathy and recognition of women's exploitation near the border is well intentioned (hence it is a *benevolent* form of sexism) and clearly causes emotional distress for men attorneys and judges but still results in differential treatment based on sex and certainly underestimates the exploitation of men, who are also frequently assaulted in crossing the border. Subjective affection for women defendants by men legal professionals creates the desire for differential treatment of women in Operation Streamline, but instead of saying Operation Streamline in general—or the current legal and immigration systems in general are problematic for *all* defendants—these men respondents focus only on how women are treated poorly.

Despite stopping short of full-system reforms for all defendants, men attorneys and judges displayed extra work-related role strain with women defendants based on idealization as well as protective patriarchy. Men respondents tended to recognize the difficulties these women had in crossing and then also idealized what the women defendants were attempting to do in crossing via gendered expectations of traditional "feminine" behavior. In an example of this idealization and how it creates more work-related role strain, Jesús, another Latino CJA attorney, said:

> Women are—I think, in my opinion, the women are particularly more heart-wrenching stories, because if you're a woman crossing that border that's so dangerous, your life has to be at a point that is—is—in my opinion, beyond comprehension, that most Americans can't ever comprehend that someone's going through that much that they put themselves through that, you know, just to work and, you know, provide for their family.

Jesús assumes that all women clients are crossing the border as a means of taking care of their families. Jesús not only explains how heroic these women defendants are but also explains that they are more heart-wrenching stories for him personally. Several men attorneys idealized their women clients in this fashion, highlighting what good mothers or daughters they must be—i.e., fulfilling a traditional feminine gender expectations. This is a specific example of work-related role strain informed by the social identity of gender, where men attorneys and judges are especially concerned about substantive justice issues in Operation Streamline based on their assumptions about the extra level of suffering women defendants undergo in Operation Streamline.

Emotional Boundaries for Women Legal Professionals

Women respondents demonstrated more emotional work and sympathy toward defendants of both genders compared to men respondents. However, they also expressed special sympathy for women clients who were mothers in particular. Many highlighted their own role identity of mother to explain these patterns. Women respondents were also more likely to describe instances of work-related role strain overall based on their feelings about their work. They were also more likely to cry on the job and in their interviews when discussing substantive justice issues for all defendants in Operation Streamline.

In courtroom proceedings, the only two women judges, Judge Pine, who is not Latina, and Judge Darrell, who is, tended to show different interactions with defendants than men judges based on their gender social identity. They were more likely than the men judges to be patient with defendants and repeat themselves as well as to be more apologetic to defendants. Judge Pine took particular care to make sure defendants were comfortable. If a defendant became confused during questioning, she would say things like, "Don't worry, it's fine. I don't have a problem repeating the question for you," and other reassuring phrases to calm defendants. She told me in her interview that she knew defendants were scared, and that the last thing she wanted to do was make them think she was "the bad guy who was going to yell at them." She may have been thinking of a particular "bad guy"— another judge who was notoriously curt with defendants—but none of the men judges discussed wanting to make defendants feel more comfortable, unless they were specifically referencing women defendants.

Women judges and attorneys alike described more empathy for defendants as well as demonstrating it more clearly in courtroom interactions. For example, women attorneys were the most likely to make physical contact with defendants. In revisiting my "tallies of touch" analysis, I found that women attorneys (64%) were more likely to engage in physical contact than men attorneys (38%). Carlita, like most Latina CJA attorneys, demonstrated higher attachment and sympathy for clients, saying she hoped to comfort them through pats on the back or rubs of the shoulder, help them with taking off the translating headphones, or guide them with soft touches on the shoulder or back.

An additional explanation for gendered patterns is that most of the women respondents in this sample are mothers. This mother role often intersected with other issues of racial/ethnic social identity, too. A conglomeration of roles (motherhood, attorney) and social identities (gender, race/ethnicity) was particularly challenging for many Latina attorneys and judges who have their own children.

Judge Darrell, who is Latina, said that seeing how frightened defendants were in the first few weeks she worked in Operation Streamline was very hard on her. She said that she kept to the minimum sentence, time served, in every petty offense. She felt she had to always give Operation Streamline defendants the chance to speak, and she continuously found the reasons people cited for immigrating heartbreaking in spite of the criminal immigration laws she was required to uphold. She recalled:

> My daughter studied abroad in [Central American country]. So, at one point, it was tough for me. I remember having this lady, this tiny little woman from [the same country] talking about her circumstances in Streamline and I just started crying. I cried almost the whole proceeding because I'm just thinking, here my daughter is in, in [Central American country] being taken care of, being treated like a little princess by these people and here's this lady coming here and we're going to send her back and God knows what's going to happen to her on her journey.

> So, being involved in Streamline, it's been very emotional. I haven't lost it like that again, but I think it was the circumstances of my daughter being there and the lady just saying something that pushed me over the edge, so you know it's really hard on the judges, too. Really hard. By Friday, we are just exhausted.

Crying on the job, which I only witnessed done by or heard about from Latina respondents, suggests more work-related role strain and the need for more identity management strategies to deal with this emotional distress. The social identity of gender particularly seems to interact with the role identity of mother as well as the social identity of race/ethnicity. This supports the conceptualization of *competing identity management* because of these overlapping systems of oppression for women of color in particular in the immigration and criminal justice systems.

Bridget, a Latina CJA attorney, remembered this incident of Judge Darrell crying, which had taken place some years earlier. The fact that Judge Darrell was crying upset Bridget very much as well. She was on the verge of tears herself, remembering that:

> [Judge Darrell] always gave them a chance to talk, and one of the people just—it was a woman, and she just started talking and she explained to the judge, you know, just her situation, and the judge just lost it. And it was very hard for her to talk again, you know? She couldn't talk, and she kept trying to talk and her voice would break up. And that was really hard and painful, I think, for all of us because it's, like, it was hard to watch her and, you know, we all felt it, but we had the benefit of being able to just be quiet; she had to keep talking.

Bridget had also cried in the courtroom, because the cut, bruised, and blistered feet of a young man who was wearing flip-flops made her think of her own son's feet. As she said:

> Something snapped, and I just thought how he had a mom who loved him and how, if she saw those feet, it would be so hard for her, and—and I thought about my own son and his feet and I just had to walk out of the courtroom. Sometimes there's nothing [you can do]; it's just a sad, horrible case, and what I'll say to them is I'll call your family, you know, make sure your kids know that I saw you today and that you said hello to them and that you love them, and that's all you can do. It's not much, but it's—that's it.

Statements like these suggest women attorneys and judges were more likely to sympathize with their migrant defendants overall than men respondents, but factors of motherhood and gender created more extreme emotional distress and subsequent work-related role strain. Women legal professionals were more likely to become emotionally involved and also to identify either with the Operation Streamline defendants and/or with the family of the defendants.

While I never observed any men legal professionals crying in court nor did any cry in interviews, Hugo, a Latino CJA attorney, acknowledged:

> When I talk [to clients] about the sentence—this is a time that gets difficult at times because when a person hears—they're in this country because they have children who are starving, they have a wife who's pregnant, they have all of these factors going on and they're here to earn money and someone says to them, you're going to be in jail for 60 days it's really hard for them to hear that. Sometimes I will hear out exactly what their story is, and it will be so close to my family's, and I will almost cry with them and then I will explain to them there's nothing I can do.

Counteracting Hugo's benevolent sexism is the fact that he mentioned the scenario in which a man wants to be in the United States to be with his pregnant wife, which suggests he may identify more closely with men clients. Regardless of the client gender, his most emotional aspect of his work is explaining the sentence, which sometimes makes him "almost cry," though he stops short of actually crying, which women legal professionals often said they did.

Estelle, a Latina CJA attorney, found women clients who were mothers particularly upsetting; she said that she often cries at work but always cries when she has a woman client who starts to cry. She identified with her clients as a mother herself, saying that she would do the same thing for her own children as her clients had done for theirs, noting, "the only difference between them and I is that I was born on this side of the border and that's the part that really is difficult because as you're looking at somebody who you know is just like me. It's like I'm looking into a mirror." Because Estelle identifies with her clients on so many identities (racial/ethnic social identity, citizenship/nationality social identity, gender social identity, and mother role identity), she feels like working with them is "looking into a mirror" and seeing a less-lucky version of herself. As such, we see how her competing identities almost all align with the less structurally advantaged identities of her clients, causing greater work-related role strain and many competing identities.

Estelle also said that she felt she had "secondary-trauma," comparing herself to people who work with refugees, but it seemed like her distress primarily came from working with mothers—regarding men, she said, "I can understand the males, I get why the males did it, but as a mom I know how difficult that decision has to be for a mother to leave her child." She dealt with her distress by spending time with her own child and practicing what she called "radical gratitude." This identity management strategy, of trying to recognize her own "luck" and privilege, was exclusive to Latina, mother respondents.

The challenge of staying engaged with Operation Streamline defendants while balancing emotions was particularly prominent for women. The intersection of various social identities (gender, race/ethnicity, and citizenship/generational status), in competition with various role identities (attorney, mother), demonstrates the profound influence of gender on legal professionals involved in Operation Streamline. In particular, the issue of emotions seems to be very much linked to gender social identity, in line with the growing literature on identity and emotions (Stets 2005).

Latina Respondents and Authority

Latina attorneys in particular were quick to bring up the fact that their gender social identity was a factor in their work-related role with clients beyond just emotional concerns. While I would have expected women attorneys in general to report that clients and others did not show respect for their authority as lawyers in equal measure regardless of race/ethnicity, the two non-Latina respondents did *not* report such difficulties while eight of the ten Latina attorneys did have these problems. This may reflect small numbers—it could be that non-Latina respondents experience the same slights as their colleagues and just happen not to take notice of them or share them. It is also possible that the traditional patriarchal element of Mexican culture commonly referred to as *machismo* means that Latinas—who share a racial/ethnic social identity with clients—experienced disrespect more often than non-Latina attorneys from their clients because of the racial/ethnic hierarchy in the U.S. immigration and legal systems. As such, Latinas would have to surmount additional barriers to be seen as competent and gain authority—the combination of social identities around gender and race/ethnicity. Latina attorneys and judges, then, experienced more work-related role strain than both Latino and non-Latino attorneys and judges. This also resulted in more intense identity competition between social and role identities when discussing Operation Streamline because Latinas were also being challenged due to their additional social identity of gender. In terms of the conceptualization of *competing identity management*, this brings in issues of patriarchy and intersectionality (Crenshaw 1989; Hill Collins 1990, 2017) for non-situationally valued social identities in competition with role identities, given the current systems of structural inequality.

Latina legal professionals described specific choices they have made to exhibit the markers of professional authority—including appropriate dress and formal means of addressing clients. Latinas were forced to account for their gender to clients more than Latinos based on structural gender inequality and, as such, Latinas were more likely to spend time and give conscientious thought to "better playing" into their attorney work-related role identity via commanding authority from clients. This means Latinas had to engage extra identity management strategies to do their work because of their gender social identity.

For example, I provided a vignette about a client becoming belligerent with his lawyer that clarifies the lawyer's gender as a man (Jason or Manuel). However, 60% of Latina attorneys suggested the lawyer's gender was a factor. Valentina, a Latina public defender, said after the vignette that men lawyers got "an automatic level of respect" that she was not given. She said she was more likely to be challenged than her men counterparts and that she was frequently addressed by clients using the Spanish familiar form of you, *tú*, while clients more frequently addressed men lawyers using the formal *usted*. *Tú* is generally used for family, children, friends, or peers, while *usted* is the default for elders, strangers, and authority figures. She explained that she personally made a point to only use *usted* with clients in order to cultivate a certain professional distance. She also said she intentionally carries a briefcase and always dresses in business attire to meet with clients, even in circumstances where she had seen men attorneys wear blue jeans. These strategies reflect Goffman's impression management strategies around dress (formal business attire), props (briefcase), and language adjustments (*tú* versus *usted*). This identity management strategy was exclusively coded for Latina legal professionals.

Another identity management strategy exclusively coded for Latina legal professionals was explaining the need for deference. Use of a more authoritative form of "you" can easily be seen as an indicator of deference in a Goffmanian sense. Valentina's conscientious use of these strategies based on her gender social identity is clear:

> I try to, I guess, know these things and use them appropriately. As a woman, I feel sometimes it's possible that I have that lack of authority problem, so I adjust as much as possible. I always dress very professionally, carry my briefcase. I expect to be treated as a professional by them.

I treat them that way. And I use those cultural norms that you would in those environments and a lot of men don't really have to do that.

Other Latina attorneys and judges described this same kind of identity management strategies around impression management and deference, though sometimes not until I asked. For example, when I asked CJA attorney Soledad about the impact of her gender identity, she said:

I think there's a—I don't want to say an inherent sexism, but there really is, culturally. Culturally, they're not used to there being female lawyers. And sometimes I think my manner is too much, uh, social worker not enough, you know, authority figure. That I—that the clients sometimes think, 'Well, you know, she's not really serious.'

She described a phone call with a client's wife that had taken place that very day in which, even though she introduced herself as the lawyer, the client's wife asked her repeatedly if she was really the "official" attorney. Soledad mentioned that she gives out business cards (a prop for identity management) on her first meeting with every client and every business contact. She also said that she always stands and shakes hands with clients to set a professional tone. Even so, she says:

Every once in a while, when I get a guy who says they don't believe me, it's like, 'Okay let's talk. I'll try to get you a boy lawyer.' And then an older male lawyer will come and talk to this guy. And it usually works. They say, 'She knows what she's talking about. You're foolish if you don't take this plea.' So, I think there's some—once in a while—some sexism that goes on with the clients.

Even though Soledad must sometimes cater to the client's sexism, she is usually able to work with them despite their initial resistance. Impression management (Goffman 1959, 1967) is very clear in explaining the importance of having to do identity work in order to define a work-related role. In the case of Operation Streamline, it was only the Latina attorneys who had to "overcome" both their gender and racial/ethnic social identities to better establish their role identity as an attorney. Props, such as business cards, having to repeatedly state and clarify work-related roles, and sometimes even having to get men attorneys to back them up to bolster authority are all identity management strategies that were unique to Latina attorneys.

Another option to garner authority was to play up an additional gender-specific role of "the mother." Five different Latina attorneys mentioned that as they aged, they could utilize their combined racial/ethnic and gender social identities to improve their work experience by expanding their attorney role to include a mothering role. CJA Latina attorney Sabrina, for example, said that she sometimes "play[s] 'the *mijo* [my son] card,' so to speak" in order to get clients' attention. Another CJA attorney Leonora explained:

> When I was younger, it was much more of a problem because they just thought I wasn't experienced. Now that I'm older, I think that my clients view me more as a mother figure, for the most part. I find myself referring to my clients as '*mijo* [son]' a lot because it turns out that I could be their mother and they could be my kid several times over [chronologically speaking]. They almost give you authority because it's like, "You know, I'm older and wiser and I know what's good for you.

This intentional use of the mother role to fulfill a certain authority position in the clients' minds demonstrates the extra level of identity management that these Latina attorneys have to do. No men respondents of any race/ethnicity mentioned any kind of fatherly connection to clients. As such, adding the mother role to their professional repertoire is an example of a role extension identity management strategy that was used specifically and only by Latina attorneys. Unlike how motherhood created an extra emotional struggle as described in the prior section, here, women attorneys try and convert what would otherwise be a gendered authority barrier into an advantage by extending their work-related attorney role to play "mom." In doing so, Latinas mitigate identity competition between professional role authority and gender social identity expectations. In other words, playing "mom" gives these Latina attorneys a unique source of authority that is based on their specific combination of gender and racial/ethnic social identities.

While none of the men, Latino or non-Latino, acknowledged the role of gender in establishing authority, Micah, very tall Latino CJA attorney, indirectly suggested gendered factors in terms of vocal pitch and physical stature when he said, "I also have a little bit of an advantage because—I think it's my size, and I sound like I speak with authority. So [clients] don't question me too much." On the other hand, Latina legal professionals knew they did not have these same advantages. Overall, then, in order to increase what is usually a lack of authority from clients based on the social identity of woman, Latina respondents in particular addressed the need to engage in the additional identity management strategies of impression management via dress, props, and language as well as role extension via the utilization of motherly behavior. This interplay of gender and racial/ethnic social identities with their attorney role identity speaks to the relevant social systems of patriarchy and structural racism within which Operation Streamline legal professionals must work.

Latina Activist Backgrounds and Altruistic Motivations

Latina attorneys were the group most likely to have an activist background; six of the ten described some of their current or previous work related to law and immigration as being "political" in nature and described themselves or their work as "activist." An even larger number, 70% of Latina attorneys, suggested they wanted to be attorneys because of altruistic reasons—such as helping others or improving equality in society. Most Latinas described their desire to help others and make changes via a career in the law as their original intent in going to law school. Sadly, many of these women then proceeded to describe how this notion of "trying to change the world" had shifted after actually practicing law. Nonetheless, most Latinas saw themselves as achieving positive social ends through their legal profession. Based on this pattern, the racial/ethnic identity of Latina and the gender social identity of woman patterned work-related role expectations and subsequent work-related role strain.

Estelle, for example, had been involved in activism-oriented immigration clubs while she was in law school and was very sympathetic to activists who oppose Operation Streamline and understood why they would stigmatize lawyers who participated. The social pressure from these activist groups had made her reluctant to sign up as a CJA attorney who participated in Operation Streamline. However, with the encouragement of more senior attorney colleagues, she came to see her work-related role in providing representation to Operation Streamline defendants as also having positive advantages. She noted, "at least I listen to them about the immigration issues because a lot of attorneys don't and that's a big deal." She acknowledged a danger of becoming "jaded" in her job, though, noting:

> Sometimes I worry, like 'Am I turning into one of those lawyers that are just here for a paycheck?' The ones who really don't care about the client? I'm not sure exactly how some of the attorney's got like that, but I don't want to be one of those jaded attorneys versus the activist kind of go-getter type of person I am. And so, I think that's something that I kind of struggle with especially in Streamline because it *is* depressing [emphasis hers] and also because I feel like I'm between a rock and a hard place in trying to help the clients because I obviously don't want them to be there in the first place, you know? But apart from trying to review the record and as far as making sure they know their rights, and what the government has to offer, there's not a lot to do. I've gotten some of them less time, you know, but yeah at least I still care, and I still try.

Estelle signaled she did not see Operation Streamline as providing substantive justice, saying that the program "doesn't really seem right or like 'real' justice, to me, in my opinion. Sometimes I feel like a traitor, and you know it's not how I like to see myself, so I struggle with that."

Estelle tried to mitigate her negative feelings and her work-related role strain by also providing "Know Your Rights" presentations for immigrants at different community organizations and giving free legal consultations to low-income clients. She acknowledged her own limitations, saying "I don't know what to do to make them stop but I can't—it's not something that I can have any control over." While recognizing the broader injustice of the "crimmigration" system, Estelle specifically took action to do the best she could both within Operation Streamline (caring about clients, making sure they know their rights, looking for immigration relief, or shortening their sentences) and beyond Operation Streamline by reaching out to the community in her legal role.

When discussing her activist past and then aligning it with her attitude of "at least I care," Estelle demonstrates her adjustment to helping the individuals ensnared in Operation Streamline, despite still having reservations about the goal and intent of the program. This is a specific example of work-related role strain brought on by continuing to describe herself as "the activist kind of go-getter type" instead of a "jaded" attorney. This identity management also identifies with the struggle to work within a broader system of social inequity in order to create positive change. Doing community presentations is an intrinsic part of her comfort with continuing to work within the system that she disagrees with in many ways.

Santana, a federal public defender (FPD), also has an activist background, claiming she went to law school specifically with a goal to fix social inequality. She says that Operation Streamline has changed her perceptions of her own work role:

> You just hear these stories from clients and feel useless. It's not like I don't know these stories, and I had already done defense work before Streamline, but there, it's really like 'all I'm here to do is to push a paper, and I'm not a real attorney,' so that's a first thing. It's like I became an attorney so I could change the world, and all I'm doing is having people sign the best agreement so that they can serve the least amount of time. Aren't I supposed to be fighting this shit? But then you fight and you're just being selfish because they just want to get out of here. And then, you're like, I don't know if I even explained something well enough so that they remember because most of them are going to come back, you know?

Santana's supposition that she is not a "real" attorney when working in Operation Streamline suggests an extreme form of work-related role strain. Santana feels she has not achieved what she wanted to when she became an attorney. As with others who have an activist background, she has not fulfilled what she thought she could do in changing the world. She suggests that fulfilling the formal justice requirements of her job (push paper, sign the plea) is not the true reason she became an attorney. This suggests she feels like her work is lacking in substantive justice, creating higher levels of work-related role strain.

While Latinas were more likely to explain that they had some kind of activist-related reason for continuing to be involved in Operation Streamline, some Latinos and non-Latinos also shared these more substantive justice-oriented perceptions of their work-related role idenity. However,

Latinas—due to their intersectional identities of being women of color who hold a legal professional role identity—were more likely to experience specific role strain based on their activist past.

Summary

This chapter examines the "gendered" interactions throughout Operation Streamline and suggests that this social identity also influences work-related role strain, interacts with the social identity of race/ethnicity, and changes the use of identity management strategies for certain respondents, specifically Latina attorneys. Men of all racial/ethnical backgrounds were more likely to express benevolent sexism toward women Operation Streamline defendants, which resulted in increased work-related role strain for them. Women were more likely to discuss issues of emotional management with Operation Streamline defendants than men. Latinas in particular discussed additional identity management strategies they used to deal with authority issues with clients who assume their gender diminishes their competence in their work-related role as an attorney. Finally, Latinas also demonstrated increased work-related role strain about being involved in Operation Streamline based on having become attorneys with activist orientations in mind. While all Latinas did not directly attribute their increased work-related role strain or emotional involvement to their gender or their activist background, these were distinct factors that were coded more frequently for these Latina attorneys than for any other group. These patterns demonstrate that gender is in fact an important social identity in the Operation Streamline context and understandably would affect attorneys' and judges' identity management strategies, given the inherent patriarchy of both U.S. legal and immigration systems.

References

Babcock, Linda, and Sarah Laschever. 2003. *Women Don't Ask: Negotiation and the Gender Divide*. Princeton, NJ: Princeton University Press.

Batton, Candice, and Emily M. Wright. 2019. "Patriarchy and the Structure of Employment in Criminal Justice: Differences in the Experiences of Men and Women Working in the Legal Profession, Corrections, and Law Enforcement." *Feminist Criminology* 14(3):287–306. https://doi.org/10.1177/1557085118769749.

Boyd, Monica. 2021. "Women, Gender, and Migration Trends in a Global World" Pp. 19–36 in *The Palgrave Handbook of Gender and Migration*, Mora, Claudia, and Piper, Nicola, Eds. New York, NY: Palgrave Macmillan.

Crenshaw, Kimberlé W. 2017. *On Intersectionality: Essential Writings*. New York, NY: The New Press.

Crenshaw, Kimberlé. 1989. "Demarginalizing the Intersection of Race and Sex: A Black Feminist Critique of Antidiscrimination Doctrine, Feminist Theory and Antiracist Politics." *University of Chicago Legal Forum* 140:139–68.

Donato, Katharine M., and Donna Gabaccia. 2015. *Gender and International Migration*. New York, NY: Russell Sage Foundation.

Glick, Peter, and Susan T. Fiske. 1997. "Hostile and Benevolent Sexism Measuring Ambivalent Sexist Attitudes Toward Women." *Psychology of Women Quarterly* 21(1):119–35. https://doi.org/10.1111/j.1471-6402.1997.tb00104.x.

Glick, Peter, and Susan T. Fiske. 2011. "Ambivalent Sexism Revisited." *Psychology of Women Quarterly* 35(3):530–5. https://doi.org/10.1177/0361684311414832.

Goffman, Erving. 1959. *The Presentation of Self in Everyday Life*. Garden City, NY: Doubleday.

Goffman, Erving. 1967. *Interaction Ritual: Essays on Face-To-Face Behavior*. Garden City, NY: Doubleday.

Golash-Boza, Tanya, Maria D. Duenas, and Chia Xiong. 2019. "White Supremacy, Patriarchy, and Global Capitalism in Migration Studies." *American Behavioral Scientist* 63(13):1741–59. https://doi.org/10.1177/0002764219842624.

Helfgott, Jacqueline B., Elaine Gunnison, Autumn Murtagh, and Bridgette Navejar. 2018. "Badasses: The Rise of Women in Criminal Justice." *Women and Criminal Justice* 28(4):235–61. https://doi.org/10.1080/08974454.2018.1468296.

Hill Collins, Patricia. 1990. *Black Feminist Thought: Knowledge, Consciousness, and the Politics of Empowerment*. New York, NY: Routledge.

Martin, Susan Ehrlich, and Nancy C. Jurik. 2006. *Doing Justice, Doing Gender: Women in Legal and Criminal Justice Occupations*. Thousand Oaks, CA: Sage Publications.

Ochoa-O'Leary, Anna. 2008. "Close Encounters of the Deadly Kind: Gender, Migration, and Border (In)Security." *Migration Letters* 5(2):111–21. https://doi.org/10.33182/ml.v5i2.47.

Pessar, Patricia. 2005. "Women, Gender, and International Migration Across and Beyond the Americas: Inequalities and Limited Empowerment." Population Division of the Department of Economic and Social Affairs, United Nations Secretariat. Retrieved January 15, 2022. www.un.org/esa/population/migration/turin/symposium_turin files/p08_pessar.pdf.

Rachlinski, Jeffrey J., and Andrew J. Wistrich. 2021. "Benevolent Sexism in Judges." *San Diego Law Review* 58:101–42. https://digital.sandiego.edu/sdlr/vol58/iss1/3.

Salerno, Jessica M., and Hannah J. Phalen. 2019. "Traditional Gender Roles and Backlash Against Female Attorneys Expressing Anger in Court." *Journal of Empirical Legal Studies* 16(4):909–32. https://doi.org/10.1111/jels.12238.

Siemsen, Cynthia. 2004. *Emotional Trials: The Moral Dilemmas of Women Criminal Defense Attorneys*. Boston, MA: Northeastern University Press.

Stets, Jan E. 2005. "Examining Emotions in Identity Theory." *Social Psychology Quarterly* 68(1):39–56. https://doi.org/10.1177/019027250506800104.

8 "THERE IS NO DIFFERENCE BETWEEN YOU AND ME"

SITUATIONALITY OF SOCIAL AND ROLE IDENTITIES FOR 1.5- AND 2ND-GENERATION LATINO/AS

Hugo, a second-generation Latino Criminal Justice Act (CJA) attorney, described the difference between his feelings about successfully enacting formal justice in his work-related role in Operation Streamline and his feelings about a known lack of substantive justice when he confronts the reproachful gaze of activists thus:

> [One time,] I was able to convince the judge—the government was asking 60 days—and I was able to convince a judge that time served was appropriate, based on the clients' immigration history, criminal history etc. And I was walking out very proud of myself. And I turned to see the gallery and it was like these people were looking at me like I was some P.O.S. [piece of shit], some piece of human waste—and it's like, whoa. After all I felt I had done for this client. Anyway, so that, to me, is harder than just the client stuff.

As seen in this description, legal professionals' social and role identities are situational. Stryker (1980) defined situationality as the "adjustment processes" between identities that is needed based on "responses to objective circumstances in which individuals and groups are embedded" (31). While Stryker focused only on adjusting different role identities, I demonstrate in this chapter that situationality applies not only to role identities but also to various social identities.

Based on the conceptualization of *competing identity management*, the reason both role and social identities are managed differently by situation is based on current systems of structural inequality that make certain identities more or less valued in a given situation. Because Operation Streamline is part of a larger criminal justice system that specifically oppresses people of color (Browne-Marshall 2013) and a larger immigration regime built on racism (Golash-Boza 2015), these different social contexts will cause respondents to play up situationally valued identities while downplaying situationally non-valued identities.

DOI: 10.4324/9781003272410-9

I focus here only on Latino/a legal professionals from the 1.5- and 2nd-generation—those who had thick/asserted racial/ethnic identities. As seen in Chapter 6, this group of 19 respondents is the most likely to feel work-related role strain and subsequent role and social identity competition. For this group, I coded for two specific types of situations in which identity management for legal professionals in Operation Streamline took different forms: (1) Talking to or about outsider critiques from activists/media/scholars and others who are not directly involved in Operation Streamline and (2) Interacting with or talking about interactions with clients in their daily work. This chapter demonstrates how these two situations (client-oriented versus activist-oriented) impact these Latino/a legal professionals in their balancing act between role and social identities. These two situations call up different levels of work-related role strain as well as increased or decreased competition between their role and social identities.

Overall, I find that client-oriented situations cause Latino/a attorneys from the 1.5/2 group to emphasize the lack of substantive justice in terms of work-related role strain as well as calling up their shared social identity of race/ethnicity with clients while downplaying their citizenship/generational status. Activist-oriented situations, on the other hand, cause Latino/a attorneys from the 1.5/2 group to emphasize the aspects of formal justice in terms of work-related role strain and to downplay their shared social identity of race/ethnicity and instead play up their different citizenship/generational status from clients. The relationship between situation and identity management suggests that situationality influences both social and role identity management based on current systems of structural inequality that value certain identities and devalue others.

Situations Matter: Balancing Competing Work-Related Role Identity and Social Identities

The concept of situationality would suggest that any change in social circumstances could affect identity management for any of the attorneys and judges involved in Operation Streamline. However, based on the social-structural lack of salience that a non-Latino/a identity carries (generally known as white privilege), I focus here on the 19 Latino/a respondents with thick/asserted identities from the 1.5/2 group who experienced the difference between situations dealing with activists and situations dealing with clients as the most likely to bring up work-related role strain as well as role and social identity competition. Non-Latino/a attorneys and judges do not have a shared racial/ethnic social identity with Operation Streamline defendants which would then compete with their work-related role and necessitate the differences in identity management strategies seen in prior chapters. Instead, this competition is strongest for those Latino/as with thick/asserted racial/ethnic identities—those who assert their Latino/a identity and feel it organizes large parts of their lives.

Thus, this analysis around situationality revolves around the 19 Latino/a attorneys from the 1.5/2 group who participate in a difficult balancing act between their work-related role identity and their social identity of race/ethnicity when discussing the different situations of working with clients and dealing with activists. As Hugo further explained, it is hard when a client's story is "close to [his] family's," which suggests the salience of his racial/ethnic identity. His voice cracks before explaining to me that "there's nothing I can do," which suggests work-related role strain based on the lack of substantive justice in Operation Streamline. When I expressed sympathy for his pain about this, he responded:

> Yeah, I'm going to tell you that what's harder than that is getting up and leaving and seeing an audience full of really hostile people. They don't understand anything about what's going on. All they see is there's a bunch of people who are being ushered to jail. They have no idea what role the attorney plays. They just automatically assume that the attorney is somehow responsible for [the defendants'] pain, and it's like it's ludicrous and it's hard for me to deal with. That's harder than the client's pain actually because it's like I'm doing my job to the absolute best that I can and I'm helping in the best way that I can in this really bad system and these people are rewarding me with frowns and total disgust is what it comes down to.

Hugo navigates a complicated relationship between the situation of working with clients—which activates his racial/ethnic social identity (their stories are "so close to my family's") and his sense of work-related role strain via substantive justice ("it's really hard for me to explain that there's nothing I can do")—and the situation of dealing with the critiques of activists—which activates his sense of work-related role strain via formal justice: "they have no idea what role the attorney plays." Hugo's inability to emphasize the formal justice pole of his work-related role to the activists in the courtroom is a larger problem for him than any of the social and role identity competition that he experiences in situations with clients. Dealing with work-related role strain and the substantive justice critiques brought up in situations with activists, he says, is actually more trying than dealing with the sad stories of his clients.

Many other Latino/as also described instances of situationality and how they struggled to manage both their social and role identities depending on their audience. Bridget, a 1.5-generation Latina CJA attorney, said that the fact that she sees the same clients more than once leads to fraught interactions with activists, who frequently confront her at the courthouse. She explains her own mixed feelings about working in Operation Streamline as a Latina and how that puts her under extra scrutiny:

> And so, there's two things that could be said about recidivism in Streamline. One is if I was talking to, like, some of those people [activists] in that group that yelled at me, I would say, 'Don't feel so sorry for

all of these people because they know they shouldn't come; I told them last time they were here.' And the other is: 'This program really doesn't work, you know? You guys were right. Let's get rid of it, I hate it.'

And when I was talking to those activists, they did yell at me and they kind of make me jump through some hoops, you know, and honestly, to be honest, there's where I feel a little bit of a—of a—of a disadvantage being Latina, because I think that—sometimes I wonder if that activist is like that with me just because I'm a Latina. I don't know. I don't know if they, you know, give me a little more trouble—if they feel like I should care more about defendants because of my background but, I have to work a little harder, you know, answer a few more questions, justify myself more to them.

Bridget swings between the formal pole of work-related role strain by acknowledging her own completion of her formal justice work-related role duties *with clients* ("I told them last time they were here") and agreeing with activists about substantive justice ("This program really doesn't work [...] I hate it"). Bridget also downplays her racial/ethnic identity because she feels that it disadvantages her in interactions with activists. Bridget feels that activists see her social identity of Latina as being in competition with the substantive justice pole of her work-related role identity, which in turn increases the work-related role strain she feels about both disagreeing and agreeing with activists.

As shown in these two examples, client-oriented versus activist-oriented situations impact the work-related role strain and social identity salience of Latino/a legal professionals with thick/asserted racial/ethnic identity in Operation Streamline. Below, I provide evidence for the two distinct patterns that became apparent in each of the situation types that I coded (dealing with clients versus dealing with activists). Each section includes information about how the situational factors interact with social and role identities.

The next section of this chapter outlines the clearest example of situationality impacting social and role identity competition: Latino/a respondents discussing their daily work with clients. In these client-oriented situations, the 1.5/2 group of Latino/as legal professionals emphasize their social identity of race/ethnicity (that they share with clients) while deemphasizing their citizenship/generational status (that they do not share with clients). In doing so, they also frequently acknowledge the lack of substantive justice in Operation Streamline *to their clients* in order to develop rapport, which highlights their work-related role strain. Additionally, in a subsection on language, I examine legal professionals' use of Spanish language, which often functions as an example of playing up their racial/ethnic social identity for Latino/as (though that also gets used by non-Latino/as in a variety of ways). There are clear identity competition patterns in how legal professionals use Spanish-language proficiency to relate to their clients.

The second pattern of situationality impacting social and role identity competition is when the 1.5/2 group of Latino/a legal professionals are faced with defending Operation Streamline *to outsiders* who are not directly involved in the program, such as activists, the media, legal scholars, or other courtroom observers of the proceeding. Latino/a respondents from the 1.5/2 group in particular have to deal with defending the program to outsiders very carefully—as their racial/ethnic social identity is assumed by these outsiders to influence their work-related role. The 1.5/2 group of Latino/as, then, must once again do extra identity management to balance their work-related role identity and their racial/ethnic social identity, but they do so in a different manner than they do with clients. In situations dealing with activists, the pattern involves this 1.5/2 group of Latino/as legal professionals deemphasizing their racial/ethnic social identity while emphasizing their citizenship/generational status social identity as well as the formal justice pole of their work-related role identity, explaining the technical legality of the program.

Client-Oriented Situations: Playing Up Racial/Ethnic Social Identity and Downplaying Citizenship/Generational Status by Acknowledging a Lack of Substantive Justice

Many Latino/a attorneys in the 1.5/2 group suggest that their shared social identity with defendants helps them build rapport with clients and helps them establish trust in the short time that they have to meet with clients. In these situations, playing up their social identity of race/ethnicity and downplaying their citizenship/generational status (which distances them from clients) assists them in their work-related role as a legal professional. They also often acknowledge a lack of substantive justice in Operation Streamline, apologizing to clients that this is what must happen based on the current system within which they operate.

There are many examples of Latino/a 1.5/2 respondents emphasizing their racial/ethnic identities, downplaying their citizenship/generational status, and bringing up issues of work-related role strain and substantive justice with clients. These legal professionals often link using their social identities to an enhanced ability to complete their work-related role (building trust, making clients comfortable, etc.). Estelle, for example, mentions her appearance as being helpful in working with clients, linking skin color with culture and language:

> A lot of people that I represent—there's not necessarily the assumption of like 'You're a part of my people' per se but, um, I think it helps because I am brown and then they do think that I know more about their situation perhaps because they know I come from a Latino/a heritage, whatever they have in mind. You know maybe they're like 'Okay well, I can understand and hear her a little bit better.' I hope they feel a

little bit more comfortable speaking to me knowing that there's perhaps a similar background and cultural connection.

A second-generation citizen, Latina CJA attorney Estelle hopes that her skin tone, heritage, and shared culture with defendants will help to relax clients, even as she acknowledges the differences between them. She further evidences work-related role strain, though, when she says:

It's still a little bit different cause they don't really believe I'm one of them—I'm still 'the other,' but not like, you know the white guy kind of 'let me sell you a car' type of attorney. I hope that they feel a little bit more comfortable or that I'm more approachable because I'm not completely different and it's not like I have no connection, even though I am helping them through this terrible system that I sort of represent. I try to let them know I'm there for *them*, [emphasis hers] not the system.

The distinction between representing "the system" and being accountable to her clients is Estelle's way of resolving her work-related role strain around the lack of substantive justice in Operation Streamline and is clearly linked to her racial/ethnic social identity.

In a similar vein, other attorneys shrug off their citizenship/generational status social identity and emphasize their racial/ethnic social identity as a way to demonstrate their proximity to their clients' situation. Latino CJA attorney Esteban explains:

I look at my clients and I see me. I tell them 'By the grace of God, I was born on this side of the line. There is no difference between you and me other than the fact that my family was here, and I was born 60 miles north of the border.' So, I'll sit there, and I'll tell them about my family history sometimes, because I think it's important for them to know that I *do* understand what they're saying, that it *is* unfair.

(emphasis his)

Esteban's parents came to the United States before his birth, making him a second-generation citizen, which is different than his client's situation. However, he uses his own family history as a way to demonstrate his personal connection with clients via his social identity of a shared race/ethnicity. As such, he describes having been born in the United States (citizenship/generational status) as only a trifling difference based on pure luck. He seems to minimize the meaning of the citizenship/generational status differences between himself and his clients, highlighting their shared racial/ethnic social identity and connection to México. Similarly, Santana says:

I like to tell [clients] that the only thing that separates me from [them] is that when my family crossed, you know, they were able to pay some pesos […] and now, we own companies, we're lawyers, we're whatever. You know, so it's, sort of like 'what the fuck? The only thing that separates us is the fact that my family could come across just by paying a couple of pesos, you know, and that was it.' And now the border is completely closed and you're talking about a group of people completely shut off.

Santana describes her own family history (her citizenship/generational status social identity) as a difference between her and her clients but frames it as an arbitrary historical fact. She is again downplaying citizenship/generational status and playing up a shared racial/ethnic social identity as a way to get clients to open up and to let them know she is on their side. She also acknowledges the absurdity of their situation and expresses her own dislike of Operation Streamline, leaning again toward the substantive justice pole of her work-related role. Santana goes on to say:

> My heritage, um, might actually help. At least I can explain the reasons behind them coming you know, and I use that sometimes for sentencing at least with the flip-flops or regular felony dockets. I can say that to a judge, when you're trying to explain why this person keeps coming over, you know what I mean? And the pattern of immigration matters over our history, um, depending on the judge. I mean, I talked about that in sentencing, but I also talk about that to my clients in Streamline.

As these examples demonstrate, in situations dealing with clients, the social identity of race/ethnicity is seen as more important than the social identity of citizenship/generational status for Latino/a legal professionals. They also highlight the shortcomings of Operation Streamline in terms of lacking substantive justice—an unfair system. Both Esteban and Santana emphasize to their clients that Operation Streamline does not deliver substantive justice using their own family history to highlight the bad timing and dumb luck that separates them from their clients with whom they share the same racial/ethnic identity. They play up their race/ethnicity and downplay their citizenship/generational status to build rapport with clients by empathizing with their plight and suggesting the process they are going through is not actually fair. In showing this work-related role strain, they use their own immigration stories to demonstrate how their shared racial/ethnic social identities with clients can build trust during their work-role interactions. The social identity that differentiates them from clients (generational status) is minimized and other factors are played up, including their Spanish language abilities.

Spanish-Language Proficiency and Racial/Ethnic Social Identity

I expected to find that Latino/a respondents' use of Spanish would be an indicator of a particularly salient (thick/asserted) racial/ethnic social identity that would be used to demonstrate a special connection with clients and build rapport. This was *sometimes* the case, as will be demonstrated below. The logical deduction from this pattern, though, would be that Spanish language usage could *not* be a social identity indicator for non-Latino/as, as they do not have a social identity that is linked to Spanish. However, I found that many non-Latino/as discussed how their higher proficiency in Spanish was a resource that built rapport with clients, too. Thus, Spanish-language usage seems to fulfill multiple functions. Latino/a attorneys certainly described their Spanish skills as something that helped them relate to clients, and more often than their non-Latino/a counterparts, but particularly Spanish-language proficient non-Latino/as also used this work-related role tactic.

Micah, a Latino CJA attorney, describes his advantage over "second-language gringos" when working with clients. As a native speaker:

> I can almost talk street Spanish, so [clients] have an easier time [under-standing]. And I have an easier time than some of these second-language gringos because I've heard how the street Spanish is, and I can throw some of that in. If you can get them to believe that there's no 'us and them,' not you're 'the other' but you're one of me, there's a lot of trust that's built up that way. Being able to speak their language, as opposed to some of the guys that learned it in college or speak it very poorly, the guy's just like, what are you talking about? Yes, they're communicating, but I found that the people that could speak the street-level Spanish have a much easier time.

Micah also says that he frequently uses a pun about his own last name in Spanish to break down barriers with clients. In referencing "street-level Spanish," some of the differentiation in Spanish skills that the attorneys discussed related to "formal" versus "slang" use of Spanish. The general consensus was that use of informal dialects not taught in school creates an automatic connection with clients. Micah suggests he can break down any barriers of "us and them" put up by his work-related role as an attorney by communicating with clients beyond the formal requirements of his legal, work-related role, but in Spanish puns and in dexterity of language that indicates their shared racial/ethnic social identity (not a "gringo").

Other Latino/a attorneys discussed this same distinction of slang/formal Spanish and being able to gain "street cred" with their clients. Solomón, a CJA attorney, noted that the fact that he learned Spanish "at home" helped him build a connection with clients. Hector, also a Latino CJA attorney, noted the same advantage:

> Especially with the men I am able to use slang and expressions, some of which they would never expect a U.S. born person to know, whether he's Chicano or Caucasian. So, I'm able to use the language and just get that smile and they say, 'All right, this dude's got some street cred here.'

Both Micah and Hector suggest that laughter and smiling relaxes their clients, and that shared language helps them to create a less stressful work-related interaction.

Jesús, a Latino CJA attorney, explicitly links his Mexican heritage with the ability to throw out "proverbs, a swear word or two" in order to get clients to trust him. He says that clients initially see him as "part of the system" and do not have confidence in him, but he explains:

> My way of approaching that is, because I'm Hispanic, I'm Mexican, I start throwing out either proverbs, a swear word or two or something like that—to, you know, to show them I understand their language and their plight. Because I don't agree with this law. I mean, it's crazy to criminalize—to criminalize just the entry. And I tell them, 'I agree with you, man. We're working with a shitty law.' But that's—that's it.

> And then they start, and I try to be as courteous as I can to them, make sure they have water and, you know, just try to establish some rapport with them to show them that I'm not a blue pinstripe suit lawyer, just— and then I show them what we're working with.

Jesús emphasizes the lack of substantive justice and his distaste for Operation Streamline, calling the law "shitty." In connecting with clients through a shared informal language that shows he understands their plight, he highlights their shared racial/ethnic social identity. However, his work-related necessity to complete formal justice duties and get clients to understand the legal options despite the substantive injustice is the last thing he discusses with clients.

Some non-Latino/as, especially those who speak Spanish more fluently, also used their Spanish-language skills to build rapport with clients. Walter, a white CJA attorney, for example, says that because he is not Latino:

> I do have to make a special effort to build rapport with clients. They may just walk in and say, 'who's this white guy? He's not on my side.' But to be honest, 95 percent of rapport is built with my Spanish. It's, it's something I've got going for me—I get told by interpreters all the time, 'you're one of the best Spanish speakers we've ever had over here.' So, I think that's always helped carry weight versus any other differences between me and my clients. I really can speak their language.

Walter's statement "I really can speak their language" relates the practical ability to speak Spanish to the more colloquial meaning of speaking someone's language to mean, understanding them. He distinguishes that he lacks the requisite shared racial/ethnic identity with his clients, but that he can overcome that identity difference through skilled use of the Spanish language.

Others non-Latino/as who do not speak Spanish as well also recognize that this creates social-structural distance between them and clients, again suggesting it might be an indicator of a social identity they do not share. Tiffany, a non-Latina CJA attorney, who had to take the Spanish-language test for all federal defense attorneys twice, explains:

> Many of my colleagues speak much better Spanish than I do, so if I'm not absolutely sure what a client is saying, I'll call over one of my colleagues, like one who looks like a traditional Spanish-speaker. Often, it's a Spanish language issue and my vocabulary isn't good enough to understand what's going on, or my comprehension.

Tiffany's indication of colleagues who look "like a traditional Spanish-speaker" implicitly recognizes the social identity of race/ethnicity that is linked to the language skills that she lacks.

Overall, both Latino/a and non-Latino/a attorneys agree that Spanish language usage affects the development of rapport with clients and that it is heavily linked to a Latino/a social identity—whether they share that identity or not. Many Latino/a attorneys in the 1.5/2-generation highlight their native-Spanish speaking skills as a way to connect with clients and as a key part of their social identity as Latino/as. They also make this language connection with clients in conjunction with demonstrating work-related role strain (expressing their distaste or dislike for Operation Streamline on substantive justice grounds). However, some non-Latino/a attorneys also use Spanish to make up for *lacking* a shared social identity of Latino/a and they tout their superior language skills as a way to make up for their non-Latino/a identity in building a connection with clients.

Activist-Oriented Situations: Downplaying Racial/ Ethnic Social Identity and Playing Up Citizenship/ Generational Status by Focusing on Formal Justice

In activist-oriented situations, many 1.5- and 2nd-generation Latino/a attorneys highlight their work-related role by emphasizing the formal justice aspects of their work. They also play up their citizenship/generational status with those who are not directly involved in Operation Streamline (such as activists, courtroom observers, the media, and legal scholars) and downplay their racial/ethnic social identity. That is to say, in situations where these extra-legal critiques would call on Latino/a respondent's shared racial/ethnic social identity with clients, they tend to downplay this social identity in favor of focusing on their social identity of citizenship/generational status, which differentiates them from clients. They also emphasize the formal justice aspects of their work-related role identity in order to avoid further scrutiny. This often results in Latino/a attorneys and judges discussing how much they dislike Operation Streamline in general, but then having to defend the program to those who are not directly involved in it (activists/media/legal scholars). 1.5- and 2nd-generation Latino/a attorneys most frequently have to explain that these outsiders "do not understand" the work-related role they must fulfill—focusing on formal justice and what they can actually do for clients given their role limitations. This often meant that 1.5/2 Latino/a attorneys and judges would become more defensive in situations involving activists. This group more often had to emphasize that their work-related role does not include the ability to broadly change the immigration system that is currently in place or to change how Operation Streamline specifically works.

Like his co-ethnic colleagues, Leo, a second-generation Latino and CJA attorney, highlights the importance of a shared racial/ethnic social identity in his client interactions. However, he also downplays this shared social identity in interactions with activists and instead emphasizes his citizenship/generational status. In doing this, he also highlights the formal justice aspect of his work-related role in Operation Streamline. This pattern means he justifies his continued participation through emphasizing formal justice and his citizenship/generational status by saying:

> Honestly, for me, I have no problem with what I do every day. I know I do the best I can for every one of my clients. But the change that really needs to happen is in the political aspect, not in the legal aspect with filing appeals and everything else. In fact, appellate courts have already said that [Operation Streamline] is okay. But I think that's a political choice. And as long as the political branches have decided that this is what's going to happen, you know, [as an attorney,] you're part of a legal system. That means that you're buying into the legitimacy of these decisions, even though you don't agree with them. So, I don't feel guilty from my—I don't feel like I, you know, lower myself or I'm a traitor or anything like that for participating in Streamline because I think it's a perfectly—it's a perfectly legal process. Whether it's politically smart or, you know, good from a policy standpoint, which I guess are two different things. I don't, you know. I think it's highly stupid and I think it's a waste of money, but as long as they do it, you know, I can have my opinions as a U.S. citizen and take those with me when I vote, but it's not my job to walk away from these clients.

Leo's discussion of his "opinions as a U.S. citizen" highlights his citizenship/generational status social identity over the racial/ethnic social identity that would subject him to more work-related role strain—he does not feel like a "traitor." In an emphasis on formal justice, he suggests he feels no guilt because the process is perfectly legal and has been approved by a higher court even if he agrees with the activists' opinions that the laws should not be there in the first place.

Next, Leo's remarks about activists suggest he respects their role in the national discourse, but they are focused on the wrong part of the system:

> I don't have a problem with the activists. I think they're doing the right thing, in the sense that they should be protesting something, but their actions are all wrong. They should be having a problem not with Streamline itself but just our immigration laws. And maybe this is a good way to call attention to what's going on with immigration, because you see a lot of people chained up together, but the problem I have is the twist where all of a sudden, we, the defense lawyers, have become the target.

This feeling of being a target led Leo to retreat from communicating with activists, even though he recognizes and appreciates their attempt to use Operation Streamline to show others how immigration laws in the United States are problematic. As he further explained:

> I used to talk to everybody. I'm more cautious about it now. I'll talk to schools. I'll talk to groups where I know someone that's involved in the group—but I don't want to talk to anyone from the press, because I think that they just start looking to sensationalize the situation. I'll definitely talk to high school or college students any time that they want to talk to me, and I'll go talk to them about it as much as they want. But I'm very wary of who brings them in. If they are with certain activist groups, I know that anything I say won't matter. And if they come in with [particular activist leader], I know I am just in for an earful of how I am a traitor to my people and how the whole system is morally corrupt.

Leo mentioned a particular activist leader he avoids because he does not wish to be accused of being "a traitor to my people." This particular activist leader is a Latina woman who has used the shared racial/ethnic identity of defense attorneys and clients to shame the Latino/a legal professionals involved in Operation Streamline. Despite his agreement with the activists about broader systematic problems with immigration—and even Operation Streamline specifically ("it's highly stupid")—Leo says he is no longer willing to talk to certain groups because he wants to avoid the scrutiny that they put him under based on his racial/ethnic social identity. Because Latino/as share a social identity with clients, many activists assume this will make them more aware of concerns about substantive justice and the structural racism in the U.S. immigration regime (Chacón 2009, 2012; Menjívar and Abrego 2012; Molina 2014; Golash-Boza 2015). Leo's reaction to the racialized scrutiny of the activists instead causes him to emphasize his completion of the formal justice aspects of his work-related role of attorney and the limits he faces in that role as well as emphasizing his U.S. citizenship.

Emiliano, another second-generation Latino and CJA attorney, also high-lighted formal justice when I asked him about activists, but, unlike Leo, he mentions both liberal and conservative critics. He plays up the importance of the Sixth Amendment and the CJA of 1964 in order to defend what he does to activists, playing on his American identity and pride in the U.S. legal system over any shared beliefs with activists:

> I always got it from the conservative groups, 'Why do you represent these criminals, these illegals? Why do you help these people out—just because you're all Mexicans?' And I tell them 'I believe in the constitution of the United States.' The thing that makes our country so much better than all the other countries in the world is the fact that we provide defense attorneys here, with CJA and the Sixth Amendment.

Emiliano's allusion to the racism of conservative groups who suggest he defends illegal immigrants because he is Mexican-American suggests his social identity of a shared race/ethnicity with clients would make him auto-matically biased. He points out that defendants in México have no legal right to a lawyer as they do in Operation Streamline. But in the United States the constitution protects even non-citizens:

> It doesn't matter if you're not an American or if you're Mexican, or if I'm Mexican, you still get these rights. So, to me, that's the most important part of what I do. Usually, my biggest defense all the time against very conservative people who really don't understand the way this country works is that this is probably the most American thing you can do as a job and I'm very proud of it and I've always been very proud of being a CJA Panel attorney.

With respect to liberal activists, on the other hand, Emiliano says:

> I finally feel attacked by people who see the world the same way I do—people who I looked up to for a long time; lawyers who I learned a lot from when I was first starting out. And so that probably hurts more than anything. Somebody that sees the world the same as you do attacks you for Streamline. Especially since I spent my whole time in school working on Chicano history and immigration stuff. I remember telling [one activist attorney] that you're seeing the world through rose-colored glasses. That if I stood up in Streamline and said, "No, we're going to fight this," that it would make a difference. It wouldn't. It would just hurt my one client that's sitting in front of me. And you can't do that. We don't represent the whole societal issue here. We represent our client sitting in front of us and if we can't represent his interests than we have no business representing him at all.

Formal justice provides Emiliano a defense of what he does as well as a sense of identity as a good American. In this activist-oriented situation, Emiliano is forced into defending Operation Streamline, emphasizing the overruling importance of formal justice ("I believe in the Constitution of the United States") over politics ("somebody that sees the world the same as you"), over his own dispositions ("this law isn't fair"), and especially over his social identity of a shared race/ethnicity with their clients ("It doesn't matter if [...] I'm Mexican"). Emiliano was one of the few Latino attorneys with an activist past, as he mentions, and his ability to shift from decrying the immigration system as a whole to defending his personal participation in Operation Streamline often felt like whiplash. However, through emphasizing formal procedural justice and his citizenship/generational status he is able to continue fulfilling the work-related role duties of a defense attorney in Operation Streamline.

Most respondents tried to avoid the impromptu confrontations of activists. However, attorneys like Leo and Emiliano, who knew some of the activists personally, were more willing to engage. In my courtroom observations, legal professionals often highlighted formal justice in such public, activist-oriented interactions and never acknowledged that they disliked the program themselves. Almost all of the observed interactions of attorneys and judges talking to activists at the courthouse took a very defensive position, as these legal professionals worked to describe their limited role and the endorsed legality of the proceeding from appellate courts. Inductive coding revealed that most comments from legal professionals to activists in courtroom proceedings conformed to the following remarks:

- "I don't make the laws; I just defend clients who are charged with violating them."
- "Streamline is better than the previous petty calendar."
- "Streamline is better now than it was at the start of the program in 2008."
- "Streamline is still better than a felony conviction for clients."
- "Streamline is basically the same as Flip-Flops."
- "All 1325s and 1326s are essentially indefensible anyway."
- "Streamline is just one part of the larger broken legal/immigration system."

That is, they were essentially the same logic as respondents used in interviews when they articulated formal justice justifications for their actions. These kinds of micro level justifications show how macro level structural inequality in the immigration system gets reproduced, even by actors who may be reluctant to endorse the system broadly.

Summary

This chapter demonstrates how situational factors influence work-related role strain, social and role identity competition, and identity management strategies. When discussing interactions with clients, 1.5- and

2nd-generation Latino/a attorneys emphasize the importance of their shared cultural and language abilities with clients (playing up one social identity), while attributing their citizenship/generational status to historic luck (downplaying another social identity). They also explain their own dislike of the legal system to their clients, emphasizing the lack of substantive justice in Operation Streamline and demonstrating work-related role strain. In sum, when these Latino/a respondents talk about or are in situations dealing directly with clients, they play up the social identity that they share with clients (race/ethnicity) and downplay the social identity they do not share (citizenship/generational status). They also lean toward the substantive justice pole of their work-related role to acknowledge the difficulties clients are experiencing in order to build trust. When 1.5- and 2nd-generation Latino/a respondents emphasize their similarities to clients and then say Operation Streamline is "unfair" they are engaging in situationally specific identity management strategies based on what identities are situationally valued.

In contrast, when dealing with activists, 1.5- and 2nd-generation Latino/a attorneys and judges focus on the procedural justice pole of their work-related role as well as their citizenship/generational status social identity and they downplay their racial/ethnic identity. Those who are not directly involved in Operation Streamline (such as activists, courtroom observers, and the media) sometimes attempt to activate work-related role strain and social and role identity competition in Latino/a attorneys and judges by highlighting their shared racial/ethnic identity with clients. In situations where they have to answer to activists or the media, then, these 1.5/2 Latino/a respondents show patterns of downplaying one social identity—racial/ethnic—and playing up a different social identity—citizenship/generational status. In terms of work-related role strain, I found that Latino/a attorneys and judges in the 1.5/2 group, in defense of the program against activists, would focus on the formal justice aspects of their work-related role and ignore concerns of substantive justice they otherwise expressed with clients or to me in interviews.

I present here some examples of patterns in 1.5- and 2nd-generation Latino/a respondents' behaviors based on situational differences in discussing Operation Streamline with those who are not directly involved in Operation Streamline (such as activists, courtroom observers, and the media) versus completing their day-to-day work. In an expansion Stryker (1980), these findings demonstrate that the concept of situationality applies not only to one's work-related role but that it also influences social identities such as race/ethnicity and citizenship/generational status (in this instance). These social identities are made relevant depending on current systems of structural inequality—in this case, the racial/ethnic and nationalist project that is the U.S. immigration system and the structural racism that is built into the criminal justice system. This integration and expansion builds on the concept of situationality as it recognizes circumstances in which certain types of social identities are highlighted or downplayed.

References

Browne-Marshall, Gloria J. 2013. *Race, Law, and American Society: 1607-Present.* New York, NY: Routledge.

Chacón, Jennifer M. 2009. "Managing Migration Through Crime." *Columbia Law Review Sidebar* 109:135–48. http://dx.doi.org/10.2139/ssrn.2033931.

Chacón, Jennifer M. 2012. "Overcriminalizing Immigration." *Journal of Criminal Law and Criminology* 102(3):613–52. https://scholarlycommons.law.northwestern.edu/jclc/vol102/iss3/5.

Golash-Boza, Tanya M. 2015. *Immigration Nation: Raids, Detentions, and Deportations in Post-9/11 America.* Boulder, CO: Paradigm Press.

Menjívar, Cecilia, and Leisy J. Abrego. 2012. "Legal Violence: Immigration Law and the Lives of Central American Immigrants." *American Journal of Sociology* 117(5):1380–421. https://doi.org/10.1086/663575.

Molina, Natalia. 2014. *How Race Is Made in America: Immigration, Citizenship, and the Historical Power of Racial Scripts.* Los Angeles, CA: University of California Press.

Stryker, Sheldon. 1980. *Symbolic Interactionism: A Social Structural Version.* Menlo Park, CA: Benjamin/Cummings Publishing Company.

CONCLUSION

Summary of Findings

Operation Streamline, a controversial criminal immigration proceeding, provides a case study of competing social and role identities for Latino/a attorneys and judges who are involved in the program. All attorneys experienced some work-related role strain but based on the differences found between racial/ethnic groups and the increased role strain for Latino/a attorneys—particularly those with a citizenship/generational status that increases the salience of their race/ethnicity—this study demonstrates that the mass criminalization of primarily Latino/a migrants indeed reproduces structural racism in both the U.S. criminal justice and immigration systems. This study suggests that the individual legal professionals involved in the program—knowingly or unknowingly—reproduce systemic inequalities through their justifications, rationalizations, and identity management strategies.

The general patterns of findings suggest:

1 Latino/a lawyers and judges involved with Operation Streamline manage their competing social and role identities differently than non-Latino/as whose social identities do not compete with their work-related role identities. That is, *between-group differences by race/ethnicity* exist because Operation Streamline represents racialized legal violence against primarily Latino/a migrants.

a *Within the Latino/a racial/ethnic social* identity *group,* some Latino/a lawyers and judges (those with higher racial/ethnic social identity salience) involved with Operation Streamline manage their competing social and role identities differently than other Latino/a lawyers and judges (those with lower racial/ethnic social identity salience).

i Other social identities, such as citizenship/generational status and gender, impact how Latino/a legal professionals experience their work, showing other structural inequities of nationalism and patriarchy.

DOI: 10.4324/9781003272410-10

2 A shared social identity with defendants seems to be useful in the daily work of Latino/a lawyers and judges but is often detrimental in their inter-actions with those who are not directly involved in Operation Streamline (such as activists, courtroom observers, and the media) who apply extra-legal critiques to the program, particularly based on the macro context and history of immigration-related racism in the United States.

Thus, initial expectations on the importance of identity competition between social and role identities as they affect identity management strategies were generally correct, but many findings suggest more nuances than originally theorized. The exact interplay of race/ethnicity, citizenship/generational status, and gender created group-specific patterns based also on situational context. In sum, I have been able to elaborate mechanisms of some iden-tity management processes while also developing grounded hypotheses on which to base future research. These are outlined below.

Tenets of *Competing Identity Management*

From this case, we can take these findings and begin to create an outline for the conceptualization of *competing identity management*, integrating prior literatures on social and role identities as well as linking these micro level identity processes with macro level structures of inequality. Basic tenets that are consistent with findings in this research include:

1 Those with non-situationally valued social identities (those oppressed by current systems of structural inequality) are more likely to experi-ence higher levels of work-related role strain resulting in competition between their social and role identities.

   • *[In this case, Latino/as experience more work-related role strain based on formal versus substantive justice causing their racial/eth-nic social identities to compete with their work-related role identity of legal professional for Operation Streamline because it is part of a long history of racialized immigration policies].*

2 Those with competing social and role identities vary in their use of identity management strategies compared to those without competing social and role identities.

   • *[In this case, Latino/as used certain identity management strategies more often than non-Latino/as as well as using some identity manage-ment strategies that non-Latino/as never had to use].*

      2a. Those with situationally valued social identities (those privi-leged by current systems of structural inequality) do not have to engage as frequently in the following identity management strategies compared to those with situationally non-valued

social identities: identity consolidation; negotiated identifications with certain times or beliefs/ideas/values; role making/
identity extension psychological compartmentalization and
fictive story telling.

- *[In this case, non-Latino/as did not have to engage in the
  above strategies as often as Latino/as because the primary
  target of legal violence in Operation Streamline is Latino/a
  border-crossers].*

3 Varieties of social identities will interact to create variation in social identity salience, work-related role strain, competition between social and role
identities, and use of identity management strategies. These various social
identities are also dependent on current systems of structural inequality.

- *[In this case, the interaction of race/ethnicity with citizenship/gener-
  ational status (because of nationalism) and with gender (because of
  intersectionality/patriarchy) created variation in social identity salience for Latino/as, which in turn affected work-related role strain,
  competition between social and role identities, and use of identity
  management strategies.]*

4 Management of competing social and role identities is situationally
dependent based on current systems of structural inequality.

- *[In this case, respondents showed numerous patterns playing up or
  downplaying their various social identities in conjunction with emphasizing certain parts of their work-related role based on talking to/about
  activists versus talking to/about clients. This links to the macro level
  based on how those who are or are not directly involved in Operation
  Streamline apply extra-legal conceptions of justice to the immigration
  and criminal justice systems.]*

With these generalized tenets, *competing identity management* can be trans-
ferred to and examined empirically in any social setting where identity competition exists based on current systems of structural inequality. Indeed,
immigration-based racism need not be the key structural inequity nor race/
ethnicity be the prime social identity for these same generalized tenets of
competing identity management to be explored. For example, how trans or
gender-nonconforming prison guards negotiate their social and role identities while working in sex-segregated prisons may be explained using these
same tenants. Continuations of this research program can more clearly
define scope conditions and help integrate additional prior theories of identity as well, such as the perceptual control research project in identity theory
(Burke and Stets 2009) and identity and emotion work by Stets (2005). As
such, this conceptualization of *competing identity management* is useful in
numerous settings.

Structurally speaking, these identity-based insights also demonstrate the oppressive and racially problematic nature of contemporary migration governance through programs like Operation Streamline. Micro level differences in identity management strategies used by legal professionals based on their racial/ethnic social identity—as well as differences within this group based on citizenship/generational status and gender—reveal the macro level, structural problems in current immigration and criminal justice systems. Latino/a legal professionals are more affected by issues of substantive justice—seeing the system as unfair even if not directly calling it racist. Latino/a attorneys and judges must do more identity management in order to participate in this program because it is a hyper-visible example of anti-Latino/a state violence.

Competing Identity Management beyond Operation Streamline

Outlining the interaction and competition between social and role identities and their subsequent identity management processes by legal professionals in Operation Streamline helps scholars understand how micro level actors manage identities that are deeply influenced by macro level forces such as racism, nationalism, and patriarchy. However, this particular case is just the beginning. Future research should include continuing to develop this conceptualization of *competing identity management* in at least two ways: (1) methodologically and (2) theoretically, including by further contextualization. Methodologically, the conceptualization of *competing identity management* should move beyond qualitative studies such as this one. In attempting larger-scale hypothesis testing of the above tenets, future work on developing survey instruments and statistical analyses may help with issues of generalizability and broader implications of *competing identity management*.

By taking the above-outlined tenets developed through the study of Operation Streamline to other contexts, this budding conceptualization of *competing identity management* can continue to define scope conditions and integrate prior theories of identity from the subfields of social psychology, culture, and legal professions. As *competing identity management* is applicable to any location where social and role identities are in competition based on current systems of structural inequality, examples of other locations for future study include police stations, prisons, and other criminal justice settings, such as the U.S. Border Patrol. These settings could also be international, considering different systems of structural inequality based on different state contexts. As such, *competing identity management* is a useful lens to critically examine institutions where individual participants actively reproduce structural inequities through their justification of participation.

Limitations

As in all research, this project was limited based on time, funding, and access. Theoretically, this book represents but one case study of *competing identity management* and is thus limited in its causal scope. There are other theoretical limitations. For example, respondents did not demonstrate all of the potential identity management strategies outlined in Chapter 2 (e.g., identity transformation). Perhaps the circumstances that would create the use of this identity management strategy were not present in this particular case, but that does not mean it would not serve as an identity management strategy to be integrated in later research.

Beyond the explored identity management strategies, this research does not include all of the existing literatures on identity. Future research should expand the theoretical contributions of *competing identity management* by comparing it with other literatures. For example, future work could integrate more thoroughly *competing identity management* as it relates to the research program in identity theory as developed by Burke and Stets (2009). Indeed, my findings relate to identity control processes given that many identity management strategies are in effect forms of identity control—specifications of the abstract general process in which inputs from outside either confirm or do not confirm existing identities. Typically, though, identity control research examines one identity at a time, while *competing identity management* adds the absolute need to examine multiple competing identities at the same time because "confirming" one may well "disconfirm" another. That then implicates hierarchies of identity salience for both social and role identity and the importance of situationality in order to know which identities in which situations best predict the identity management strategies most likely to be used.

Empirically, this is a study of Operation Streamline in Tucson, Arizona, a specific and limited sector of this program. Other federal districts' versions of this program may have different contexts that impact identity management and I do not claim to know what occurs in other sectors.

Additionally, even within the Tucson Sector, there were limits to data collection surrounding Operation Streamline. For example, as discussed in Chapter 3, no government prosecutors were interviewed due to access issues and also because defense attorneys provide a stronger test of significant work-related role strain and *competing identity management*, especially Criminal Justice Act (CJA) panel attorneys compared to federal public defenders, given their choice to participate in Operation Streamline. Future research involving government prosecutors and non-Operation Streamline attorneys, both in Tucson and in other federal districts, could check my findings and add to them. However, given the consistency of findings between both the judge and attorney respondents in dealing with identity management based on their legal involvement with Operation Streamline, additional analysis of other courtroom players may prove to be redundant.

Finally, this book only focuses on the theoretical area of identity management within Operation Streamline. Future research on other aspects of the program, such as judicial variation or systems of discipline and race/ethnicity in Operation Streamline, may provide additional insight.

Broader Contributions

Beyond the development of the conceptualization of *competing identity management,* this study can help contribute to a more equitable society in a variety of ways, from micro level identity management practices to macro level policy implications. The oppressive nature of Operation Streamline impacts both the front-line workers tasked with implementing this program day after day and those who are subjected to the legal violence and immigration-based racism (Chacón 2009, 2012; Menjívar and Abrego 2012; Molina 2014; Golash-Boza 2015). It also represents the contemporary "crimmigration" regime that has become all too common in the United States, which has proven to be both morally indefensible (Greene, Carson, and Black 2016; Finch 2021), and, quite frankly, ineffective (McCombs 2007a, 2007b, 2009, 2010; Buentello et al. 2010; Lydgate 2010; Robbins 2010a, 2010b, 2010c; Grassroots Leadership 2012; Corradini et al. 2018). Ending Operation Streamline permanently and beginning to dismantle structurally inequitable immigration and criminal justice systems would be advisable to promote a more just system of dealing with migrants.

Best Practices

At the micro level, it is possible to extract from this study some best practices for attorneys, judges, or other legal professionals who wish to decrease their work-related role strain, lessen identity competition, and serve clients better. Generally speaking, respondents who were more aware of their competing role and social identities had developed better coping strategies, while those who denied or were oblivious to potential work-related role strain and role and social identity competition were less likely to have healthy identity management strategies in place. For example, Latino/a attorneys and judges who highlighted their racial/ethnic social identity felt they could better relate to Operation Streamline defendants and more quickly develop rapport with them, improving their day-to-day work. Additionally, those who were able to employ more identity management strategies had an easier time discussing their personal unease about being involved in Operation Streamline. This may be due to practice in justifying their involvement, but it also meant they were better at thinking about what aspects to improve not only for Operation Streamline specifically, but also criminal immigration proceedings in general. Indeed, many of the legal professionals who used a variety of identity management strategies supported more intense reforms to the contemporary crimmigration regime that Operation Streamline represents.

My research suggests that making attorneys and judges aware of these competing identities and helping them to see how some of the larger social systems of race/ethnicity, citizenship/generational status, and gender inform their work is a good start to helping them cope with work-related role strain and opens to them a larger variety of identity management strategies. An interaction with Dean, a Latino CJA panel attorney whose family had been U.S. citizens since the nineteenth century when the United States annexed Mexican land, bore out this prediction. While he claimed in a lunchtime interview that Operation Streamline had no racial/ethnic component, hours later after that day's proceeding, he approached me and said:

> I had another thought. I had a client once and I forget what we were talking about, but she was in Streamline, and she made this comment about darker skin being subject to more prejudice. If you came from the South and you were darker than the rest of México [you were seen as less than]. And so today, after our talk, I started looking at the clients, like you said, racially, and they are all darker. So, if you look at any of the TV programs, any of the TV stations like Univision, they're all, well, they're mostly men and very light-skinned, fair skinned. And a lot of Mexicans in the North, along the border, are very light skinned. And I thought, wow, this is really interesting. So maybe there is, at least, ancestor-wise, a racial part about who is migrating and getting caught.

While Dean personally identifies as an "American-Mexican," he begins here to acknowledge that complexion correlates with racial/ethnic bias. It seemed to him that it might be the case that darker-skinned people have been more likely to be stopped at the border for generations.

Thus, recognition of racialized immigration and criminal justice inequities, especially *within* the group of Latino/as based on skin tone, helped Dean to think more broadly about systematic racism (Bonilla-Silva 1997, 2014; Cobas, Duany, and Feagin 2009; Feagin 2010) as a contributor to inequality. Thus, helping those in the field of Operation Streamline (and others, for example, in other law enforcement agencies) to understand these larger factors and thus better manage identities might improve their own well-being as well as their promotion of substantive justice and reform, specifically as extra-legal critiques from those who are not directly involved in Operation Streamline (such as activists, courtroom observers, and the media) impact their work-related role identities causing work-related role strain. Once activists or the media call out injustice in programs such as Operation Streamline, signaling work-related role strain or social and role identity competition to respondents' attention, legal professionals will better be able to grapple with these broader questions of structural racism and their own role in upholding these systems. Those who are aware of certain identity management strategies and/or recognize problems of substantive justice are better able to perform their work-related role to the best of their ability and even harness the power of their competing role and social identities in order to better serve their clients while still managing their mental health, perhaps avoiding burnout at the micro level while also promoting more equity and justice at the macro level.

Policy Implications

From a macro perspective, though, Operation Streamline is only one part of a complicated immigration regime in the United States that is based on existing racial/ethnic hierarchies (Chacón 2009, 2012; Menjívar and Abrego 2012; Molina 2014; Golash-Boza 2015) and has increasingly focused on "governing immigration through crime" (Dowling and Inda 2013). It is also part of a global network of crimmigration systems (Koulish and van der Woude 2020)—with similar trends in racialized legal violence developing in diverse national contexts from Russia (Kubal and Olayo-Méndez 2020) to Australia (Sharples and Briskman 2021) to India (Mishra 2021) to the United Kingdom (Parmar 2020). There is, however, hope in shifting the decades-long trend of crimmigration (Miller 2021; Wonders and Jones 2021) and there are policy changes that can be made to improve the way justice is actually served to migrant populations.

While Operation Streamline has survived through a diverse set of political players—starting under Republican President George W. Bush, developing further under Democratic President Barak Obama, weaponized to separate families by Republican President Donald Trump (American Bar Association 2018), and paused but not forgotten by Democratic President Joseph Biden—the globally impactful COVID-19 pandemic put a major hold on the program for the first time since its inception. In March 2020 as the world began to grapple with what was just the beginning of the effects of the COVID-19 pandemic, Operation Streamline proceedings in Tucson were indefinitely paused due to public health concerns. Having 70 migrants and 20-some odd lawyers, judges, translators, U.S. Marshals, and Border Patrol agents in one courtroom suddenly posed not only a threat to civil rights but also to everyone's immediate health and safety. As of the writing of this book in early 2022, the program had not resumed, based on continued guidance from the Center for Disease Control and Prevention and other federal recommendations.

This study of Operation Streamline shows that legal professionals of different social identities (race/ethnicity, citizenship/generational status, and gender) pattern their identity management differently because of inherent power differences based on existing social inequalities (structural racism, nationalism, and patriarchy). As such, beginning to dismantle these broader oppressive social systems begins with permanently ending programs like Operation Streamline, which clearly reproduces social disparities in a variety of ways. Not bringing back Operation Streamline, though, is just the beginning of re-envisioning our current immigration system—moving away from criminalization and racialization and toward greater global justice for all people.

While it is my sincere hope Operation Streamline never returns from its COVID-19 hiatus, there are structural reasons to believe it might. For example, Operation Streamline makes money, linking criminal justice to capitalism. Corporate interests via private prisons (Gilman and Romero 2018; Jefferis 2019) effectively lobby for programs such as Operation Streamline in order to keep occupancy rates high. Broader trends in mass incarceration (Alexander 2010; Kohler-Hausmann 2018) show that imprisonment for petty offenses results in high profits for these corporations, even more so if it is not impacting U.S. citizens (Ryo 2020). Federal and local disinvestment in the private prison industry is a must.

There are also federal government budgetary incentives for court districts along the México-U.S. border in sustaining the number of judges, pre-trail officers, U.S. Marshals, etc., that participating in Operation Streamline has created. Terminating Operation Streamline may mean some legal professionals find themselves out of work. However, if broader reforms were implemented in both the immigration and criminal justice systems, the goal would be to allow these legal professionals to find work that does not include racializing and criminalizing migrants.

Policymakers who wish to improve how the criminal justice system deals with sensitive racial/ethnic issues like those surrounding immigration crimes and *en masse* proceedings such as Operation Streamline can use these findings to guide new policies that focus not on criminalization and deterrence, but on expanding legal options for migration and creating broader economic reforms that mitigate "push" factors from the global south (Donato and Massey 2016; Miller 2021). There would also need to be new policies developed to allow those who have been prosecuted through mass criminal immigration proceedings like Operation Streamline to have new, legal options for re-entry (Sarabia 2012; Martínez and Slack 2013). Other political emphases on welcoming DREAMers and creating pathways to citizenship, as well as buoying protection programs for asylum seekers, play into these complicated structural concerns around immigration reform.

Because previously proposed "comprehensive immigration reform" has sometimes included expanding programs like Operation Streamline, my research to understand the broader effects of the program on legal professionals is especially important not only to social scientists but also to society at large. Structurally speaking, the racial/ethnic, gender, and citizenship/generational status social identity differences that speak to structural inequalities in Operation Streamline that are likely also present in other justice professions such as with local law enforcement, the Border Patrol, or Immigration and Customs Enforcement. The fact that there is a difference in identity management strategies for Latino/a and non-Latino/a respondents helps demonstrate there is in fact underlying patterns of structural racism, as well as nationalism (based on differences in citizenship/generational status social identities) and patriarchy (based on gender identity differences) that are reproduced—even unknowingly or reluctantly—by legal professionals who participate in Operation Streamline. Ending Operation Streamline permanently may be a first step in beginning to dismantle larger systems of crimmigration and structural racism.

References

Alexander, Michelle. 2010. *The New Jim Crow: Mass Incarceration in the Age of Colorblindness*. New York, NY: New Press.

American Bar Association. 2018. "Family Separation and Detention." americanbar.org. Retrieved January 15, 2022. https://www.americanbar.org/advocacy/governmental_legislative_work/priorities_policy/immigration/familyseparation/.

Bonilla-Silva, Eduardo. 1997. "Rethinking Racism: Toward a Structural Interpretation." *American Sociological Review* 62(3):465–80. https://doi.org/10.2307/2657316.

Bonilla-Silva, Eduardo. 2014. *Racism without Racists: Color-Blind Racism and the Persistence of Racial Inequality in the United States*. Fourth Edition. New York, NY: Rowman and Littlefield Publishers.

Buentello, Tara, Sarah V. Carswell, Nicholas Hudson, and Bob Libal. 2010. "Operation Streamline: Drowning Justice and Draining Dollars Along the Rio Grande." Grassroots Leadership. Retrieved January 15, 2022. http://grassrootsleadership.org/sites/default/files/uploads/operation-streamline-green-paper.pdf.

Burke, Peter J., and Jan E. Stets. 2009. *Identity Theory*. New York, NY: Oxford University Press.

Chacón, Jennifer M. 2009. "Managing Migration Through Crime." *Columbia Law Review Sidebar* 109:135–48. http://dx.doi.org/10.2139/ssrn.2033931.

Chacón, Jennifer M. 2012. "Overcriminalizing Immigration." *Journal of Criminal Law and Criminology* 102(3):613–52. https://scholarlycommons.law.northwestern.edu/jclc/vol102/iss3/5.

Cobas, José A., Jorge Duany, and Joe R. Feagin. 2009. *How the United States Racializes Latinos: White Hegemony and Its Consequences*. Boulder, CO: Paradigm Publishers.

Corradini, Michael, Jonathan A. Kringen, Laura Simich, Karen Berberich, and Meredith Emigh. 2018. "Operation Streamline: No Evidence That Criminal Prosecution Deters Migration." Vera Institute of Justice. Retrieved January 15, 2022. https://www.immigrationresearch.org/system/files/operation_streamline.pdf.

Donato, Katharine M., and Douglas Massey. 2016. "Twenty-First-Century Globalization and Illegal Migration." *Annals of American Academy of Political and Social Science* 666:7–26. https://doi.org/10.1177/0002716216653563.

Dowling, Julie A., and Jonathan X. Inda, Eds. 2013. *Governing Immigration Through Crime: A Reader*. Stanford, CA: Stanford University Press.

Feagin, Joe R. 2010. *Racist America: Roots, Current Realities, and Future Reparations*. Second Edition. New York, NY: Routledge.

Finch, Jessie K. 2021. "Racialized Habitus in Criminal Immigration Defense Attorneys" Pp. 165–84 in *The Logic of Racial Practice: Explorations in the Habituation of Racism*, Bahler, Brock, Ed. Lanham, MD: Lexington Books.

Gilman, Denise, and Luis Romero. 2018. "Immigration Detention, Inc." *Journal on Migration and Human Security* 6(2):145–16. https://doi.org/10.1177/2331502418765414.

Golash-Boza, Tanya M. 2015. *Immigration Nation: Raids, Detentions, and Deportations in Post-9/11 America.* Boulder, CO: Paradigm Press.

Grassroots Leadership. 2012. "Operation Streamline: Costs and Consequences." Retrieved January 15, 2022. http://grassrootsleadership.org/sites/default/files/uploads/grl_sept2012_report-final.pdf.

Greene, Judith A., Bethany Carson, and Andrea Black. 2016. "Indefensible: A Decade of Mass Incarceration of Migrants Prosecuted for Crossing the Border." Retrieved January 15, 2022. https://grassrootsleadership.org/sites/default/files/reports/indefensible_book_web.pdf.

Jefferis, Danielle C. 2019. "Private Prisons, Private Governance: Essay on Developments in Private-Sector Resistance to Privatized Immigration Detention." *Northwestern Journal of Law and Social Policy* 1(15):82–97. https://scholarlycommons.law.northwestern.edu/njlsp/vol15/iss1/3.

Kohler-Hausmann, Issa. 2018. *Misdemeanorland.* Princeton, NJ: Princeton University Press.

Koulish, Robert, and Maartje van der Woude. 2020. *Crimmigrant Nations: Resurgent Nationalism and the Closing of Borders.* New York, NY: Fordham University Press.

Kubal, Agnieszka, and Alejandro Olayo-Méndez. 2020. "Mirrors of Justice? Undocumented Immigrants in Courts in the United States and Russia" Pp. 198–224 in *Crimmigrant Nations: Resurgent Nationalism and the Closing of Borders*, Koulish, Robert, and van der Woude, Maartje, Eds. New York, NY: Fordham University Press.

Lydgate, Joanna Jacobbi. 2010. "Assembly-Line Justice: A Review of Operation Streamline." Chief Justice Earl Warren Institute on Race, Ethnicity, and Diversity at the University of California, Berkley Law School. Retrieved January 15, 2022. http://www.law.berkeley.edu/files/operation_streamline_policy_brief.pdf.

Martínez, Daniel E., and Jeremy Slack. 2013. "What Part of 'Illegal' Don't You Understand? The Social Consequences of Criminalizing Unauthorized Mexican Migrants in the United States." *Social and Legal Studies* 22(4):535–51. https://doi.org/10.1177/0964663913484638.

McCombs, Brady. 2007a. "Jail Time in Store for All AZ Crossers." October 25, 2007. *Arizona Daily Star.* Retrieved January 15, 2022. http://azstarnet.com/news/local/border/jail-time-in-store-for-all-az-crossers/article_b10a5bc4-a1d0-564d-b0b5-fc8d1048d757.html.

McCombs, Brady. 2007b. "Bp May Have to Rein in Its Zero-Tolerance Plan." November 23, 2007. *Arizona Daily Star.* Retrieved January 15, 2022. http://azstarnet.com/news/local/crime/bp-may-have-to-rein-in-its-zero-tolerance-plan/article_4d83c082-7537-56e1-b919-2fa8365900e5.html.

McCombs, Brady. 2009. "Hearings for Entrants Taking More Time." December 13, 2009. *Arizona Daily Star.* Retrieved January 15, 2022. http://azstarnet.com/news/local/border/hearings-for-entrants-taking-more-time/article_b141f49b-8d5d-5106-bdcb-8eedf6c170d8.html.

McCombs, Brady. 2010. "Border Boletín: A Close Look at Operation Streamline (Updated Again)." September 13, 2010. *Arizona Daily Star.* Retrieved January 15, 2022. http://azstarnet.com/news/blogs/border-boletin/article_2f2d7ea8-bf5e-11df-a3ef-001cc4c002e0.html.

Menjívar, Cecilia and Abrego, Leisy J. 2012. "Legal Violence: Immigration Law and the Lives of Central American Immigrants." *American Journal of Sociology* 117(5):1380–421. https://doi.org/10.1086/663575.

Miller, Todd. 2021. *Build Bridges, Not Walls: A Journey to A World Without Borders.* San Francisco, CA: City Lights Books.

Mishra, Amlan. 2021. "From Foreigners Tribunal to Tablighi Jamaat: Elusive Bail in India's Colonial Crimmigration Regime." University of Oxford Border Criminologies Blog. Retrieved January 17, 2022. https://www.law.ox.ac.uk/research-subject-groups/centre-criminology/centreborder-criminologies/blog/2022/01/foreigners.

Molina, Natalia. 2014. *How Race Is Made in America: Immigration, Citizenship, and the Historical Power of Racial Scripts.* Los Angeles, CA: University of California Press.

Parmar, Alpa. 2020. "Arresting (Non)Citizenship: The Policing Migration Nexus of Nationality, Race, and Criminalization." *Theoretical Criminology* 24(1):28–49. https://doi.org/10.1177/1362480619850800.

Robbins, Ted. 2010a. "Border Patrol Program Raises Due Process Concerns." September 14, 2010. npr.org. Retrieved January 15, 2022. http://www.npr.org/templates/story/story.php?storyid=129780261.

Robbins, Ted. 2010b. "Claims of Border Program Success Are Unproven." September 13, 2010. npr.org. Retrieved January 15, 2022. http://www.npr.org/templates/story/story.php?storyid=129827870.

Robbins, Ted. 2010c. "Border Convictions: High Stakes, Unknown Price." September 14, 2010. npr.org. Retrieved January 15, 2022. http://www.npr.org/templates/story/story.php?storyid=129829950.

Ryo, Emily Q. 2020. "Introduction to the Special Issue on Immigration Detention." *Law and Society Review* 54(4):750–4. https://ssrn.com/abstract=3886005.

Sarabia, Heidy. 2012. "Perpetual Illegality: Results of Border Enforcement and Policies for Mexican Undocumented Migrants in the United States." *Analyses of Social Issues and Public Policy* 12(1):49–67. https://doi.org/10.1111/j.1530-2415.2011.01256.x.

Sharples, Rachel, and Linda Briskman. 2021. "Racialized Citizenship: Challenging the Australian Imaginary" Pp. 202–21 in *Handbook of Migration and Global Justice*, Weber, Leanne, and Tazreiter, Claudia, Eds. Cheltenham, UK: Edward Elgar Publishing.

Stets, Jan E. 2005. "Examining Emotions in Identity Theory." *Social Psychology Quarterly* 68(1):39–56. https://doi.org/10.1177/019027250506800104.

Wonders, Nancy A., and Lynn Jones. 2021. "Challenging the Borders of Difference and Inequality: Power in Migration as a Social Movement for Global Justice" Pp. 296–313 in *Handbook of Migration and Global Justice*, Weber, Leanne, and Tazreiter, Claudia, Eds. Cheltenham, UK: Edward Elgar Publishing.

APPENDIX A
RESEARCH DESIGN, DATA
COLLECTION, AND METHOD
OF ANALYSIS

This study uses multiple data sources (legal documents, media reports, and activist publications; ethnographic observations; and interviews) to explore the identity processes involved in everyday experiences of lawyers and judges who participate in Operation Streamline proceedings. I analyze these data using strategic narrative, a systematic and theory-driven interpretive approach after the methodology elaborated by Stryker (1996). The various concepts and mechanisms are elaborated in the theoretical framework in Chapter 2 (e.g., work-related role identities and role strain, social identities of race/ethnicity, citizenship/nationality and gender, identity construction, thick versus thin and assigned versus asserted identities; and impression management). These functioned as key sensitizing concepts and mechanisms that provided an initial set of coding categories to empirically examine the expectations I had developed about how and under what circumstances legal professionals manage work-related role strain and competing social and role identities in Operation Streamline.

The three sources of data collected (documents/text, ethnographic fieldnotes, and interviews) were coded and analyzed interpretively through strategic narrative according to first the prior theoretical frameworks, while still allowing for the inductive creation of additional coding categories and sub-categories that in turn led to a more fully elaborated conceptualization of *competing identity management*. Through this kind of iterative "back and forth" between my starting sensitizing framework of concepts and mechanisms and my data, I was able to further classify the strategies of identity management used by respondents as well as the specific conditions under which work-related role strain and competing social and role identities became relevant to the work of Operation Streamline legal professionals. This allowed me to modify and build from the conceptualization of *competing identity management* to offer further empirically grounded conclusions via strategic narrative analysis.

Research Design

My basic research design is a study of Operation Streamline as a strategic case (as explained in Chapter 1) to explore identity management strategies in a setting of work-related role strain and competing social and role identities. Coming from a method of strategic narrative analysis and because my goal was to recognize and analyze previously unexplored strategies of negotiation between social and role identities, a qualitative design was particularly advantageous. The research strategies I used to collect data were threefold:

1 Documents/Textual Data (legal documents, media reports, and activist publications) that served as a collection of extra-legal critiques (perspectives from those who are not directly involved in Operation Streamline, such as activists, courtroom observers, the media, and legal scholars) on the identity of Operation Streamline lawyers and judges to contrast with their own descriptions and enactments.
2 Extensive ethnographic observations of lawyers and judges at the Evo A. DeConcini U.S. Courthouse in Tucson, Arizona.
3 In-depth interviews of both Latino/a and non-Latino/a lawyers and judges who participate in Operation Streamline.

The use of several data sources allowed for more conclusive results and a better understanding of identity-related issues in the Operation Streamline context. I explain how/for what I used each data source below in the data collection section.

In designing my project, it was infeasible to conduct qualitative research in each of the eight federal court districts along the México-U.S. border that have had some version of Operation Streamline in place. In addition to being practical, I limited my scope to the Tucson Sector, as defined by the U.S. Border Patrol, because it is one of the most substantively relevant locations to study Operation Streamline. This sector covers about 90,000 square miles of eastern Arizona, including 262 linear miles of the México-U.S. border, beginning at the east edge of Yuma County, and extending to the Arizona-New Mexico state line. The most recent trends in border security (building fences in easily accessed land and increasing protection at urban crossings) have greatly increased the flow of migrants through the Tucson Sector. This phenomenon of moving the migrant stream from urban areas to the desert is known as the "Funnel Effect" (Rubio-Goldsmith et al. 2006). As the number of border-crossers in this sector has increased, so too have the number of federal prosecutions for immigration-related crimes (U.S. Department of Justice 2010). In addition, recent Arizona legislation on immigration—such as the controversial S.B. 1070, dubbed the "show me your papers" law—has highlighted the racially charged undertones surrounding immigration in this area (Anderson and Finch 2014).

Focusing on Operation Streamline proceedings only in the Tucson sector also helped with access, depth of data collected, and completing the project in a timely manner. First, concentrating on Operation Streamline in Tucson facilitated ease of entry in attending legal proceedings and into the social circles of lawyers and judges. Second, limiting my data collection to Tucson allowed for thicker and more in-depth data collection on one specific site. This avoids a problem of "thin" data over a variety of sectors or district courts. Thin data would be particularly troublesome in developing a deep understanding of how multiple competing identities interact in particular settings. Third, concentrating on Tucson allowed for enough in-depth information to adequately address the theoretical and empirical questions posed while not overextending available resources, including time and funding.

Data Collection

Documents/Textual Data

The first research component included the collection of scholarly, media, and activist coverage of Operation Streamline in Tucson (as well as in other locations). I collected over 80 documents though various systematic online searches related to Operation Streamline. I also received copies of some documents from the attorneys and judges involved as well as from activists who I met at the ethnographic observations. I believe I found nearly every media and scholarly article related to Operation Streamline, at the time of this books' publication, though I cannot be certain of this fact.

These external documents/textual data allowed me to investigate how external viewpoints—sometimes referred to as the source of reflected appraisals (Cooley 1902) or identity confirmation/disconfirmation (Burke and Stets 2009)—affect identity management strategies around work-related role strain and competing social and role identities. That is, examining the broader discursive context of Operation Streamline both nationally and specifically in the Tucson community allows insight to how judges and lawyers manage their various identities in the face of identity attribution by others. Interviews with judges and lawyers revealed that they were very familiar with these external representations of Operation Streamline; interviewees even shaped some of their responses to my questions around these critiques. These legal professionals often counterposed themselves against activists' descriptions or corrected the media's conceptions of their work, allowing me to see which external attributions have been especially relevant (either positively or negatively) for respondents. In short, being familiar with the "outsider" or extra-legal perception of Operation Streamline allowed me to better see how these external influences affected work-related role strain and competition between social and role identities for legal professionals involved in the program.

Overall, the analysis of documents/textual data and views from outsider communities provide a unique look at Operation Streamline through the lenses of three communities who are not directly involved in Operation Streamline: (1) legal scholars; (2) Tucson media outlets; and (3) humanitarian activist groups. While the Tucson media sources highlight historical changes of Operation Streamline, the legal resources and activist groups provide the strongest critiques and suggested improvements to the program. The activist groups also emphasize the racialized nature of immigration and specifically Operation Streamline, which relates to the social identities of lawyers and judges, while the legal documents highlight lawyer and judge work-related role identities.

One extreme example of activists involves a group known as the "End Streamline Coalition." This group's actions have bordered on harassment—emailing Operation Streamline defense attorneys up to 40 times a day with the same letter outlining their complaints about the program. As described in previous chapters, these activists use the language of role identities to call forth two poles of justice that create work-related role strain. Activists suggest that Operation Streamline is in violation of the work-related role expectation of providing Operation Streamline defendants with substantive justice (as opposed to formal justice that attorneys and judges perform when participating in Operation Streamline). By calling upon their work-related role (in the form of rules of conduct and professional responsibilities), these activists highlight the importance of identity assignment done by those who are not directly involved in Operation Streamline.

Similarly, other documents have questioned the racialized nature of Operation Streamline, suggesting that the "brown skin" of the defendants is what makes them more likely to go through an *en masse* proceeding (Langston-Daley 2011). One organization, "Grassroots Leadership," wrote a report critiquing Operation Streamline and the broader criminal system by pointing out that while (at the time) only 16% of the U.S. population is Latino/a, half of the prison population is now Latino/a (Grassroots Leadership 2012). Other scholarly publications have also made this connection (Boyce and Launius 2013; De La Rosa 2019; Finch and Stryker 2020; Finch 2021; Sarabia and Perales 2021). While not always specifically calling on the social identities of the lawyers and judges, these types of documents highlight the racialization of immigration proceedings, bringing the overlapping social identities of race/ethnicity, citizenship/generational status, and gender all into play in the Operation Streamline context.

Ethnographic Observations

Over 18 months of fieldwork, I observed 66 Operation Streamline procedures at the U.S. Courthouse in Tucson, seeing over 4200 defendants processed, prosecuted, and sentenced. In line with Stryker's structural view of role identity, observation of the lawyers and judges in the court setting provides insight into the meanings and behavioral guides for the roles played by these actors from a larger organizational and structural vantage point. This work setting allowed me to observe lawyers and judges in the company of a variety of other people—creating situational combinations of Latino/a lawyers and judges, non-Latino/a lawyers and judges, activist audience members, and numerous defendants/undocumented border-crossers—highlighting various situations that affect identity management processes. This moves the data from the individual level to a more interactional basis where setting and situation influence how lawyers and judges deal with both work-related role strain and competing social and role identities.

My observations focus on recognizing and categorizing processes of identity management that occur for lawyers and judges on the job, specifically examining processes that highlight work-related role strain and competing social and role identities. For example, instances of identity management strategies such as embracement, social-structural distancing, amplification, consolidation, extension, and transformation were examined in work behavior *a la* strategic narrative analysis. The lawyers and judges (as well as U.S. Marshals and Border Patrol agents) controlled the professional setting and I conducted unobtrusive observation. Due to external situational constraints—needing to complete their jobs as usual in a courtroom proceeding—lawyers and judges were not noticeably influenced by the presence of a researcher along with other audience members in the courtroom. Being in a comfortable and routine setting for lawyers and judges provided a more accurate representation of regular, routine behavior. Through these observations, I also built rapport with numerous lawyers and judges, and gained access to less superficial or managed impressions of on-the-job life in non-courtroom settings. For example, I joined participants in lunches, meetings, presentations, and other events that expanded my ethnographic observations.

The lawyers and judges I observed are both of Latino/a and of non-Latino/a origin, which provides comparative insight into identity processes as they specifically implicate the social identity of race/ethnicity. Though all lawyers and judges might deal with work-related role strain, Latino/a lawyers and judges dealt with more intense work-related role strain based on their competing identities of race/ethnicity and citizenship. It is, however, important to have the comparison of both Latino/a and non-Latino/a respondents in order to make any claims of variation based on social identity. Chapter 3 begins with instances of work-related role strain for both social identity groups and then explains how the addition of a competing social identity for Latino/a respondents intensifies this work-related role strain. Later chapters explore of the social identities such as citizenship/generational status and gender.

I use the term Latino/a to refer to a diverse group of people previously colonized by the Spanish—including people from any part of North, Central, or South America. I asked about the various countries of origin of Latino/a lawyers and judges in my research and Latino/a respondents' backgrounds were mostly Mexican. However, analysis of the data reveals significant similarities in terms of identity management strategies with Mexican lawyers and judges compared to those from other national backgrounds such as Perú, Chile, or Guatemala. Instead, variation in citizenship/generational status based on immigration history (naturalized and born generational statuses) accounted for the bulk of within-group differences, as discussed in the section on differences within Latino/a lawyers and judges in Chapters 6–8. As such, to protect the confidentiality of respondents, I use the two very broad categories of Latino/a and non-Latino/a.

Additionally, the different circumstances under which attorneys and judges find themselves describing Operation Streamline also influence their identity management strategies. Being able to do courtroom observations of the legal proceedings as well as interactions around the proceeding allowed me to see this situational variation in identity management. Dealing with clients in their formal work-related role, as opposed to dealing with those "outside" observers who are not directly involved in Operation Streamline (such as activists, courtroom observers, the media, and legal scholars) before or after court, is a situational distinction that affects identity management as explored in Chapter 8.

Interviews

Finally, the project also included interviews with Operation Streamline lawyers and judges to examine conditions that lead to work-related role strain and competing social and role identities as well as to examine how respondents manage their various identities through different identity management strategies. My ethnographic setting proved successful for recruiting respondents for interviews as I continued to attend hearings on a weekly basis both to observe and to sustain my contact with lawyers and judges. I scheduled interviews with attorneys and judges soon after observations, in order to question lawyers and judges on specific incidents that may have occurred during the previous observations and to use this material to support or question my findings from observations. At the time of field observations, I informed participants of the general nature of my research about "Operation Streamline, everyday experiences, and identity." I remained somewhat vague so as not to prime participants or make them defensive about racial/ethnic concerns related to their work. If pressed, I suggested that "identity" includes, but is not limited to, their work life, their citizenship/generational status, their gender, and their race/ethnicity. Additionally, all lawyers and judges who decided to participate were informed of the minimal risks and benefits of participating in my research and made aware of how I intended to keep individual respondents' data confidential. All interviewees signed an informed consent form, as approved by the University of Arizona's Institutional Review Board.

Interview questions addressed attorneys' and judges' experiences in the Operation Streamline program and asked about how their experiences had been shaped, influenced, or differentiated by any of their various role or social identities (see Appendix B for the full Interview Guide). Lawyers and judges provided open-ended responses and expressed their views in a secure space of their choosing. In giving descriptions of their work, respondents articulated how they saw their professional, work-related role and how committed they were to it within the Operation Streamline context. They also discussed instances of work-related role strain in their work. Additionally, they talked about their personal work histories, often bringing up social identities in the process. Strategic narrative analysis of the interview data illuminated conditions for work-related role strain and competing social and role identities as well as how these were managed. I included an embedded "quasi-experiment" vignette, but this feature did not incite clear enough results for its original function and instead ended up serving as a gateway to solicit discussion of race/ethnicity as it applies to Operation Streamline if respondents had not already talked about this topic.

In what was meant to serve as an embedded quasi-experiment, every interview included a vignette about a hypothetical lawyer's handling of a belligerent Operation Streamline defendant. The vignette is identical in all interviews except for the treatment of the race/ethnicity of the hypothetical lawyer (who varied between the name of Manuel Martínez/Jason Johnson and the identity of Mexican/white), which was randomly assigned to different lawyers and judges. The race/ethnicity of the lawyer is mentioned twice in the vignette, once at the start through the lawyer's surname and once in conversation with a defendant (for the full vignette, see the Interview Guide in Appendix B). The interviewee was asked to evaluate the performance of the hypothetical lawyer in the vignette. This vignette came at the end of the interview, and I did not specifically ask about racial/ethnic issues until this time unless the respondent had broached these issues on their own. After this vignette, I opened the conversation to racial/ethnic social identity issues. This was an excellent way of looking specifically at the importance of racial/ethnic identity and bringing it up with lawyers and judges in a casual and non-defensive way near the end of an interview and after I had established rapport.

The use of this randomly assigned vignette was originally intended as a way to manipulate race/ethnicity to check for the responses of lawyers and judges of all races/ethnicities to the racialized vignette. That is, because the lawyers' and judges' races/ethnicities cannot be manipulated as an experimental treatment, the use of the vignette was to help to examine any differences present when a lawyer of a certain race/ethnicity interacts with a defendant. However, due to the attorney and judge's responses to this quasi-experiment, most did not really imagine themselves as the attorney in the vignette—i.e., representing self. Instead, respondents generally just talked about their own experiences with belligerent clients, and this became a jumping off point for talk about the relevance of the social identity of race/ethnicity. Instead of examining an interaction between race/ethnicity of respondent and race/ethnicity of lawyer in the vignette, I use these discussions more broadly as a way to explore the relevance of race/ethnicity in attorneys' interactions with their own clients.

Interviews were primarily conducted in English; however, I also asked about individuals' acquisition and use of Spanish-language skills. As described in Chapter 8, Spanish is often conflated with, or seen as a signal of, one's racial/ethnic identity (Roth 2012), but it is not a specific identity on its own—"Spanish speaker." Due to its proximity to the México-U.S. border, there are a very large number of immigration-related cases and non-U.S. citizens processed through the Tucson Federal Court District. As such, to be a federal public defender (FPD) or a Criminal Justice Act (CJA) panel attorney in the Tucson Federal Court District, every lawyer must pass a Spanish-language test. I am fluent in Spanish and have been able to use it as needed both in the field and in interviews. I ask all my interviewees how they learned Spanish and how they use Spanish on the job as a way of getting at what influence language plays in social identity and in *competing identity management*. Using Spanish was a cue toward emphasizing a shared social identity with border-crosser defendants for Latino/as, but only in certain contexts, as elucidated in the findings in Chapter 8.

Overall, I interviewed 45 defense attorneys and seven magistrate judges with interviews lasting anywhere from 45 minutes to three-and-a-half hours. None of the Special Assistant U.S. Attorneys (government prosecutors) would agree to interviews as they had specific directions from the Border Patrol to direct any and all inquiries received from the public to the Public Information Office. However, my inability to interview representatives of this role has minimal bearing on the theoretical questions at hand, as none of the government prosecutors involved in Operation Streamline at the time of my fieldwork were Latino/a. Perhaps Latino/as self-select out of this work-related role precisely because the conceptualization of *competing identity management* would suggest that work-related role strain and competing social and role identities would be exacerbated for Latino/as in a prosecutor legal work-related role.

I was able to interview seven out of the eight judges who presided over Operation Streamline during my fieldwork. One judge retired at the end of 2013 and simply did not respond to multiple requests for an interview via email or requests from other respondents I had interviewed. All other judges, including the replacement for the retired judge who began in 2014, participated in my study. The racial/ethnic and sex/gender breakdown of judges is shown in Table A.1. Non-Latino/a men made up the majority of respondents, while every other category was represented only once. This lack of diversity in higher-level legal positions was interesting given the larger diversity that was present in the lawyers who practiced in Operation Streamline but is not surprising given the broader context of the U.S. criminal justice system (Browne-Marshall 2013).

Table A.1 Judge Interview Respondents by Race/
Ethnicity and Sex/Gender

	Latino/a	*Non-Latino/a*	
Men	1	4	**5**
	(14%)	(58%)	**(71%)**
Women	1	1	**2**
	(14%)	(14%)	**(29%)**
	2	**5**	
	(29%)	**(71%)**	

The 45 attorneys interviewed were a more diverse group than the judges, partly based on the abovementioned Spanish language requirement for Operation Streamline attorneys. Nationally, throughout 2006–2010, only 4.2% of lawyers, judges, magistrates, and other judicial workers were categorized as Hispanic or Latino/a, while Arizona has a slightly higher rate at 6.6% (U.S. Census Bureau 2014). The Tucson Metro Area has a 5.9% rate of Hispanic judicial workers. Strikingly, for my respondents involved in Operation Streamline, the breakdown was 64% Latino/a. This suggests that a larger proportion of Latino/a attorneys end up working in federal criminal defense generally and in Operation Streamline specifically.

This over-representation of Latino/a attorneys in Operation Streamline may be because Latino/a lawyers have fewer alternatives for legal work, and they are perhaps thought to have a competitive advantage for Operation Streamline work. Predictions based on the conceptualization of *competing identity management* would suggest that Latino/as should be less likely to want to work in Operation Streamline. However, though Latino/a attorneys may be less likely to want to do Operation Streamline because of anticipated work-related role strains and competition between social and role identities, they are also more constrained in their choices because of their race/ethnic social identity based on structural racism and they are valued in Operation Streamline for their language skills. The racial/ethnic and sex/gender breakdown of all lawyer respondents is shown in Table A.2.

Table A.2 Attorney Interview Respondents by Race/
Ethnicity and Sex/Gender

	Latino/a	*Non-Latino/a*	
Men	19	14	**33**
	(40%)	(33%)	**(73%)**
Women	10	2[a]	**12**
	(22%)	(4%)	**(27%)**
	29	**16**	
	(64%)	**(36%)**	

a Smallest N represents all available respondents in category.

The 45 attorneys interviewed represent approximately 70% of the panel defense attorneys who regularly participated in Operation Streamline and about 15% of the FPDs who regularly participated in Operation Streamline during my fieldwork period. Every CJA panel defense attorney (that is, private attorneys who are contracted by the government to defend indigent clients) who was on the regular schedule for Operation Streamline during the 18 months of my fieldwork was asked to participate in at least two different formats (face-to-face and either by email or by phone). Only four panel attorneys outright refused interview requests. Another 17 panel attorneys said they would be interested but after at least two attempts failed to schedule interviews with me. Characteristics of all non-respondents are discussed below.

There are approximately 35 defense attorneys at the FPD office in Tucson. The FPD's office, however, has long been reticent about participating in Operation Streamline and, as of 2014, sent only one attorney a week to participate. Thus, 98% of the attorneys who participate in Operation Streamline on a regular basis are panel attorneys. I was able to meet FPDs at the court infrequently (as they only attend Monday's procedures). To make up for this lack of interaction, I was able to send out a blanket email request for interview participants to the entire FPD staff with the assistance of a key informant. Between this email, which garnered some participation, and face-to-face requests, I interviewed a total of five public defenders. It should be noted that several CJA panel attorneys had previously been employed by the FPD's office and had been "let go" because of budgetary issues or had retired over the years and now did part-time CJA panel work. Generally, responses from the FPDs were fairly similar to CJA attorneys. Overall, by primarily making in-person face-to-face contact at court proceedings and having other lawyers and judges vouch for me, I minimized non-response bias to the best of my ability.

There were attorneys who regularly participated in Operation Streamline that I was not able to interview. However, my main demographic variable of interest—race/ethnicity—was relatively consistent between respondents and non-respondents for CJA attorneys. I was not able to obtain demographic data on FPDs. Table A.3 shows that the relative racial/ethnic and sex/gender categorical proportions of CJA attorneys who were on

Table A.3 Non-Respondent Criminal Justice Act (CJA) Panel Attorneys by Race/Ethnicity and Sex/Gender

	Latino/a	*Non-Latino/a*	
Men	11	7	**18**
	(52%)	(33%)	**(86%)**
Women	3	0	**3**
	(14%)		**(14%)**
	14	**7**	
	(66%)	**(33%)**	

the Operation Streamline schedule during my fieldwork but did not participate in interviews is relatively similar to those who were interviewed. Latino/as represented 66% of non-respondents compared to the slightly lower 64% of respondents.

Though I have no way of knowing if non-respondents experienced more or less work-related role strain or competing social and role identities based on working in Operation Streamline, I can say that there does not seem to be a racial/ethnic pattern in those who did not participate compared to those who did. In any case, I am not attempting to generalize my findings to a population of broader Operation Streamline attorneys but instead I generalize to concepts and mechanisms in the conceptualization of *competing identity management*. Resulting empirically grounded theoretical propositions about variability in conditions and identity management processes due to work-related role strain and competing social and role identities must be tested in further research, as described in the Conclusion.

Method of Analysis: Strategic Narrative

This study examines identity processes in a natural setting, with the goal of constructing a thorough account of how and under what circumstances work-related role strain and competing social and role identities may cause variation in identity management strategies for lawyers and judges in their Operation Streamline work. Instead of explicitly testing one or more extant theories, I investigate how research participants manage the problem of balancing their multiple identities in order to formulate an empirically grounded conceptualization of *competing identity management*. This work, being the first of its kind in this setting, develops systematic interpretive assessment of the conditions that result in variations of work-related role strain and competing social and role identities as well as mechanisms that respondents use to manage work-related role strain and competing social and role identities. These assessments may then be used as beginning points for further interpretive research. They can also be used to help construct appropriate measures for future quantitative, hypothesis-testing research (Stryker 1996).

The various qualitative data collected were analyzed according to the method of strategic narrative (Stryker 1996). Though initially designed for historical work, strategic narrative's analytic methodology—allowing for the "concurrent construction and mutual adjustment" of theory with empirical observations—is broadly appropriate for qualitative-interpretive analysis (Stryker 1996: 304). It requires the explicit and precise operationalization of concepts, measures, and coding techniques as they inform—but do not preclude—further theoretical development. The use of coding categories created based on prior theory and the creation of new categories/modifications of prior categories based on the empirical analysis allows for and operationalizes the idea of iterative mutual adjustment of theory and data and of theoretically informed and delimited field research.

I originally had informed expectations based on prior theories as outlined in Chapter 2, but this analysis differs from traditional, strict hypothesis testing in that I was also able to inductively find new identity management strategies and tactics that resulted in additional concept formation for the conceptualization of *competing identity management*. This type of iterative analysis gives the benefits of qualitative analysis for new discovery without being so open-ended as to be unsystematic or imprecise. Interestingly, Burawoy's extended case method (2009), though not so focused on precision in measurement, shares the same general philosophy about relation of theory and data as strategic narrative analysis.

Qualitative data analysis for documents/textual data (legal documents, media reports, and activist publications), ethnographic observations, and interviews was a multi-step processes, as I iterated between new observations, inductive coding, and writing analytical memos—a standard approach in qualitative data analysis (Emerson, Fretz, and Shaw 2011). My preliminary results from observations and documents helped me further develop a coding scheme that branched out from various identity theories, mechanisms, concepts, and categories. This coding scheme was then applied and expanded to remaining fieldnotes, interview transcripts, and documents. Due to the large volume of documents, fieldnotes, and transcripts, I used computer-aided qualitative data analysis software, ATLAS.ti. This program facilitates iterative and inductive coding, as well as a plethora of other "epistemic orientations" (Abramson 2011), and thus represented an effective way for me to make analyses more systematic.

The issue of selection bias is present, but accounted for, in this work. That Latino/a lawyers and judges have already selected into a specific work-related role may make any problems with work-related role strain and competing identities less prevalent. In other words, despite the numeric over-representation of Latino/as, those who had even thicker racial/ethnic identities that would too seriously compete with their work-related role in Operation Streamline or cause too much work-related role strain may have opted out of or withdrawn from participation in Operation Streamline. That I nonetheless observed work-related role strain and identity competition in Latino/a judges and attorneys who selected into Operation Streamline suggests this is a real phenomenon and that without selection processes, I would have observed more rather than less work-related role strain and identity competition between social and role identities. This selection bias, then, makes my work a more robust examination of the conceptualization of *competing identity management* because to the extent that work-related role strain and identity competition between social and role identities is present in the group of Latino/as I studied, it has already survived one "opting-out" stage.

In terms of over-time reliability in analysis, as I further refined my coding scheme, I went back to the documents and observations I had coded previously and I recoded, applying the further developed coding scheme. As mentioned, while coding fieldnotes, interviews, legal documents, media reports, and activist publications, I used a coding scheme that began with my theoretically derived sensitizing constructs but was further developed inductively based on my empirical data.

The validity of this research is further fortified by four factors. First, with respect to the issues of researcher bias, I was extremely reflective of my own social location as it influenced my interpretative inclinations. Though any researcher's social location has influence on interpretation, I tried to be aware and prevent this type of bias. I kept numerous memos (examples available upon request) in which I detail any potential influences that my own social location may have had on the research at hand. Second, in terms of data depth and thickness, I was intensively involved in this research for a substantial time over many years, and this allowed exposure to competing explanations of behavior beyond perspectives emphasizing identity and identity management. Third, I use multiple data sources on social and role identities in Operation Streamline (documents/textual data, ethnographic field observations, and interviews). I compared these potentially different means of looking at findings in a way that makes the overall results more accurate to the nuanced and complex research question at hand. Finally, it is relevant to validity to discuss the constraints of the field. My work follows in line with Becker (1970), who suggests "the presence in the observational situation of the very social constraints the sociologist ordinarily studies makes it difficult for the people he [sic] observes to tailor their behavior to what they think he might want or expect" (47). That is, there is no reason to expect that my presence at Operation Streamline proceedings hindered or changed any of the interactions that I was observing.

References

Abramson, Corey M. 2011. "Qualitative Research in the Positivist-Behavioral Tradition: Resources for Addressing Type I and Type II Errors in Code Associations Using Atlas.TI." *The QDA Newsletter* 3:5–9.

Anderson, Kathryn Freeman, and Jessie K. Finch. 2014. "Racially Charged Legislation and Latino/a Health Disparities: The Case of Arizona's S.B. 1070." *Sociological Spectrum* 34(6):526–48. https://doi.org/10.1080/02732173.2014.947452.

Becker, Howard S. 1970. *Sociological Work: Method and Substance*. Chicago, IL: Aldine Publishing.

Boyce, Geoffrey, and Sarah Launius. 2013. "Warehousing the Poor: How Federal Prosecution Initiatives Like "Operation Streamline" Hurt Immigrants, Drive Mass Incarceration and Damage U.S. Communities." Retrieved January 15, 2022. https://dspace.hampshire.edu/bitstream/10009/935/1/popdev_differentakes_082.pdf.

Browne-Marshall, Gloria J. 2013. *Race, Law, and American Society: 1607-Present*. New York, NY: Routledge.

Burawoy, Michael. 2009. *The Extended Case Method: Four Countries, Four Decades, Four Great Transformations, and One Theoretical Tradition*. Berkeley, CA: University of California Press.

Burke, Peter J., and Jan E. Stets. 2009. *Identity Theory*. New York, NY: Oxford University Press.

Cooley, Charles Horton. 1902. *Human Nature and the Social Order.* New York, NY: Scribner's.

De La Rosa, Bill. 2019. "Criminalization, Social Exclusion, and Punishment: The United States Prosecution of Migrants Under Operation Streamline." MSC Criminology and Criminal Justice, 2018-19, Dissertation Submission. https://www.law.ox.ac.uk/sites/files/oxlaw/bill_de_la_rosa_msc_dissertation.pdf.

Emerson, Robert M., Rachel I. Fretz, and Linda L. Shaw. 2011. *Writing Ethnographic Fieldnotes, Second Edition.* Chicago, IL: University of Chicago Press.

Finch, Jessie K. 2021. "Racialized Habitus in Criminal Immigration Defense Attorneys." Pp. 165–84 in *The Logic of Racial Practice: Explorations in the Habituation of Racism*, Bahler, Brock, Ed. Lanham, MD: Lexington Books.

Finch, Jessie K., and Robin Stryker. 2020. "Competing Identity Standards and Managing Identity Verification." Pp. 119–48 in *Identity and Symbolic Interaction: Deepening Foundations; Building Bridges*, Serpe, Richard T., Stryker, Robin, and Powell, Brian, Eds. New York, NY: Springer.

Grassroots Leadership. 2012. "Operation Streamline: Costs and Consequences" Retrieved January 15, 2022. http://grassrootsleadership.org/sites/default/files/uploads/grl_sept2012_report-final.pdf.

Langston-Daley, Paul. 2011 "Reflection on My Trip to the Border" Standing on the Side of Love: Unitarian Universalist Association Blog. Retrieved January 19, 2014. http://standingonthesideoflove.org/blog/reflection-on-my-trip-to-the-border/.

Roth, Wendy D. 2012. *Race Migrations: Latino/as and the Cultural Transformation of Race.* Stanford, CA: Stanford University Press.

Rubio-Goldsmith, Raquel, Melissa Mccormick, Daniel E. Martínez, and Inez Magdalena Duarte. 2006. "The 'Funnel Effect' and Recovered Bodies of Unauthorized Migrants Processed by the Pima County Office of the Medical Examiner, 1990-2005." *Report Submitted to the Pima County Board of Supervisors.* Tucson, AZ: Binational Migration Institute, October 2006. http://dx.doi.org/10.2139/ssrn.3040107.

Sarabia, Heidy, and Maria Perales. 2021. "Operation Streamline: Producing Legal Violence, Racialized Illegality, and Perpetual Exclusion" Pp. 403–415 in *Race and Ethnicity in the U.S.: The Sociological Mindful Approach*, Brooks, Jacqueline, Sarabia, Heidy, and Ida, Aya Kimura, Eds. San Diego, CA: Cognella Academic Publishing.

Stryker, Robin. 1996. "Beyond History Versus Theory: Strategic Narrative and Sociological Explanation." *Sociological Methods and Research* 24(3):304–52. https://doi.org/10.1177/0049124196024003003.

U.S. Census Bureau. 2014. "EEO 10w K. Detailed Census Occupation by Industry (Services-Professional, Scientific 54, Management 55, and Administrative and Waste Management 56), Sex, and Race/Ethnicity for Worksite Geography, Total Population; Universe: Civilians Employed at Work 16 Years and Over; EEO Tabulation 2006-2010 (5-Year ACS Data)" Tables for Geographic Regions: United States; Arizona; Tucson, AZ Metro Area. Retrieved Jan 20, 2014. http://factfinder.census.gov/faces/tableservices/jsf/pages/productview.xhtml?pid=eeo_10_5yr_eeoall10wk&prodtype=table.

U.S. Department of Justice. 2010. "Immigration Offenders in the Federal Justice System, 2010." Retrieved January 15, 2022. http://www.bjs.gov/content/pub/pdf/iofjs10.pdf.

APPENDIX B
INTERVIEW GUIDE

This first section includes questions about you and your background.

1 Tell me about the town/city that you grew up in.
2 What is your educational and legal background?—high school, college, and law school?
3 How did you decide on your current law career [federal public defender, Criminal Justice Act panel attorney, or judge]?—how did you get interested in this path?—what do your friends/family think?—was this ever a difficult decision or a trying path to follow?
4 How did you learn Spanish [required for Operation Streamline defense attorneys]?—how useful has that been in your career?—how often do you use Spanish on the job now and in what contexts?

This section is about your specific work with Operation Streamline.

5 How often do you work on Operation Streamline?—which days of the week?—how many days a week or weeks per year?
6 How did you become involved/hear about Operation Streamline?—what do you see as your role [federal public defender, Criminal Justice Act panel attorney, or judge] in Operation Streamline?
7 What were your first experiences with Operation Streamline?—what was it like on your first day?—were you prepared for this different kind of proceeding?—was it what you expected it to be?—was it easier or harder than you thought it would be?—any really big learning experiences the first few times?
8 Please walk me through your day-to-day work with in Operation Streamline—what is an average day on the job like for you?—what do you do to prepare?—what do you do each hour of the day?—what do you do during the proceedings?—what do you do after the proceedings?—any regular routine or is each day different?—is there anything you always do every day?
9 What do you like and dislike about Operation Streamline?—any outstanding experiences?—what is the best/worst part for you?—do you

find it hard/rigorous?—do you feel your legal background prepared you
for your work with Operation Streamline?

10 What are some of the most outstanding experiences you have had?—
best or worst cases?—easiest/hardest cases?—what is the most difficult
or challenging part of the job?—what is the best part of the job?

11 How does your job affect your home life?—what does your family
or friends think of your job?—have you ever had any conflicts about
your job?

This section asks about my experience observing some of your work in the
Operation Streamline proceedings in the past months.

12 Was the time I spent [with you/today/on a given date] relatively repre-
sentative of a typical day?—if not, how did it differ?—what was special
or unique?

13 [Any questions about specific incidents observed with this person]

Now I am going to ask you about a hypothetical situation on the job and
what you think about it:
Vignette: [a: Manuel Martínez/b: Jason Johnson] is a panel defense
attorney. He is working with a client going through Operation Streamline.
The client is a 25-year-old man and a Mexican citizen who was apprehended two days prior and is going through proceedings today. As the
lawyer begins to speak, the client becomes defensive and belligerent. The
client refuses to answer questions asked by the attorney, saying: "C'mon,
man, you are just a [a: Mexican/b: white] guy on a power trip, give me a
break here." The attorney explains his services are for the client's benefit
and, after some cajoling, the lawyer is able to establish that the client
wishes to take the standard plea. The attorney sees the client through the
rest of the procedure.

14 What do you think of this situation?—has something like this ever hap-
pened to you?—what did you think of the lawyer's reaction?—did he
follow proper procedure?—what would you have done differently? [prod
on race/ethnicity if they do not get there]

[Hopefully, a section on race/ethnicity following the vignette]

15 Do racial/ethnic issues often arise for you at work?—do other people
bring up race/ethnicity?—when has it ever been a problem?—do you
have any specific examples of racial/ethnic tension?

16 What do you consider to be your race/ethnicity?—do you prefer the
term Latino/a or Hispanic or Mexican/Guatemalan/whatever country?—were you born in the United States or are you a naturalized citizen?—if you are naturalized, what is your country of origin?

17 How do you handle this personally?—are you ever offended by what others say about race/ethnicity as it relates to Operation Streamline?—are you ever asked about race/ethnicity by others outside of work?

This concludes our interview.

18 Is there anything else you want to add at all?
19 Are there other people involved in Operation Streamline who you think I should talk to or contact?—can you introduce me or provide me with their contact information?

Index

Note: Page numbers in *italics* indicate a figure and page numbers in **bold** indicate a table on the corresponding page.

176   *Index*